EDITH STEIN

EDITH STEIN

by Sister Teresia de Spiritu Sancto, O. D. C.

EDITH STEIN

TRANSLATED BY *Cecily Hastings* AND *Donald Nicholl*

SHEED AND WARD

NEW YORK · 1952

EDITH STEIN

Part I : THE WORLD

I.	HOME	3
II.	SCHOOL	12
III.	THE STUDENT : BRESLAU AND GÖTTINGEN	16
IV.	ASSISTANT TO HUSSERL	56
V.	THE CONVERT	64
VI.	" FRÄULEIN DOKTOR "	69
VII.	BEURON	83
VIII.	THE " WAY OF KNOWLEDGE "	90
IX.	THE " WAY OF LOVE "	95
X.	MÜNSTER AND THE *MARIANUM*	104
XI.	THE ROAD TO CARMEL	116

Part II : CARMEL

I.	THE SCHOOL OF HUMILITY	135
II.	THE NOVICIATE	144
III.	THE BRIDE OF CHRIST	165
IV.	THE WAY OF LOVE AND KNOWLEDGE	177
V.	ECHT	186
VI.	PLANS OF ESCAPE	196
VII.	THE WAY OF THE CROSS	211
VIII.	THE LAST NEWS	224
	POSTSCRIPT	233

THE WORLD

I

HOME

WEEK by week, usually on Friday morning, there was a knock at the door of my cell. At my " Come in ", Sister Benedicta would enter with a letter addressed to " Frau Auguste Stein, Breslau, Michaelisstrasse 38 ". These few words summed up everything that was dearest on earth to Edith Stein : her parents' house, her own city, and the name of the woman who had brought her into the world.

Edith Stein travelled much about the country, saw her own age with a clear vision and formed her judgment and intellect through contact with many people, but it was her home which was, and remained, the soil that nourished her heart. While that house in the Michaelisstrasse was not actually the place of her birth, it was there that she spent the greater part of her youth. It was a solid stone-built house with a plain and unadorned exterior. If you knocked at the door and stepped into the large hall, you were at once surrounded by the atmosphere peculiar to years of a consciously cultivated Jewish tradition. Big engravings, illustrating scenes from the history of Israel, beautiful carving on cupboards and chests displaying exclusively biblical motifs, gave one a sense of having been carried back into the Old Testament. The whole house, down to the smallest articles of furniture, bore evidence of a most highly cultured and decorously stable pattern of life. But everything was attuned to a dominantly religious note, so that one might have thought oneself in the house of a devout Rabbi. The vast spaces of the living rooms also, lacking ornament or stucco, and too big to be really comfortable, were all arranged in accordance with this same Hebrew pattern. They would be best compared to some of Rembrandt's interiors. This was the home of Frau Auguste Stein, née Court; here it was her outlook, her taste, and her spirit which reigned. Frau Stein was Jewish and proud of the fact. She set an irreproachable example in her observance of the rites of Israel, and saw to it that her·children strictly followed her example. For instance, grace was said in Hebrew, and every appropriate ceremonial prescription of the Talmud was precisely carried out. And so a reverent fear of God formed a deeply serious background to the children's natural gaiety.

Frau Stein had not found it at all easy to achieve this comfortable and cultured standard of life for her family. She had been thrown early into the hard struggle for existence. Her very happy marriage with Siegfried Stein had been of short duration. Edith, the youngest of her seven children, was only three years old when the sudden death of her husband—he died of sunstroke when away on business—left her to take care of the family and the growing timber business. We may catch a glimpse of what Frau Stein accomplished during those early years of widowhood from the following description by Frau Ruben, Edith's godchild, which also throws a significant light on young Edith.

' " Whoever lies once is never believed, even when he speaks the truth! " I can still hear young Edith saying that ; she would then have been in her fourth year at the most ; she and her sister Erna, eighteen months older, were speaking as one. It was Erna who was my real friend at that time. We were just the same age, and regarded little Edith, " Jitschel " [1] as she was called, with proper contempt. Besides, she was much too small and pale and delicate, and since Erna and I were often complimented on being big and strong for our age, we behaved condescendingly towards her. I did not even know, then, that " Jitschel " had another name. The reason why I

---

[1] This was probably Edith's own name for herself, before she could speak properly. It was then adopted by her brothers and sisters, and persisted for a time.

remember this moral lesson administered by the two sisters so clearly is that I strongly resented it because it was thoroughly unjust. I had *not* told a lie.

Our mothers came from the same little town in Upper Silesia, Lublinitz, and had been girlhood friends. After their marriages, they met again in Breslau, but their relationship was polite rather than intimate. Their children, on the other hand (I had a brother and sister much older than myself, just as Edith's brothers and sisters were much older than she) became close friends and even for a time inseparable.

We lived very close together, " just round the corner " in the same part of the town, and at this period we used to play together a lot. Now my mother used to go for a walk with me every afternoon, usually on the " Promenade ", the old crumbling ramparts, beautifully laid out as a garden, which encircled a large part of the centre of the town. But poor Frau Stein, a widow with seven children, ambitious, compelled by necessity to develop her husband's timber business, and occupied over and above this with baking bread and a thousand other household matters, could find no time to take her two small daughters for walks. One morning my mother had promised me some little expedition which I looked forward to with great delight. She then sent me to play with Edith and Erna, and in my excitement I told them about this expected treat, asking them if they would like to come too. They would. I told them we should be going at 3 o'clock, and ran off home. But they didn't come, and I said nothing about it to my mother. But when I came to see the Steins next day, I was greeted with the accusation I have already quoted. They had waited all the afternoon, dressed up in their best clothes, and had been so disappointed. And the worst accusation was the one my mother made when she heard what had happened : " Poor Frau Stein, she had to waste all that time getting the children ready."

This remark shows how overworked Edith's mother was at that time. All her children except the eldest boy, who was probably serving his apprenticeship, were still at school, and of little help to her. Everything rested on her seemingly fragile shoulders. She must have been extraordinarily intelligent.

She was the first person I knew to instal a telephone for business purposes : and the glorious thing was that she let me use it, and I made my first telephone calls under her supervision. By that time things were improving for her. She had taken her eldest son into the business, and had moved to a new timber-yard for the third time. And this one was a really large yard.

Oh that timber-yard ! It was heaven for us children. What games we could play there ! Edith was then perhaps about eight, or a little less. We no longer lived so close together, and, more important, we did not go to the same school. Frau Stein's three elder daughters had gone to a private school, but she sent the two youngest to the town's *Viktoriaschule*, which was considered much better but meant a quite considerable journey to school, on which they had to cross a long bridge. The two of them now had a very high opinion of themselves. Meanwhile Edith's whole character had developed noticeably.

As she was the youngest member of a large family, it was not to be wondered at that she was a precocious child. She read a great deal, and the great mental stimulus provided by her reading and the company of her brothers and sisters was no doubt a desirable thing. A less desirable result was that she acquired an ungovernable ambition, a source of tension liable to break out into tears of rage if she did not get what she wanted and if she did not always occupy the centre of the stage. And yet her brothers and sisters were in part to blame for this, too, for they made a sort of infant prodigy of her and idolized her. Moreover she was her mother's favourite, though I never noticed that her mother showed this by spoiling her or giving her any special privileges.

At this time I no longer used to go very often to the Steins', but when I did go she used to make much of me, and never refused me anything. But however rare my visits were, I never missed one of the Birthdays. Birthdays at the Steins were a very special kind of festival. They had a host of relations in the town, all with several children. All these children were invited, and even though these parties were of the very simplest, none of the children gave that a moment's thought : they were all aching for the games to begin. Lotto was one of our favourites. Edith preferred those games which gave an opportunity to show one's brilliance, such as " How, where and why ? " For this you had to be pretty cunning and skilful, in order to find out what the thing was, if you were sent out, or to conceal it with clever answers, if anyone else was trying to discover it. Afterwards we redeemed our forfeits, which meant more fun. In fact it was all pure bliss, and I am certain that is how we all felt.

Then came the day when my parents sent me to school, and I went into the same class as Edith. She was an excellent pupil, and I must say that it was her real interest in the subject which made her so attentive and hardworking. But like every human being she had her limits, and I shall never forget how deadly pale and worried her face used to become in the arithmetic classes. During the last three years of my school life we always sat together. We were now Seniors, and Seniors did not have to sit at benches like Juniors, but at real, slope-topped desks with chairs. There were three pupils to a desk, whereas the benches were always for two, and as she was now always second and I third in class, until I left school, we were always next to each other. Now I was just as bad at languages as I was good at arithmetic and science, while with her it was the other way round. So we quite spontaneously began a sort of (illicit) cooperation, in which each of us was prompted by the other, or copied from the other whatever she did not know. We formed a perfect team. But we were both equally good at German, and did not write our essays together.

However, though our intellectual concerns brought us together in this way, in our private affairs we were no longer so intimate. It may partly have been because of the great distance between our two homes—we had moved to suburbs which lay in diametrically opposite directions. And things were now going so well with Frau Stein that the house she lived in was her own, and she probably also owned the site of her greatly expanded timber-yard. I never saw this, the last of her houses in Breslau. But the estrangement was due more to Edith's character, which was so dominated by fierce ambition that it left no room for warm feeling. She was obsessed with the aim of being first—an aim, moreover, which she never reached during the time I was at school with her. The fact that she never realized it was perhaps due less to her than to a certain latent anti-Semitism from which our German schools were not free even then. Edith herself considered that our Headmaster, Professor Roehl, whom we always called " Rex", was an anti-Semite, and I am glad to be able to remember the following little scene, which probably took place about 1904. Prizes were distributed to celebrate the centenary of Schiller's death. Edith was doing particularly well at this time, and everyone expected her to get the prize. But instead of her, it was given to one Martha Ritter, the head of our class. (She was always first and also, as it happened, the daughter of a widow.) We did Geography with Rex, at which I was especially good. I was also personally in high favour with him. So it was not a very heroic act to come forward and ask why Edith Stein had not got the prize, when the whole class considered that she deserved it rather than Martha Ritter. He laughed, but with the faintest touch of embarrassment—of course it was quite impossible that " Rex " should really be embarrassed—and said that the head of the class had to have it. It was the rule. There was of course no such rule, because it was an altogether exceptional occasion, since Schiller anniversaries were not regular events—but Edith's honour was saved !

It was with tears of bitter regret that I eventually left school, after reaching Class Ib. I had loved the place passionately.'

There is little to add to this very illuminating account. We are introduced to the strenuous and courageous struggle of the young widow, who succeeded in spite of her difficulties in providing for her young family a childhood filled with sunshine and warmed by the love of a real mother. She had always been the pivotal point for the whole family, and after the father's death she had become the undisputed authority to whom everything must be referred. She undertook the management of the business in a spirit of virile determination and complete trust in God.

A quick look at the books showed her that the business was not in good shape financially. But she was undismayed and had the strength and energy to surmount this crisis. Several times she went to Agram, in order to renew and maintain her personal contacts with business friends there. She had acquired such knowledge on the technical side that she had only to pass by a wood to make an accurate estimate of its value as timber. She bought up whole forests in Croatia, had the wood sawn up on the spot and then brought to Breslau as it was needed. Her untiring energy, judgment and competence brought the business added prestige.

The family reached a level of prosperity which the children, indeed, attributed rather to their mother's goodness than to her business efficiency. The poor craftsmen and " small men " could all have told how Frau Stein used to sell them the wood they needed and then not infrequently return the purchase money. She bought up whole lots of timber to give as winter fuel to the poor. Frau Stein handed on this characteristic of warm love for her neighbour especially to Edith over whose development she had watched with devoted care. " With us ", Sister Benedicta was later to say, " it was not a matter of education exactly. As children we read right conduct in our mother's example as if in a mirror of the virtues." There was only one thing that this God-fearing Jewess tried to impress deeply in her children's hearts : a horror of sin. When their mother said " That is a sin ", they all knew that she meant to convey the idea of all that is hateful and unworthy. Edith was the acknowledged favourite of this serious, austere, unworldly woman. Frau Stein felt that the fact that she had brought this child into the world on one of the great festival days of the

Jews was the omen of a special blessing upon her youngest
daughter's future.[1]

At the same time the valiant services of her eldest sister,
Else, ought not to be overlooked. As soon as she left school
she began to bear some of that year's endless worries single-
handed. Whilst her mother took charge of their complicated
business-affairs—an impossibility according to everyone else
in the family—Else kept house and looked after the children.
Previously their father used to go to the forest every Monday ;
now it was mother who had to go, leaving everything in charge
of this slip of a girl—including even the sales in the timber-
yard. In this way Else came to watch over her two youngest
sisters like a second mother ; though, as a matter of fact, that
heavy responsibility had been laid upon this mature child on
the very Day of Atonement that Edith was born. Her father
had come to her with the good news during the night, and had
brought along Erna, then aged eighteen months ; Erna had
been used to sleeping with mother and was now so upset that
nothing Else said could comfort her. Else was probably the
person who influenced the formation of the two children most
directly. She herself says of Edith :

' We used to stick together a great deal, and she was also
more like me than any of my other sisters and brothers. Her
first introduction to literature she received from Paul ;
holding her on his arm he used to cram her with poet's names,
their dates and their main works, which he himself had just
learnt from his new illustrated history of literature. I can still
see her as she used to sit beside the large table at which her
elder sisters and their friends used to hold poetry-competitions.
Every now and again they used to shoo her away for butting
in, " You can't join in, little Edith, you can't read yet ! " But

[1] " Whatever did not fit in with my plans did lie within the plan of God. I have
an ever deeper and firmer belief that nothing is merely an accident when seen in the
light of God, that my whole life down to its smallest details has been marked out for
me in the plan of divine Providence, and has a completely coherent meaning in God's
all-seeing eyes. And so I am beginning to rejoice in the light of glory wherein this
meaning will be unveiled to me." (Sister Teresia Benedicta a Cruce.)

why did she need to ? Whilst the rest of them were puzzling out the answer she would reel it off by heart. (Many people used to annoy me by saying that she was too forward.) Her first literary venture was made under my direction when she was ten years old, a composition in honour of Paul's marriage. Yet how different those two inseparable youngsters were ! For example, after leaving school and before attending the training-college I had been obliged to spend four years helping my over-burdened mother ; consequently, despite being first in my class, I was trembling at the thought of my teacher's Examination. I had promised Edith that if I passed I would register her at our *Viktoriaschule*, even though it was October and the middle of the school year. But in my excitement I had also said in front of the children, " If I don't pass, I shall jump into the Oder ! " It was late in the evening when I arrived back home after the last day of the Examination, and Erna lay fast asleep in bed. Edith had gone to sleep in mother's lap. Mother now woke her : " Edith, darling, Else has failed ! " She leaped up immediately and put her arms round me : " But you won't jump into the Oder ! " (I cannot give you any idea of her voice as she said it.) Mother now set her down beside Erna and said : " Erna, darling, Elsa has failed." Back came the sleepy reply, " Not really ? "

For my own part I gladly leave it to my mother to complete this picture of their childhood. It was during my first year of teaching ; I was at Preussisch-Oderleug and had asked mother to come and bring " our two little ones " for a visit. She came alone for just one day, but to make up for my disappointment at not seeing the children she proudly brought me a delightful picture of them.'

II

SCHOOL

JUDGING from the photographs, Edith must have been a most attractive child. She was naturally vivacious, with a quick intelligence and a precocious critical faculty. Her sister Erna, who was her inseparable playmate, tells us :

' Overburdened with activity as she was, Mother could devote little of her time to us. We two little ones were quite used to going out together and keeping ourselves occupied, at least in the mornings before the older ones came back from school. So far as I know, from what my mother and family have said and from my own recollection, we were fairly good and seldom quarrelled. One of my earliest memories is of my eldest brother Paul carrying Edith round the room on his arm and singing student songs to her, or showing her pictures in a History of Literature and lecturing her on Schiller, Goethe, etc. She had a tremendous memory and forgot nothing of all this. Several of our numerous aunts and uncles [1] used to tease her and try to catch her out, suggesting that Goethe wrote *Maria Stuart*, for instance. It was always a failure. She began to get a grasp of literature when she was between four and five years old.'

It was no wonder that such a mature child should have wished to go to school along with her beloved elder sister as soon as the latter began to go. But in this, alas, her mother

---

[1] Frau Stein had twelve brothers and sisters, whose names the children had to recite as if naming the twelve tribes of Israel.

refused to allow her to have her way. Prayers and tears were of no avail. The only consolation granted to the four-year-old was a promise to send her to a nursery-school. But to this proud little seeker after learning, whose life-long desire for knowledge was already awakened, such a solution was an intolerable insult. She tried everything she could think of to alter her mother's decision. But Frau Stein was firm. The dreaded first day arrived. It was pouring with rain. Edith tried a forlorn hope by declaring energetically, " I can't go to Kindergarten, my shoes will get dirty." No use. Paul, who was to accompany her, picked up his baby sister and firmly carried her off to the nursery-school. But the experiment was soon abandoned, for Edith was so inconsolably unhappy and so far in advance of all the other children that there was obviously no point in keeping her there.

After this Edith looked forward to the 12th of October, her sixth birthday, when she hoped to get permission to go to school. Chance was on her side. Out walking one day with her eldest sister Else she met one of the teachers. He took a fancy to the intelligent child, and Else told him her small sister's birthday wish. The good man gave her an examination on the spot, and found her perfectly fit to go to school. Edith was thrilled. Though she was exceptionally small and often taken for less than her six years the Head Master of the Breslau *Viktoriaschule*, which Erna was already attending, gave in to her earnest request. Her school days began on her sixth birthday, October 12th, 1897. " As it was not the custom in those days to begin the school year in the autumn, she was in the lowest form only half a year. All the same, she was one of the best in it by Christmas. She was hard-working as well as gifted, and possessed an iron will. But she was never a ' go-getter ' in the bad sense, and always friendly and helpful." This is from Erna, who goes on :

' Though she continued to shine throughout her school years, and we all assumed that she would go on from the School to complete the newly-introduced course in the

College, she surprised us by deciding to leave. As she was still undersized and delicate my mother consented and sent her, partly for a rest and partly as " help ", to my eldest sister, Else, who had married Dr. Max Gordon of Hamburg and had three small children. She stayed there eight months and carried out her tasks conscientiously and without flagging, though housework was not to her taste.

When after about six months my mother went to visit them, she hardly recognized Edith. She had grown greatly and looked radiantly healthy. But she confided to my mother that she had changed her mind and wanted to go back to school, and after that to the University. She came back to Breslau, worked at Latin and Mathematics with two students to help her, and passed the entrance examination brilliantly.'

A girl who was at school with her at this time writes :

' Edith Stein was my school-fellow in the Breslau Girls' College, and as we used to go to school together for a long time I got to know her well. Though at that time the College was closed to most girls due to the stiff entrance examination, and therefore most of the pupils were extremely gifted, she was way above the others in ability and knowledge. Even then she already possessed great modesty, which is not a characteristic typical of the Jewish people as a whole. As a matter of fact it was only when I saw this sketch of her life that I realized that she was the same age as myself ; I had always believed that she was our superior in age as well as in knowledge, probably just because she was more mature and serious than the rest. I remember her as a quiet, withdrawn, and at the same time very lovable person. One thing she said I shall never forget, when she once gave her reason for an unfavourable criticism of a very free translation : " A translator must be like a pane of glass, which lets all the light through but is not seen itself." It was a very characteristic saying.'

SCHOOL

Erna concludes her account as follows :

' For the rest, nothing remarkable happened during her time
there. As always, Edith was high in the class and was excused
the *viva voce* at the final examination. At the leaving ceremony
the Headmaster used to speak of the individual personalities
of the graduates who were going on to the University, trying
to characterize them in an apt phrase. When it came to Edith's
turn, he said, after a moment's thought, punning on her name,
" Strike the stone[1] and wisdom gushes out." At school she
always took a lively part in social amusements ; she was never
a spoil-sport. You could tell her all your troubles and secrets,
she was always ready to advise and help, and anything was safe
with her. Our years there (I had begun to study medicine in
1909, while Edith was studying German language and literature) were a time of hard work and wonderful happiness.'

[1] *Stein*, in German, means "stone ".

III

THE STUDENT: BRESLAU AND GÖTTINGEN

AMONGST the lecturers at that time in the Experimental Psychology Department of the Philosophy School at Breslau were Professor Stern and Professor Hönigswald, a man of outstanding intellect. Both were of Jewish origin. Of one of them Edith herself says, " As I was the only feminine member of the audience, the Herr Professor once said smirkingly in the middle of his lecture, ' When I say " *Gentlemen* ", I naturally include the *lady* present, too ! ' "

Frau Stein had followed her youngest daughter's intellectual development with justifiable pride, but also with a secret anxiety. Edith was clever but not pious. Up till now she had not acknowledged any religious convictions, and she showed little interest in Judaism. She herself said she was an atheist until her twenty-first year, being unable to believe in the existence of God. She was also at that time a thorough-going feminist. In the vacation, it is true, she went with her beloved mother to the Synagogue whenever she so desired. But more impressive to her than the religious ceremonies was the deep devotion of her mother, who used to lose herself completely in God. Frau Stein feared, then, that the study of philosophy, to which Edith wished to devote herself exclusively, would sweep her child more and more into the liberalist current and so away from her religious influence.

This fear was by no means unfounded. Sister Benedicta said later : " To study philosophy is to walk perpetually on the edge of the abyss." Frau Stein at first offered some opposition to her daughter's plans. But in this battle, too, Edith won the victory over her mother's love. For two years she studied at the university in her home-town, and then transferred to Göttingen which she herself so charmingly outlines.

' I had been studying for four terms at Breslau University. Few students had taken such an intimate part in the life of this " alma Mater " as I had, and it might have seemed as though I had grown into it so much that I would not break away of my own free will. But now, as so often in later years, I was able to snap seemingly secure ties with one easy movement and to fly off like a bird from a snare. I had always intended to study at some other university. Whilst I was at secondary school my plan had been to go with Erna for my first university term to Heidelberg, whose magic is so enchantingly evoked by the old student songs. This plan did not materialize because Erna was in the middle of her Physics during that term and so could not leave Breslau. The next summer it was the same ; she was too near to her State Examination and must therefore stay at home. A more powerful attraction, no doubt, was Hans Biberstein ; he had been studying in Freiburg im Breisgau during the summer before my matriculation and would not be going away again. I saw now that I could not hang onto my sister. Nor did I wish to delay and find myself having to stay just because examinations would soon be upon me. During my fourth term I had the impression that Breslau had nothing more to offer me and that I needed some fresh stimulus. Actually this was by no means true. There were more than enough unexplored possibilities, and I would still have been able to learn a great deal. But something was drawing me away. However, the poetry of the student-songs no longer played the decisive role in my choice of a university ; a quite different factor was determining that. During the summer of 1912 and the winter 1912–1913 Stern's seminar was devoted to problems in the psychology of thought, mainly with reference to the works of the " Würzburg School " (Kulpe, Buhler,

Messer, etc.) In both terms I undertook to produce a thesis, and time and again as I was working away at the recommended books I came across quotations from Edmund Husserl's *Logische Untersuchungen* (" Logical Investigations "). One day as I was working on my thesis in the Psychology Seminar Dr. Moskiewicz came up to me. " Throw all that rubbish away," he said, " and read this ; if there is anything in the other people they get it all from here." He handed me a thick book—it was the second volume of Husserl's work. I could not delve into it immediately because the term's programme did not allow me time, but I noted it for my next vacation reading. Mos knew Husserl personally, having studied under him for a term at Göttingen, where he was always longing to return. " In Göttingen you do nothing but philosophize—day and night, at meal-times, in the streets, everywhere. All the time you just discuss 'Phenomenen '." [1] One day the illustrated newspapers showed a picture of a Göttingen student who had won a philosophical award—it was Husserl's extraordinarily gifted pupil, Hedwig Martius. Mos knew her as well and had heard of her recent marriage to another old pupil of Husserl's, Hans Theodor Conrad. When I came home late one evening I found a letter for me from Göttingen on the table. Not long before my cousin Richard Courant had become a tutor there in mathematics. He had just been married to his student-friend Nelli Neumann from Breslau, and this letter was from Nelli to my mother, thanking us for our wedding-present. After a description of how the young couple were finding their new life, the letter went on, " Richard has brought a lot of men-friends into our married life but very few young ladies. Could you not send Erna and Edith here for their studies ? They would balance things a bit." After this letter I did not need any more persuasion. The next day I informed my astonished family that I wanted to go to Göttingen for the coming summer-term. Since they did not know what had been going on in my mind previously the announcement came like a peal of thunder out of a clear

[1] A technical term of Husserl's phenomenological philosophy.

sky. My mother said, "If it is necessary for your studies I shall certainly not stand in your way." Nevertheless she was sad—much sadder than the separation for a short summer-term warranted. " She doesn't like being with us any longer," she said to little Erika [1] on one occasion and in my presence. The child was very attached to me, and loved to sit beside me in the room as I was working. I used to sit her down on the carpet and give her a picture-book, then she would remain perfectly quiet and not disturb me. You could give her the very best books—she never damaged one. And she did not need entertaining, but sat there contented and peaceful until someone took her away.

The first step towards putting my plan into operation was a letter to my cousin asking for information about the lectures to be given next term by the Göttingen philosophers. Soon afterwards he sent me the proof-sheets of the lecture-programme. I took advantage of the Christmas holidays to study the *Logische Untersuchungen* ; since it was then out of print, however, I had to use the copy in the Philosophy Seminar, and there I passed my days. Professor Hönigswald often used to come in and eventually one day he asked me what I was studying so eagerly throughout the whole vacation. " Well ! Nothing less than Husserl ! " was his exclamation when I informed him. Then my heart beat faster. "In summer I shall be going to Göttingen," I told him, my eyes shining with joy, " oh, if only one had got so far as to be able to do work along those lines oneself." He was rather taken aback. During that winter, for the first time, he gave a lecture on the psychology of thought ; it was his first attempt to make an assessment of phenomenology of which he later became a resolute opponent. At that time his disapproval was not so marked, but he was not altogether pleased to discover one of his pupils going over to that camp with flags awave. I had scarcely thought of it in that way, for, despite admiring Hönigswald's acute mind, it had never struck me that he would dare to set himself on a level with Husserl—so sure was I that Husserl was

---

[1] Daughter of her sister, Frieda Tworoga.

the philosopher of our age. From then on, whenever phenomenology was being discussed in Hönigswald's seminar I
was always called upon as " the expert ".

On New Year's eve Lilli Platan and Rese and Hede Gult-
mann recited some playfully satirical poetry for us. About
each of us they had composed a verse to the well-known
refrain, Aren't you standing on your head ? They sang from
behind a screen over which only their heads were visible ; but
each time they came to the refrain they would bob down and
up would come a pair of feet (actually they stuffed shoes and
stockings fitted over their hands). The verse for me said that
whereas other young ladies dreamed of kisses [German
Busserl] Edith dreams only of Husserl, and that Edith would
really " see him in the flesh " at Göttingen. But a deeper note
was struck in our New Year magazine which contained a legend
about a little blue " stone " ; its tender symbolism revealed
to me that my friends and acquaintances felt my pursuit of
pure learning as a loss to themselves on the human level. It
had been written by Lilli.

Gradually all my preparations for leaving were completed,
but an idea had come into my head when once my own
summer-term in Göttingen was fixed. Göttingen was a
paradise not only for philosophers but also for mathematicians
and so I suggested to Rese that she should come with me.
Naturally my suggestion appealed to her greatly, but she had
to think it over to see if she could afford it. She used to pay
for her own studies by private coaching ; this was out of the
question at a strange university, where she would have to use
every minute to drink in the new learning for which she was
thirsting. That was precisely what I wanted for Rese. This
constant overwork by someone so young in years worried me,
and I would have been very glad to take her away from all this
business if only for a couple of months. One day when I was
alone with my mother I asked her jokingly, " Mummy, are
you a rich woman ? " In the same tone she replied, " Yes,
child ; what are you wanting ? " Immediately I confessed
what was at the back of my mind, that perhaps she could

provide Rese with the means to study for a term at Göttingen. Straightaway she agreed to do so. When I passed the news on to my friend she decided to go with me ; then after discussing it with her relations it turned out that she could manage on her own means and did not need to rely on mother's generosity. Our decision also clinched Georg Moskiewicz's plans for going back to Göttingen once again. This was very pleasant for us since he was already known there and could introduce us to the circle of phenomenologists.

I had never thought of staying there for more than one term. If it was a cheap luxury in those days to study at one of the smaller universities, still it did cost more than living at home. And the habits of economy which had been bred in me from my childhood scarcely allowed me to express my desire to stay for a longer period, with the extra expenditure involved. Therefore my mother's concern over the short separation ahead of us seemed to me exaggerated. In the depths of my heart, all the same, I had a secret premonition that this separation was going to go deeper than appeared. Almost as if to fight against this half-conscious suspicion I did something which would compel me to come back : I went along to Professor Stern to ask him for a theme for a doctorate on psychology. The reason why I went to him rather than to any other Professor was because my previous dealings with him had made me imagine he would give me a free hand. There I was mistaken. In his seminar he had accepted our criticism of his methods in a kindly fashion and without the least resentment ; but his ideas were so rigidly fixed that nothing could move him from them ; moreover he wished to use his pupils' works as material for his own. That also was very obvious to me after our conversation. He received me as kindly as ever and also agreed readily to my request, although I was still very young. But I could not take seriously what he suggested to me : amplifying the thesis which I had written during the winter I should work out the development of child-thought, and that, indeed, by means of those very questionnaires with which poor tormented Mos had been forced to experiment for years. Since I had it in mind to travel to Göttingen by way of Berlin and Hamburg I should pay a visit to the Institute of Applied Psychology in Klein-Glieneke near Potsdam ; there Stern's collaborator, Dr. Otto Lipmann, would be glad to show me whatever pictures he had on hand, to see if they contained anything suitable for my work. The visit to Klein-Glieneke was the only step I ever took towards the psychological doctorate. Since Mos was friendly with Dr. Lipmann he sent word that all three of us (himself, Rese and I) would be arriving one afternoon. The doctor and his charming little wife received us with overflowing hospitality and invited us to stay for coffee and dinner. After being introduced to the sweet children we were shown over the whole house and then went for a stroll along the Havelsee which was very near by. Meanwhile we had been taken to look at the brightly-lit cellars in which the Institute was housed. The collection of pictures, which was kept in a set of drawers, did not prove in the least entrancing, and the shrewd Dr. Lipmann assured me that there was nothing there worth working on. I took away with me the memory of a nice afternoon and the conviction that I could make nothing of that sort of work. From now on I abandoned all thought of my psychological thesis. All my psychological studies had led me to the view that this science had not got beyond its infancy, that it still lacked the essential, clear, basic concepts, and that it was in no condition to work out these basic concepts for itself. And what I had so far learnt about phenomenology had captivated me precisely because it set itself this task of classification and was fashioning the very conceptual tools one needed. For a time when I was first in Göttingen the memory of my psychological doctorate used occasionally to burden my mind, but I soon shook it off.

Dear old Göttingen ! I don't believe that anyone who did not study there between 1905 and 1914, during the short spring-time of the Göttingen phenomenology school, could ever imagine what that name conjures up for us.

I was twenty-one years old, and keyed up in anticipation

of what was to happen. During the holidays I paid a visit to Hamburg. No lectures were held before the end of April, although the term began officially on the 15th, when all the university offices became hives of industry. I had no need to go through matriculation ceremonies and other incidentals but could get down to work as soon as the lecture-rooms became the centres of activity. And so it was the 17th of April before I left Hamburg. My brother-in-law, Max, became rather worried at the thought of sending me off alone into strange surroundings, and asked whether I should not stay with the Courants, for the first night at least, rather than at the students' lodgings which they had booked for Rese and myself. Naturally I declined the suggestion. I simply sent them a note about my arrival, and Richard picked me up at the station, although he was suffering from an injured foot. It was already evening as he led me though the darkened streets to my new home. Rese was not due to arrive from Berlin until a few days later. I was overjoyed when the door was opened for me by a young woman with a pretty, friendly face. Later she admitted that she was herself pleasantly surprised at my own appearance, because this was the first time she had taken in students, and she had been frightened that they would all be old and ugly. Almost all the householders in Göttingen take in students, but many landladies refuse to take female students on principle. A lot of them had moral scruples, others feared that their kitchens would be commandeered for washing, cooking and ironing or that spirit-stoves would be set up and ruin their rooms. It was very miserable to go searching for rooms and be met by a surly face which squinted through an opening in the door and muttered a few words of refusal. Therefore we had been in luck. The house was situated in a long, narrow little alley, the Geismarstrasse, which led out from the centre of the town to the Albanikirchhof—" Kirchhof" is the name given in Göttingen to the church-square, and our lodging was No. 2, immediately next to the square. The Albanikirchhof lies on the boundary of the old city, and stretching beyond it is the residential area where the professors and well-to-do people live. St. Albani is the oldest church, with a perfectly smooth façade and a massive tower. Three times a day the bells used to ring out the Angelus, that sign of its Catholic past which I heard but did not understand. On the very day following my arrival I set off on a tour of inquiry. Ever since my earliest childhood it had given me great joy to go exploring. Whenever Erna and I went out for a walk in Breslau or Hamburg on our own I used to say, " Today let's go where we have never been before ". And now I had a whole city to conquer, besides the surrounding countryside ! There was certainly enough to see. You need only go down the stretch of Geismarstrasse, turn right at the corner, and there you were in the market-place. Facing you was the beautiful Gothic town-hall, at the windows blossoming red geraniums which stood out so delightfully against the old grey stones. In front stood the Goose-Girl fountain by Schaper. Set a little away in a side street was the loveliest old house in Göttingen, the " peak " house as it was called, an old-German inn with carvings and bull's-eye window-panes. Leading directly northwards out of the market-place to the Weender Gate ran the main street of the city, the Weenderstrasse, which was filled by a throng of strollers in the afternoons. On the right-hand side towards the middle rose the great church-tower of St. James's, the very symbol of Göttingen—when viewed from a distance this tower, along with the two less stately towers of St. John's, set off the picture of the city. On the opposite side of the street are the famous confectioners, Kron and Lanz, where the best cakes are to be had, where professors and students (providing their grants are sufficient) take their afternoon coffee and read the newspapers. The last building on the right-hand side before coming to the Weender Gate is the centre of university life ; there the lectures are held. It is by no means a great monument and cannot be compared either with our old Leopoldina in Breslau or with the splendid modern buildings in Jena or Munich ; a simple, modest building, rather, with simple, modest work-rooms. It lies back a little from the street and is sheltered by green groves where the students wander for a few minutes in between lectures smoking their cigarettes. The adjacent Seminar building, both more modern and more elegant, stands on the corner of the Nikolausburgweg ; in those days it was completely new. Most of the seminars took place there—the philosophy Seminar right up under the roof, where I have found it in almost every other university I know. The Psychology Institute was entirely separate, being situated in the area of St John's church a little west of the market-place ; it was an old house with worn steps and narrow rooms. This spatial separation in itself indicated clearly that philosophy and psychology had nothing to do with each other in Göttingen. The Nikolausberg road ran eastwards from the city out of the Weender Gate and wound its devious way up the mountain-side. Once you had the last houses of the city behind you the charming little hamlet of Nikolausberg was visible above you on the mountain-top. Those in the know could tell you about the wonderful waffles which were baked by the hostess of the inn ; if you let her know beforehand you could walk up there after the burden and cares of the day and find a delicious and refreshing evening meal waiting for you. This I only discovered later. Rising up to the left of Nikolausberg is a bare hill with three wind-swept trees on it, which always reminded me of the three crosses on Golgotha. All this I caught a glimpse of during those first days, but on my first walk I was not able to go up the mountain ; instead I wandered on the plain, through the meadows, and got to know the peculiar properties of the Leineberg soil ; for you seldom return from there without thick lumps of clay sticking to your shoes. Even the paving in the streets is peculiar—a sort of asphalt which is alternately churned up by the rain or dried up by the sun—more often by the rain, for it rains a great deal in Göttingen. At that date the population was about 30,000. There were no tram-cars, and although their introduction was constantly under discussion until the outbreak of war, it became out of the question afterwards. The city's life centred round the university and the students ; it was a genuine university city, and not, like Breslau, a city which amongst other things had a university.

I was very much struck by the memorial-plates which were fixed up on almost every old house, recording the names of previous famous inhabitants. At every step one was reminded of the past ; the Grimm brothers, the physicists Gauss and Weber and the others belonged to the " Göttingen seven ", all of whom had lived here and made their mark, and were constantly brought to the minds of their successors. Also the ancient city ramparts have survived, covered with strong, tall lime-trees ; their fragrance used to waft into the lecture-rooms in summer-time (the lecture-hall being immediately next to the ramparts). And whenever I heard Heine mentioned in the lecture-hall I used to call to mind how he himself had once sat at these very benches, and how the ramparts of Göttingen must have come before his mind's eye when he spoke in his poetry about the " Ramparts of Salamanca ". I was always glad to go for a walk along the ramparts ; there was such a lovely view on one side towards the old houses within the city, and on the other side towards the villas and gardens stretching far outside. At one spot on the wall stood the little wooden hut in which the student Bismarck had lived.

Some days after my arrival Rese also came, and we arranged our accommodation. Between us we had two rooms, one in which we both slept and a larger one which we used as a common living and work-room. Early in the morning our landlady used to bring in hot milk and fresh slices of bread, and we would make up the cocoa ourselves. We used to meet again for lunch, which we usually took in a vegetarian restaurant kept by a South German lady and her three nice daughters. It was always very crowded. Several tables were pushed together to make one long table at which the English and American students sat ; their noisy yet innocent exuberance used to make the whole place rock. Whichever of us arrived home first in the evening from lectures would prepare a meal of tea and bread-and-butter, and so the one who came late would find the table set for her. I do not remember a single occasion during that whole summer of living so close together when any quarrel or disagreement sprang up between us. So far as her time allowed Rese used to attend my philosophy lectures, and I tried to interest myself a little in her mathematics. Still our courses of study were very different. In Göttingen it was the tradition to have no lectures on Wednesday and Saturday afternoons because the students, and occasionally even the professors and their daughters, used to go out for the dancing to Maria Spring. Only the philosophers, Nelson and Husserl, ignored this tradition. On Wednesday afternoon Husserl held his seminar, but on Saturday afternoon even we were free. All the same we did not go to Maria Spring, but out into the country, so long as the weather permitted. Beforehand we would write our weekly letters home as well as replying to our various friends' letters. If it was fine on Sunday we used to spend the whole day in the country, often staying there, as a matter of fact, from Saturday evening till Sunday evening. We wanted to get to know the countryside of central Germany, and Göttingen was a wonderful place from which to do so. On the south-east side the city nestles against a hill crowned by the Bismarck tower. From the edge of the city beautiful parkland stretches away towards the Göttingen forest ; one can walk for a whole day through the forest without coming to the end, and perhaps without meeting another soul. Göttingen people themselves do not go in for long walks. As we were setting off on a Sunday we used to see them drifting out in large numbers, but their destination was no further than one of the two large coffee-houses which lay some distance apart up on the broad sweep of hillside, " Rohn's " and " Kehr's " as they were called. If they wished to go further than Kehr's they would drive out in carriages. One could easily distinguish the townspeople from the students because they always wore hats, whereas the students went bare-head. But everyone would be loaded with a hamper of food ; because everyone took cakes out with them the inns did not provide any, and one had to be content with coarse country-bread and Göttingen sausages.

On longer expeditions we took our provisions with us in a rucksack and had our meals in a wood ; a loaf of black bread, a packet of butter, a slice of cold meat, fruit and chocolate—it tasted better than a dinner in the hotel.

Göttingen is also surrounded by woods and hills in other directions. There are beech-woods which used to glisten red and gold in autumn when we returned for the winter term. And from the surrounding hills the ruins of old castles look down into the valley. I had a special liking for the " twins ", two peaks standing close together, each of them crowned with a ruined castle. On the ridge between them was a modest inn with a chronicle of the counts of the " twins " who had once dwelt up there. Whenever I looked down into the valley I used to feel that I was in the very heart of Germany ; a dear countryside, the fields on the slopes carefully cultivated, the neat little villages and around them a wreath of green woods. It was almost as if any moment a marriage procession might emerge on the edge of the wood, as in Ludwig Richter's etchings.

On our longer journeys we got to know Kassel, and Weserland, Goslar and the Harz. At Whitsun we spent several days wandering through Thuringia. We climbed up from Eisenach to the Wartburg, went through the Dragon's Gorge to Hohen Sonne and later up the mountain-track to Inselsberg. On some stretches we used to go by train in order to be able to cover more ground. Of course Weimar was included in our programme, and that visit we were supposed to round off by inspecting the Free School Community at Wickersdorf. For the first few days we had glorious weather, and then on the third day (if I remember rightly) it began to rain in the evening. We had been on the road since morning and before nightfall we wanted to reach Illmenau, our last stop before Weimar. The rain came down harder and harder, the road stretched out further and further in front of us, our feet were refusing to go another step, and there was no sign of habitation. Rese was silent and depressed through sheer weariness, and so I did everything I could to remain in good humour. It must have been easily eight o'clock by the time we eventually reached a straggling village. Judging by the boarding-houses on the road-side it seemed to be a summer resort, but wherever we knocked it was the same—there was no room for us to stay. I screwed up courage to repeat our request at every house, but each time in vain. We spent a good half hour there going from door to door before we finally found a hotel which could take us in. The rooms for lodgers were actually in a separate building opposite the hotel itself. Whilst the beds were being made up we went into the guest-room where a good hot meal brought back our spirits. We asked our friendly host where we actually were. The name of the hole was Manebach. Manebach—it sounded so stretched-out, like the endless rain and the endless road. Already we had regained sufficient good humour to have a hearty laugh over it. As soon as our rooms were ready we slipped out of our sopping clothes into the warm beds. Now a new plan of campaign would have to be worked out. We pulled out Richard's beautiful military map—the relic of troop-manœuvres in Thuringia—which until this evening had guided us superbly. Whereabouts was Manebach ? Yes, there it was ! We were only one railway-station distant from Ilmenau. But we could not make up the loss of time now, and so we decided to cut out Ilmenau and Gickelhahn, and go to Weimar the next morning. Having our railway timetable with us we were able to make sure of the next train.

In Weimar we visited the stately Goethehaus at the Franenplan and the charming garden-cottage at Stern, and then Schiller's house with the heart-rending miserable little room in which he died. It was a Sunday, and crowds of sight-seers were strolling out there. As we were rather beat and foot-sore from the previous day's march we thought we were crawling like snails, but all the same we soon left the citizens of Weimar behind us. In the beautiful park of Tiefurt we had to sit down on a bench in order to transact a little poetic business : to count our cash. Before setting off I had drawn enough money out of the bank to last me the journey, but Rese had tried to be economical, and so had not brought enough with her. Now we reckoned that the common exchequer could no longer stand a visit to Wickersdorf, so we had to telegraph to cancel it. With what was left we had just enough to travel to Jena that evening and return straight to Göttingen the following day. I was very thrilled at seeing Jena, and felt much more at ease than in Weimar. You could search for its memorable places in complete peace, without great crowds pressing around you ; and you did not run into devoutly staring girls' boarding-schools at every turn.

After our return, when we went to deliver his military map back to Richard, we naturally had to give an account of our wanderings. We would have gladly held our peace about its unflattering ending, but Richard asked immediately about our visit to Wickersdorf. He had an uncanny knack of always asking about whatever we did not want to mention.

Rese and I had ventured on this journey on our own, but we almost always had a companion with us, Dr. Erich Danziger, an assistant in the Chemical Institute. Rese had made his acquaintance during her Chemistry Studies at Breslau, which was his home-town. He was a small, inconspicuous and somewhat awkward man, but Rese said that he had the most skilful hands in the whole Institute, and his help was always asked for whenever something required especially delicate handling. There was always an oppressed atmosphere about him, the result, no doubt, of his very sad home-circumstances ; his mother had been in a home for neurasthenics for many years, which meant that he and his young sister had grown up almost like orphans. Now he doggedly attached himself to us, since he had scarcely any other contacts. He was a good-hearted and faithful soul. It always depressed him a little that he had no entry into the philosophical world in which we lived.

Georg Moskiewicz arrived somewhat later than ourselves. He was considerably older than us ; in May we all had a celebration for his thirty-fifth birthday. Instead of living in student-quarters he rented two spacious and well-furnished rooms in the quiet church walk near the clinics ; which corresponded to his status as doctor of medicine and philosophy, and as a coming young tutor. Yet we also acted as his human supports. He seldom joined us on our expeditions because such ventures involved making decisions and he was not able to bring himself easily to do that. When he did come with us, however, he was as gay and frolicsome as a young boy, and it was very obvious that he had conceived a deep affection for Rese. But how could he ask her to attach herself to him when his own future was so uncertain ? He and I had in common a good friendship and similar philosophical interests.

With that, after many digressions, I have at last come to my main reason for setting out to Göttingen : phenomenology and the phenomenologists. In Breslau they had given me this piece of advice : when you arrive at Göttingen you go first of all to Reinach,[1] then the rest will look after itself. Adolf Reinach was a philosophy tutor. He and his friends, Hans Theodor Conrad, Moritz Geiger and several others, had originally been Theodor Lipps' pupils in Munich. After the publication of *Logische Untersuchungen* they had all insisted on Lipps ' discussing this work with them in his seminar ; and when Husserl was called to Göttingen they all followed him in a body (the year 1905) in order to be initiated by the master himself into the secrets of the new science. Such was the beginning of the " Göttingen school ". Reinach was the first of them to receive permission to lecture in Göttingen, and had thereby become Husserl's right-hand man, acting, above all, as a link between him and the students ; for Reinach had a wonderful way of dealing with his fellow-men whereas Husserl was helpless at it. Reinach was thirty-three years old at the time.

I carried out Mos' good advice to the letter. The very day after my arrival, I believe, I made my way along to No. 28 Steinsgraben ; this street takes you right to the edge of the city, and the Reinachs lived in the last house of all. Beyond it lies a great stretch of corn-fields through which a narrow foot-

[1] He joined up in 1914 as a volunteer and in 1917 died in battle. His wife and sister later became Catholics.

path leads to the Kaiser-Wilhelm Park, along the route up to the Bismarck Tower and the Göttingen forest. When I asked for Herr Dr. Reinach a fair-haired servant girl showed me into his study and took my visiting-card before calling him. It was a beautiful, large room with french windows, dark wall-paper and brown oak furniture. The two walls to the left of the entrance were entirely covered, almost up to the ceiling, with book-shelves ; to the right, opening into the next room, was a big sliding-door with panes of multi-coloured glass. The large corner between this door and one window was completely occupied by a massive writing-desk, beside which were easy-chairs set for the visitors. In the angle between the two walls of books was a pleasant corner set out with a table, a settee and several chairs. Hanging on the wall behind the writing-desk was a reproduction of Michael Angelo's " Creation of Man ". It was the most comfortable and tasteful study I had ever seen. Reinach had been married some six months previously, and it was his wife who had lovingly planned the whole arrangement of the spacious house, and supervised the work on it. Nevertheless I do not believe that I took in all these details on my first visit, for I had only been waiting a few minutes when I heard a voice calling out in joyful surprise from the end of the long passage. Someone came dashing along, the door was flung open, and there was Reinach standing facing me. Somewhat below medium height, and not strong, despite his broad shoulders, he had no beard but a short, dark moustache ; his brow was broad and high ; the intelligent brown eyes looking through his rimless pince-nez were, above all, kindly. He greeted me with winning affection, helped me to a seat, and then took a seat at his desk opposite me. " Dr. Moskiewicz has written to me about you. You have already gone into phenomenology ? " (He spoke with a pronounced Mainz accent.) I gave him a short summary of what I had done. He was immediately ready to let me take part in his " Exercises for advanced students ", but could not give me any more precise information about the day or the hour, because he wished to fix that with his students. He promised to mention my name to Husserl. " Would you like to meet some of the people in the Philosophical Society ? I could introduce you to the ladies." I asked him not to put himself out on that score, because Dr. Moskiewicz would take me there. " Quite ! Then you will soon get to know them all."

After this first conversation I was most thrilled and filled with deep gratitude. It seemed to me that no one had ever received me with such sheer goodness of heart. The affection displayed by near relatives and friends who have known me for years seemed self-explanatory ; but here was something quite different, it was my first glimpse into a completely new world. A few days later I received a friendly note to say that the exercises had been fixed for Mondays between 6 and 8. Unfortunately these hours were already occupied with something which I did not wish to miss, Max Lehmann's history seminar. Therefore I had to decline, though very unwillingly.

I did not immediately visit Husserl's house in order to introduce myself, because he had put up a notice on the board to say that he would be holding a preliminary discussion in the philosophical seminar which newcomers were expected to attend. There, for the first time, I saw " Husserl in the flesh ". There was nothing striking or overpowering about his appearance ; he was a typical distinguished professor. Of average height and dignified bearing, with a well-shaped, impressive head, his speech betraying his Austrian origins (he came from Mahren and had studied in Vienna). His cheerful kindliness also had in it something of old Vienna. He had just reached the age of fifty-four.

After the general discussion he called for the newcomers one by one. When I told him my name, he said, " Hm—Dr. Reinach has spoken to me about you. Have you already read some of my stuff ? " " The *Logische Untersuchungen* " [1] " The

---

[1] The first volume of the *Logische Untersuchungen* appeared in 1900 and proved epoch-making on account of its radical critique of the current psychologism and all other forms of relativism. The second volume followed in the next year. Both in scope and importance it went far beyond the first volume ; here, for the first time, logical problems were dealt with by means of that method which Husserl was later to perfect as the " phenomenological method ", and apply to every province of philosophy.

whole of *Logische Untersuchungen* ? "—" The second volume "
—" The whole second volume ? Really ! That is heroic "
he said smilingly. That was how Husserl welcomed me.

Shortly before the beginning of term Husserl's great new
work appeared, *Ideas towards a pure phenomenology and
phenomenological philosophy*.[1] It was to be discussed in the
Seminar, but, in addition, Husserl announced that he would be
" at home " regularly one afternoon each week so that we could
come and put our questions and opinions to him. Naturally I
bought myself the book immediately (i.e. the first volume of
the *Jahrbuch für Philosophie und phänomenologische Forschung* ;
it was the first volume of this journal, which was founded in
order to publish collections of studies by the phenomenologists). For the first " at home " I happened to be the
earliest arrival, and gave him my opinions. Soon the others
began to appear, all of them bursting with the self-same
question. The main reason for the tremendous excitement
caused by the *Logische Untersuchungen* had been its apparently
radical aversion from critical idealism either of the Kantian or
the neo-Kantian variety. It was regarded as a " new scholasticism ", because it did not begin from the subject and then
proceed to things : knowing was once more a process of
reception whose laws were received from things, and not—as
in Critical Idealism—the imposition of laws upon things. All
the young phenomenologists were convinced Realists. The
Ideen, however, contained certain passages which strongly
suggested that the " Master " was leaning back towards
Idealism. Nor did his explanations in discussion relieve these
suspicions. It was the beginning of that development in
Husserl's thought which led him to regard what he called
" Transcendental Idealism " as the kernel of his thought, and
to the implications of which he devoted all his energies
(though it is not to be confused with the " Transcendental
Idealism " of the Kantian School). This was a line which his
old Göttingen pupils, to both his and their sorrow, were
unable to accept.

[1] Usually referred to in German simply as *Ideen*.

Husserl's own house was situated on the edge of the town, on the road up to the " Rohn's " (the " Rohn's " played a great part in his philosophical discussions, for the place had often to serve as an example when Husserl was talking about how we perceive things).   The house was built in accordance with his wife's instructions to meet the needs of the family. In the upper storey was the Master's study, which opened out onto a small balcony where he used to retire to " meditate ". Its chief piece of furniture was an old leather sofa which he had purchased when he was a tutor in Halle after he had just been given a scholarship.   Usually I found myself sitting in a corner of the sofa ; and later, in Freiburg, our conversations about Idealism used to flow backwards and forwards between one corner of the sofa and the other.   Amongst his pupils, so long as he was not there himself, he was known as " the Master " ; he was aware of this and found it hard to tolerate. His wife was called Malwine and amongst ourselves we used to refer to her by this poetic name.   She was small and lean, her shiny black hair brushed smoothly back over her head, and her lively brown eyes, full of curiosity, used always to gaze out onto the world with a certain astonishment.   When she spoke her voice sounded sharp and hard, always as if she were calling you to task ; yet signs of good humour were rarely lacking and this somewhat reassured one.   But when she was there you were always rather on edge about what would happen, for she frequently caused embarrassment by what she said ; and people whom she could not stand fared very badly.   She also developed a pronounced liking for some people, however, and I personally have never received anything but friendliness at her hands.   How I came to deserve it, I do not know.   In later years it might perhaps have been attributed to the valuable services I was able to do for her husband ; but as a matter of fact she had always treated me kindly, even when I was a little, insignificant student.   Normally when I was with her husband she used to come in and exchange greetings with me.   She would regularly go along to Husserl's lectures ; though she later admitted to me that it was in order to count the number in his audience (as we had all known for long enough) ; philosophy left her cold. She considered it the greatest misfortune of her life that Husserl had had to live as a tutor in Halle for twelve years before receiving a chair. And even then he was not a regularly-established professor in Göttingen, since it was the Minister of Education, Althoff, an energetic and far-seeing though somewhat autocratic man, who had intervened personally to create the post for him ; consequently his position in the Faculty was extremely uncomfortable.[1] On account of these experiences Frau Malwine was determined to keep her three children away from philosophy. The oldest of them, Elli, was about my age, and she was studying the history of art ; in appearance she resembled her mother but her make-up was much gentler and more tender. Gerhart was a lawyer, but in later years would not tolerate the attempt to keep him from philosophy. Wolfgang was still at the grammar-school at that time, and wished to study languages, for which he had an extraordinary gift. He was his mother's favourite, and it was later that one got to know what a motherly heart she had—when she spoke about him after he had fallen in Flanders as a volunteer at the early age of seventeen. She once told me that she had never worried about Wolfgang's future, because she had always known that wherever he went he would bring happiness to those about him.

Both the Husserls were Jewish by birth, but had gone over to Protestantism early in life, and so his children were brought up as Protestants. The story goes—though I cannot vouch for it—that when Gerhart was six he was going to school one day with Franz Hilbert, the only child of the great mathematician ; Gerhart asked his young friend what he was (i.e. which denomination he belonged to). Franz did not know.

[1] *Translator's Note.*
No attempt has been made, throughout this translation, to reproduce the fine shades of meaning involved in such words as *Privatdozent, Dozent,* etc., which express academic gradings rather different from those common in Britain. Readers familiar with German academic life will appreciate the nuances without prompting ; those unfamiliar with it would require an explanatory treatise for which this biography is not the place.

" If you do not know, then you must certainly be a Jew."
The conclusion was incorrect, but very typical. Later Gerhart
very often used to refer to his Jewish ancestry.

During that summer Husserl lectured upon " Nature and
Spirit ", examining the foundations of the natural sciences and
the humanities. He was to deal with the same subject in the
second part of his *Ideen*, which had not yet been published.
The master had already drawn up a rough outline at the same
time as he did the first part, but had put off the job of preparing
it for the press to give himself time to bring out the new
edition of the *Logische Untersuchungen*. This was the more
urgent task since the book had been out of print for years and
was in constant demand.

Soon after Moskiewicz had landed in Göttingen the Philosophical Society held its first meeting for the summer term.
This was a select circle of Husserl's own pupils who gathered
together one evening every week to thresh out specific
problems. Rese and I had no idea how bold it was of us to
join this select group immediately ; but since Mos took it for
granted that we should go with him we thought the same.
Otherwise it might have been terms and terms before we were
admitted to this institution, and even then one was expected to
sit there listening for months before daring to open one's
mouth. But I chirped up straight away. Since Moskiewicz
was by far the oldest of us the chairmanship was entrusted to
him for this term ; but no one in the whole circle felt himself
so unfitted for the chair as he did. At the meetings it was
obvious how unhappy he felt in this rôle ; true, he did
preside at the table, but it was never long before the thread of
the discussion slipped out of his hands. Our meeting-place
was at the house of Herr von Heisler, a young landowner who
delighted in living at Göttingen, attending philosophical
lectures and enjoying personal contact with the philosophers.
He was very pleased to have us in his home, and not in the
least disturbed that his own contributions to the discussion
were allowed to pass unobserved because they were irrelevant.
His gentle, fair-haired wife endeared herself to us all much

37

more than he did. She was a daughter of the Düsseldorf painter, Achenbach, whose numerous paintings adorned the house. Whenever we arrived—often enough in real Göttingen weather with soaking coats and shoes—the servant would help us off with our clothes in polite silence ; but it was perfectly obvious that he was secretly shaking his head over these strange guests. He must have noticed many no less unusual incidents as he was handing out tea or wine (according to choice) in the feudal dining-room. I shall never forget how Hans Lipps, during a heated discussion, kept knocking his cigar-ash into the silver sugar-basin, until our laughter made him notice what was amiss.

The founders of the Philosophical Society were not all in residence at this time. Reinach had not been coming since being made a lecturer and getting married. Conrad and Hedwig Martius, now that they were married, used to live alternately in Munich and Bergzabern (Pfalz). Dietrich von Hildebrand [1] had moved to Munich ; Alexander Koyré [2] to Paris ; Johannes Hering [3] had to take his State Examinations sometime the next summer and had retired for peace and quiet to his home at Strasburg. However, there were still some people there who for terms had worked alongside these ideas and who were able to hand on the tradition to us newcomers. A leading light was Rudolf Clemens, a language-expert. His fair brown beard and his cravats, his soft voice, and eyes that were both emotional and roguish, all reminded one of the Romantics. His manner was friendly, but with a friendliness that did not inspire complete confidence. Fritz Frankfurter, a native of Breslau, was studying mathematics. His brown eyes expressed his child-like openness, his deep loyalty and goodness. Most of us found philosophizing a joy, but his joy had a specially amiable quality. Once he was telling me about Husserl's course on Kant, which I had not yet heard, when he suddenly stopped himself and said, " No, what follows is too

---

[1] Later a member of the Franciscan Third Order.
[2] He and his wife later came very near to the Catholic viewpoint.
[3] Now Professor of Protestant Theology in Strasburg.

wonderful for me to spoil it. You must hear it for yourself".
But the one who most deeply impressed me was Hans Lipps.[1]
He was then twenty-three years old, but looked much younger.
He was tall and slim, but strong, and his fine, animated face
was as fresh as a child's, as well as serious, his big round eyes
questioning like a child's. Normally he expressed his viewpoint in short but very firm sentences ; and if asked to amplify
his statement he would explain that there was nothing more to
be said since the truth was its own justification. Consequently
we had to be satisfied with that, and we were all convinced that
his insights were both profound and genuine, even though we
were not in a position to accept them entirely. Though he
found difficulty in expressing himself in words, his eyes and
his animated, unself-conscious gestures spoke all the more
eloquently. Unfortunately he could not attend our meetings
regularly that summer because he was both taking his Physics
Examinations and completing his doctorate in philosophy—
with a work on plant physiology. He was taking medicine
and natural science in order to fill in the time when philosophizing was not possible. He already had a varied career
behind him ; he had begun life as an interior decorator and
art-dealer but that could never have satisfied him. Still he
loved pottering, and his personality betrayed his unmistakably artistic qualities. Whilst doing his year's military service
as a dragoon in the life-guards at Leipzig he had become
acquainted with the *Logische Untersuchungen*, and that had
meant the beginning of a new life for him. That was what
brought him to Göttingen. He was the only one in the circle
who used to spend much time with Mos and really befriended
him—the others used secretly to make fun of his nervousness
and his eternal unsolved problems.

All those named so far were entirely absorbed in philosophy,
even though they were also studying other subjects. Some
others used to attend of whom the reverse was true ; their
special sciences were their main interest, but they managed to
fertilize them by means of phenomenology. For instance,

[1] Killed in the World War 1939-45.

there were the experts in German studies, Friedrich Neumann and Günther Müller, who were later to receive chairs in German studies at a comparatively early age.

The Philosophical Society for several terms included two ladies amongst its members, Greta Ortmann and Erika Gothe. They were considerably older than myself, both of them having spent some time teaching before deciding to come to the university. Both from Mecklenburg, Fräulein Gothe's home was Schwerin and Fräulein Ortmann's an estate on the land. The latter was a slim little creature, but she stamped around so ponderously that her coat was generally splattered high up with Göttingen mud. Similarly weighty strokes punctuated her conversation, and her pronouncements always sounded like solemn declarations, but what she had to say often seemed trivial to us. However, she rarely spoke, usually listening both in the seminars and at the Philosophical Society with an expression of misty piety in her big blue eyes. In her this seemed to me comical, though on the other hand I found Erika Gothe's attitude of reverent silence quite attractive. Fräulein Ortmann soon made it known that I did not enjoy her favour. Once later she became confidential and told me that Reinach had asked her in deep concern why she behaved in such an unfriendly way towards Fräulein Stein, who was so nice. The reason she gave, " She always talks as if it were simple, when these matters are really very difficult ". Even worse, Mos had asked me at the first meeting if I would look after the minutes, which I accepted without a second thought. None of the others seemed to take offence at my doing so, but were always friendly towards me and respected my remarks in discussion. Nevertheless Fräulein Ortmann's behaviour meant at first that my personal contacts with the whole circle remained rather restricted, because she and Erika Gothe seemed to be inseparable and it should have been the ladies' duty to put me into the swing of things. I did not mind this much during that summer because my Breslau acquaintances supplied my need for personal contacts. Besides it was only later that I learnt of the activities outside the Philosophical

Society and the University, and so I could scarcely tell that I was being excluded.

There were other recently introduced members of the circle besides Rese and myself. Betty Heymann was a Hamburg Jewess, small and somewhat stunted in her growth, her fine, gentle face rather spoilt by too large teeth ; her beautiful eyes were uncommonly clear and intelligent. She was a pupil of Georg Simel and intended to do her doctorate under him, but had come for just one term to get to know Husserl. Fritz Kaufmann was another with a philosophical past upon which he was prone to dwell with a certain pride. He had been studying under Natorp at Marburg and already had so much neo-Kantianism in his system that he found difficulty in adapting himself to the phenomenological method. He was the eldest son of an obviously well-to-do Jewish business-family from Leipzig, and since he had his younger brothers to take over the family business, he could devote himself entirely to philosophy and concentrate immediately upon advanced studies. Certainly he was the only one amongst us who had no need to plan his studies with an eye to his daily bread. In a circle such as ours, where no one bothered much about appearances, his elegant clothes quickly caught one's eye. We were all secretly amused once when the man beside him in the seminar, an American, very vigourously squirted the ink out of his fountain-pen, and Kaufmann was visibly concerned for his light grey suit. He spoke faultless pure high German without the slightest suggestion of his Saxon origins, whereas Lipps to his great mortification betrayed the Saxon in him with his very first words. (He was not proud of the fact, but always insisted that he was Prussian since he had inherited Prussian citizenship from his father.)

The day that we had our preliminary discussion with Husserl Rese and I set off in the afternoon for the Bismarck tower. As we were on our way, and were busy picking violets, Kaufmann caught us up ; he recognized us from our meeting in the morning and greeted us in a friendly way. " What a host of violets here ". And straightaway we began a conversation. I was amazed when he informed me that on his first visit Reinach had " almost thrown him out ", and had firmly refused to take him for his " exercise ". It had never struck me that the kindliness with which he had received me might be a personal favour. When I later took part in Reinach's " exercise " I realized the explanation. For all his kindness and friendliness Reinach was really revolted whenever he encountered signs of arrogance, and Kaufmann might have given such an impression on account of his self-consciousness. He spoiled himself by this attitude and a certain affectation in his speech, but I noticed fairly quickly that this was only superficial. So I made a point of teasing him mercilessly and ignoring the façade which he presented to the world. He used to look startled, as if something unusual had happened, but he gradually thawed out and ended by being quite unpretentious and affectionate.

There were also people in Husserl's seminar who were working personally with him but did not come along to the Philosophical Society. Soon after term began I was spending the evening with the Courants when Richard said, " If you are in Husserl's seminar then you must have met Bell". He was a Canadian. I had indeed noticed one or two Americans and Englishmen but did not know which one he meant. " He is the nicest student in Göttingen. You must certainly get to know him." Some time afterwards I saw a student standing on the drive in front of the lecture-building ; wearing sporting clothes and hatless, he seemed to be looking out for someone. There was something very attractive in his free and easy attitude, and I thought, " That is Bell ". And so it was. He was not often in the company of the other phenomenologists, because the Americans and English in Göttingen formed a colony of their own and kept very much together. Besides, he had a circle of friends who did not all specialize in his own subject—my cousin, for instance, who told me Bell's previous history. A native of Halifax and originally an engineer he had started philosophizing during his journeys into the Northern Arctic. He came over to study first of all in England and then in Germany. I remember Bell himself telling me that a review by Moritz Schliek put him onto the *Logische Untersuchungen*, and this drew him to Göttingen. He had already been there three years and was working under Husserl on his doctorate thesis about the American philosopher Royce. Although thirty-one years old, he looked very much younger.

In the Philosophical Society that summer we chose as our subject for discussion the second great work that had appeared in the *Jahrbuch*, and which had perhaps exercised a more powerful influence upon recent intellectual life in general than Husserl's *Ideen*. This was Max Scheler's work on ethical formalism (*Der Formalismus in der Ethik und die materielle Wertethik*). The younger phenomenologists had fallen very much under Scheler's influence, and many of them—such as Hildebrand and Clemens—adhered to him rather than to Husserl. Scheler himself was in a very bad state at that period. His first wife, from whom he was separated, had involved him in a court scandal at Munich. The damaging facts which came to light compelled the university to withdraw the *venia legendi* from him. Having lost his teaching post he was left without any assured income, and was living on his writings—generally in a modest boarding house in Berlin, with his second wife (Märit Furtwängler), though he was frequently away on travels.

Each term the Philosophical Society used to invite him to come and lecture for a fortnight in Göttingen. But he was not permitted to talk in the university, nor were we even allowed to publicize his addresses by putting a poster on the notice-board. We could only pass round the information by word of mouth, and we had to book a large room in some hotel or café for the meeting. Towards the end of term Scheler came. Originally his addresses were fixed for certain evenings of the week, but he did not understand how to divide up time, and it eventually turned out that we had to meet every day. When the official time was up he used to remain in the café for hours and hours talking to a smaller group. I only took part in these nocturnal sessions once or twice ; for despite my eagerness to seize on every stimulating thought something about them put me off ; it was the way they spoke about Husserl. Scheler naturally was sternly opposed to the idealistic deviation and was almost pontifical on the subject ; but many of the younger ones also indulged in ironic remarks, and such irreverence and ingratitude angered me. Relations between Husserl and Scheler were not altogether smooth. At every opportunity Scheler would insist that he was not a pupil of Husserl's, but had discovered the phenomenological method for himself. Certainly he had not sat under him as a student, yet Husserl was quite convinced of his dependence. They had known each other for many years. Whilst Husserl was still a tutor in Halle Scheler was living nearby in Jena, and they frequently met and carried on a lively exchange of ideas. Anyone who knew Scheler, or has even read his works closely, will know how open he was to suggestions from other people. The ideas flew in and fermented inside him without his realizing that he was being influenced ; and so he could say with a clear conscience that it was all his own doing. Husserl's reaction to this dispute over priority was an even deeper concern for his pupils. He took the greatest pains to instil in us precision and thoroughness, to cultivate a " radical intellectual integrity ". Scheler's way of throwing out stimulating suggestions, without ever following them up systematically, had something dazzling and misleading about it. As a result, whereas he was always discussing vital questions of importance to each individual personally, and especially calculated to move young people, Husserl dealt soberly with abstract matters. Yet in spite of this tension they each treated the other in a friendly manner during that time at Göttingen.

The first impression which Scheler made was one of fascination. Never again in any man have I experienced so unmistakably the " phenomenon of genius ". Out of his big blue eyes shone the light of a higher world ; his face was beautiful and his features nobly cut, although his life had left its scourge upon them. Betty Heymann used to say that he reminded her of the portrait of Dorian Gray ; that mysterious portrait in which the wasted life of the original draws its disfiguring lines whilst the man himself retains his unspoiled youthful beauty. He spoke with great emphasis, sometimes with dramatic gestures. He dwelt reverently and tenderly upon certain words of which he was particularly fond (e.g. " pure whatness "). If he was arguing about his supposed opponents he would adopt a contemptuous tone. Just then he was dealing with the questions which formed the theme of his recently published book, *On the phenomenology and theory of sympathy*. (*Zur Phänomenologie und Theorie der Sympathie- gefühle*). These were of particular interest as far as I was concerned because I had just begun to struggle with the problem of " empathy ".

Scheler in practical matters was as helpless as a child. I once saw him standing in the cloak-room of a restaurant and gazing at a row of hats ; he did not know which was his. " I think it's your wife you need ? " I said smiling. He nodded his agreement. When one saw him like that one could not hold anything against him—not even when he had done something which one would have condemned in other men. Even the victims of his waywardness used to stand up for him.

For myself, as for many another, his influence during those years was of great importance outside the bounds of philo- sophy. I do not know in which year Scheler returned to the Catholic Church, but it cannot have been long afterwards. In any case this was the time when he was overflowing with Catholic ideas, was propagating them with all the brilliance of his intellect and his powers of expression. This was my first contact with a world which had so far remained entirely unknown to me, and even though it did not lead me to the faith it did open up for me a whole region of " phenomena " which I could no longer blindly pass by. It was not in vain that we were continually being disciplined into gazing squarely at things without prejudice and learning to cast aside our " blinkers ". I was now freed from the strait-jacket of rationalist prejudice in which I had unconsciously grown up, and the world of faith suddenly stretched out before me. In that world lived people with whom I was in contact every day and whom I admired, and therefore it must at least be worthy of serious consideration. Yet I did not make any systematic enquiries into questions of belief because my mind was occupied with so many other things. I contented myself with remaining open to suggestions from my surroundings, accepting them and being affected by them almost without noticing it.

This account of my early Göttingen days needs to contain rather more details about my relationship with my kinsfolk. My cousin Richard Courant was then twenty five years old, recently married and now a tutor. His wife, Nelli Neumann from Breslau, was rather older than he ; she had studied mathematics with him, had gained her doctorate in that subject and had later taken her State Examination. Justice Neumann had hesitated for a long time before entrusting his only child to this young man with no secure income. Old Neumann was a thoroughly good and noble man, his very appearance dignified and inspiring confidence. Tall, slim, with light fair hair and blue eyes, he struck one as a typical German autocrat rather than a Jew from Posen (which he was). Nelli's mother having died when Nelli was only two years old, he had been both a father and mother to her ; he surrounded her with the tenderest affection and worked alongside her like a comrade. Their blissful life together was only disturbed by his mother-in-law whom he took into the house after his wife's death, although she was constantly tormenting him and the child with her moods. She died soon after Nelli was married. I have previously mentioned my cousin's hard upbringing ; he had risen entirely by his own energy and all of us harboured a profound admiration for his extraordinary gifts and his character. His wife's fortune afforded him an opportunity to lead the untroubled, joyful life of a young man for the first time. Like Anne Reinach, Nelli had taken the greatest pains to plan a beautiful and comfortable household for her husband.

THE STUDENT : BRESLAU AND GÖTTINGEN

The little house in the Schillerstrasse, where they occupied two storeys, lay on the southern edge of the city, looking out over gardens and fields. Their lovely home was thrown open to the most varied company. Richard loved to bring home unexpected guests, and he had a very wide circle of friends among both lecturers and students. He would even bring his pupils home with him when there was something they wanted to discuss. It was Nelli who had suggested my coming to Göttingen and she took me to her heart. Often I was invited round to dinner ; and the bathroom was placed at my disposal whenever I wanted it, for Nelli's greatest joy was to allow others to share the goods she possessed. She was cheerful and talkative, and yet the sort of person who really wants to get to the bottom of things. Ethical questions interested her particularly, and she never ventured on any undertaking without carefully weighing the reasons for and against it. She still attended occasional lectures, including one course at which we used to meet each week and afterwards walk home together. On the way she would enquire about all my activities, eagerly following the progress of my studies and visibly rejoicing that here was someone pursuing the career for which she was cut out. Housekeeping did not come easy to her, her whole upbringing having unfitted her for it. Soon after her wedding, when she came to Breslau for her grandmother's funeral, she recounted her many mishaps in housekeeping with great gusto, explaining that, " Things become more complicated the further removed they are from mathematics, and housekeeping is the furthest removed of all from mathematics ". Richard used to banter with her in that playful manner so typical of him. He and I were firmly united by our kinship, because although he would never admit it he was very much attached to the family, and was always asking how different members were faring. He was also glad to talk to me about his worries over his parents, just as he used to discuss them with my mother in Breslau. Like Nelli he showed a lively interest in the progress of my studies.

I had come to Göttingen for the sake of philosophy and

wished to devote most of my time to it ; but since I only intended to stay one term I wanted to make the best of it and meet historians and German experts other than the Breslau ones. Richard Weissenfells' course on " Börne, Heine, and the new Germany ", proved more of an entertainment than a task, and I even enjoyed the severe and greatly feared Edward Schröder by gaily regarding him as a " phenomenon ". He was a large, powerful man with a wide, greyish, beard, parted in the middle. It was his boast that he could speak a " natural language "—that of his native Hessen : though I myself thought he could with more reason be proud of his middle high German or old high German, and was always pleased whenever he read out to us one of the set texts. Like his brother-in-law in Berlin, Roethe, he was opposed to women studying and had so far refused to allow any women into his seminar, but I was present at his " conversion ". At the beginning of that term he was giving out seminar keys to the members of his seminar (each of us had to go out individually and solemnly promise never to take·a book home from the seminar library) when he announced publicly that from now on he would allow the ladies into the senior section of his seminar ; they deserved it for their industriousness and their excellent performances. He was an emotional person ; once in a lecture when he recalled a dead colleague the tears began to flow.

Another philosopher whom I went to hear, apart from the phenomenologists, was Leonard Nelson. Despite his youth— he was scarcely over twenty—he was already famous or rather notorious throughout Germany for his book on " the so-called problem of knowledge ". In this book he had " liquidated " every outstanding spokesman for modern theories of knowledge by incisively proving them all guilty of formal contradictions. When I attended his course on the " Critique of Practical Reason " his procedure was no more indulgent. He had two schematic diagrams to expose the contradictions ; they were chalked up on the board almost every period for some new victim, and were described by his ·classes as the " guillotine ". The only survivor on the battle-field was the post-Kantian Fries, after whom Nelson named his own philosophy. The net result of his ethics was a somewhat diluted categorical imperative. His every lecture was primarily a faultless series of deductions from several presuppositions, and although his conclusions were very difficult to refute I always had the impression that his presuppositions contained fatal errors. The great danger arose from the way in which he unhesitatingly put his abstract ethical theories into practice and demanded the same of his pupils. He had gathered around him a circle of young men who allowed him to lead them and directed their lives according to his axioms. Richard Courant, who had been strongly influenced by him at one time, used to say, " Just as the student corps goes for its meeting point, so the volunteers go to Nelson's courses ". He was a leader to his finger-tips ; his strong character, his unbending will and the silent passion of his ethical Idealism gave him power over others. There was nothing startling about his appearance. He was big and broad-shouldered, and walked ponderously ; the lids of his light blue eyes were heavy ; even his speech sounded heavy and rather weary despite the emphatic, decisive way he expressed himself. His face was ugly yet interesting, though most attractive was his thick wavy fair hair. In his speech he was very simple and dry ; he used to sketch his main arguments on the board, and both his handwriting and his diagrams showed that he had an artist's touch. There were few people whom he deemed worthy of his company unless they subscribed unconditionally to his philosophy and manner of life. Amongst these few was Rosa Heine, a Russian Jewess who had already been studying psychology in Göttingen for some years. I had made her acquaintance in the Psychological Institute, and one day as I was walking down the street with her we met Nelson. She greeted him, introduced us, and then said that we must have a talk. At which she went off and left us to go on alone. Nelson had noticed me at his course and was very anxious to hear my opinion of it because he knew that I was a pupil of Husserl's, and it was not often that anyone came over to him from that camp. He himself did not know

Husserl's writings in detail because, as he explained, it took too much time to get accustomed to their difficult novel terminology. I asked him whether he had not thrashed the matter out with Reinach, because that would be simpler. " Reinach is clearer, but less profound in consequence ", came the terse reply. With that our conversation was closed since we were by now in front of the Vandenhoeck and Ruprecht publishing house which he was heading for. Not until years afterwards did I meet him again in person.

At the Psychological Institute I heard Georg Elias Müller on " Psychophysics of visual perception ". He was a veteran from the old school which swore by the methods of the purely natural sciences. He worked with a precision which attracted me and seemed sounder than what I had learnt from Stern ; but this was a subject which I only enjoyed in the same way as theoretical physics or mathematics—I was glad of the instruction but knew that the work offered no scope for me personally. Müller was a rabid opponent of phenomenology because he held that there was no science but empirical science. Husserl on the other hand recommended us to go and hear Müller so that we should be familiar with the methods of the positive sciences. David Katz, who was working as a lecturer in the Institute alongside Müller, had devoted some time to phenomenology in his student-days, and from his lectures one could see that it was bringing its rewards. I came to know him personally through Moskiewicz and Rosa Heine (whom he later married). The set-up in the Institute was extremely curious. Müller had a whole string of pupils who were wanting to do their doctorates under him, although this was no easy matter, for months went by sometimes before you were given your experiments and the necessary apparatus. No one told anyone else what sort of work they were doing, and they used to watch furtively over their instruments in the laboratories at the old building in the Paulinenstrasse. At one time I acted as the " guinea-pig " for a Danish psychologist. I sat in a darkened room in front of a tachystoscope whilst various illuminated green shapes were passed in front of my eyes for a moment ; and then I had to describe what I had seen. Consequently I knew that it was something to do with recognizing shapes, but I was never given any further explanation. We phenomenologists used to laugh over this petty secrecy and were always glad to exchange our thoughts with each other ; we did not fear that someone might steal off with our results.

Apart from philosophy my most important work in Göttingen was with Mark Lehmann. In Breslau I had read through his great study on Baron von Stein and was very pleased to meet Lehmann in person. I attended his wonderful course on the Ages of Absolutism and Enlightenment, as well as one lecture on Bismarck, and was very greatly impressed by his European outlook. This he had inherited from his master, Ranke, and it made me proud to become Ranke's grandchild in scholarship. Yet I could not agree entirely with his viewpoint ; coming from old Hanover meant that he was strongly anti-Prussian, and his idea was English liberalism. This came out particularly in his lecture on Bismarck, in which his onesidedness prompted me to defend the opposite standpoint, so I became more conscious of the Prussian's good points than I had been at home, and was confirmed in my Prussianism.

I have already mentioned that I cut out Reinach's exercises in order to go to Lehmann's seminar with which they clashed. However, I soon regretted it when I discovered how much work it involved, because I had no desire to devote so much time to History in Göttingen. Our task for that whole term was to compare the present German constitution with the proposed constitution of 1849. The recommended books for this question were kept in a little study leading off from the History class-room, and there I spent many hours. But, most disconcerting of all, every newcomer had to undertake to write a most lengthy essay. The subjects were handed out in our very first period, two people (if possible a man and a woman) being set to work on each of the subjects. Even the time for delivering them was fixed on the spot ; our essays would be discussed at the seminars during the second half of the term. On these occasions the two victims had to take their places at the horseshoe table facing Lehmann and deal with the questions that arose. This was his chance to get to know each of us personally, because his eyes were so weak that he could not see us when we sat further away. At the beginning of every term he used to have the table marked out, with the name of each student fixed to a particular seat, so that he came to know us as functions of that seat, which we were not to change at any cost. My essay was entitled, "The realization of the party-programmes in the proposed constitution of 1849"; and my partner and I had our turn at the very end of term. Previously we had not known each other, but now that we were groaning under the same burden he used sometimes to accompany me home to talk the matter over on the way. He was an able and industrious person whose work I respected. Our task was a heavy one. One had to dig out precise information about the play of parties in the Frankfurt National Assembly and summarize their programmes, not all of which were easily accessible; most of them had been published in handy collections but there was one which I only got hold of in an old volume of newspapers from the Heidelberg library. And then one had to introduce some order into it all. During the whole term it rather oppressed me. Finally it came to our turn to have Lehmann shooting at us. However he did so in a most friendly way and declared himself very satisfied this time with the course of the discussion. But a tragi-comical difficulty arose—he had been unable to decipher all of my essay because the ink was too pale for his weak eyes. Another colleague (a student-teacher) gave me the good advice to visit Lehmann and ask him whether I should not give him another copy in typescript. So I made my way to his private house in Bürgerstrasse, an ancient house in the middle of a garden. There I was shown up to his study on the top-storey, where even the passage-way was piled high with book-shelves. Lehmann welcomed me most pleasantly. No, it would not be necessary to have my essay copied out; he had gathered enough about it from the discussion and was very satisfied.

Bless the ladies ! What would his seminar be like without the ladies, who are so industrious and conscientious ! This seemed to me rather exaggerated and I felt obliged to stand up for my male colleagues, saying that some of the men also worked. He was rather taken aback by this rejoinder, but then agreed, " Oh, yes, an odd one. Your partner, for instance, also turned in a good essay." And then came a great surprise. Lehmann acknowledged that the essay was good enough for him to accept as a thesis for the State Examination ; I would only need to amplify it here and there. This was not an exceptional privilege, because Lehmann used to allow good seminar essays to be counted for the State Examination ; but I knew nothing about it, since it had never occurred to me to do my examinations in Göttingen. What is more, I had always thought of the State Examination as something very remote, because I intended to do my doctorate first. Besides, I had only come to Göttingen for one term and counted on doing my State Examination in Breslau, although I must admit that as we drew nearer to the term-end I found it more and more difficult to imagine leaving Göttingen and not returning. These last months had not just been an episode but the beginning of a new lease of life. Help had now come from a quarter where it was least expected, since you could hardly abandon a completed thesis acceptable for the State Examination—even the people at home would see that. I believe that my plans were already laid out before I arrived home on the strength of this successful visit. First of all I had to clear up any possible misunderstanding with Professor Stern. After giving an account of the term I explained that I had done no work for my psychology thesis ; actually I had become more and more absorbed in phenomenology, and now my chief desire was to write a doctorate under Husserl's supervision. This was all received in good part, and Stern advised me to carry on with my plans. Nor did my relatives offer any objections. Now came the decisive step. I went to Husserl and asked to do a doctorate. " Are you ready for it by now ?" he asked in amazement, since he was accustomed to people's studying under him for years before they dared even suggest independent work. All the same he did not refuse outright ; he simply placed all the difficulties in front of me ; he demanded very high standards for a doctorate and reckoned on its taking three years. If I had the State Examination in mind, then he would strongly advise me to take that first, otherwise it meant having one's special subject too soon. It was worthless just to philosophize, because this demanded a solid foundation which one could only acquire through mastering the methods of other disciplines. That really spoilt my cherished plans and depressed me a little ; however, I did not show myself to be frightened off, and said that I wanted to go on under any condition. With that " the Master " became rather more accommodating. He would not object to my choosing a theme and beginning to work on it. If I was already so far advanced in my preparations for the State Examinations he would be glad to arrange my thesis for the State Examination so that it could be developed with a doctorate. The only question was what I should work on. About that I was not in doubt. Husserl in his course on Nature and Spirit had maintained that an objective external world can only be experienced intersubjectively (i.e. by a plurality of individual knowing subjects) who are in a position to exchange information with each other ; which means that such an experience presupposes other individuals. Husserl, following Theodor Lipps, named this experience " empathy ", but did not explain what it consisted of. Here was a gap which was worthwhile filling ; I wanted to discover what empathy meant. This did not displease the master, but at the same time he gave me another bitter pill to swallow. He insisted that I should work the thesis out as a commentary upon Theodor Lipps. He was very keen for his pupils to use this work as a means of classifying the relationship between phenomenology and other important philosophical movements of the day. He rarely did this himself, being too pre-occupied with his own thought to spend time commenting upon other people's. But this demand evoked no more enthusiasm in me either. As he used to remark smilingly, " I bring my pupils up to systematic philosophy, and then I wonder why they cannot settle down to works on the history of philosophy." For the first time he was adamant. I must take my medicine, i.e. apply myself to studying the lengthy series of works by Theodor Lipps.

This visit had proved a turning point. New plans must now be drawn up, but I was not long in doing that. If I had to pass the State Examination before my doctorate then I would get it off my chest as soon as possible. I had already kept five terms, but that was too few for me to present myself for examination, since the prescribed minimum was six. Nowadays most people took 8–10 terms because the regulation dated from a time when there was less material to be coped with. But my mind was made up ; in the coming winter I must have the outline of my work on empathy completed, and must have myself sufficiently prepared for my oral examination so that I could propose myself as a candidate by the end of term.'

IV

ASSISTANT TO HUSSERL

AFTER the summer vacation Edith returned to Göttingen without Rese Guttmann. In the course of the following terms her relations with Erika Gothe seem to have become friendlier, and here is what Erika Gothe says in remembrance of the lovely time which she and Edith Stein spent together :

' We went for many walks together and Edith was a lovable, quietly happy companion. We talked philosophy together and often argued over religious matters, being specially moved by such questions since our teacher, Adolf Reinach, had been converted to Christianity during the war ; moreover he had stated in black and white that he would only teach philosophy in future as a means of showing men the way to faith.

Besides, the Munich phenomenologist Max Scheler was at that time giving evening-lectures in Göttingen on religious questions, on the essence of holiness, for example. They were a real event in the little university town and must have given an impetus to the movement towards the Catholic Church which was then unmistakably taking place in the circle around Husserl and Reinach. This affected us a great deal, but both of us were still children of our world, and we never seriously considered being converted. Nevertheless for me, and probably for her also, this was the first impulse towards conversion.[1] '

[1] According to Edith herself her first meeting with Christianity was the Gothic Old High German " Our Father ", which was then included in the ordinary linguistics course. Afterwards, whenever she took this text with her pupils, she used always to speak of the deep impression it had made on her.

Edith's sister Erna modifies a little the almost frightening picture of the vast programme of work which the thirst for learning imposed upon her sister.

' We had both gathered around us a crowd of friends of both sexes in Breslau, with whom we used to spend our vacations in what was, for that time, great freedom from restraint and conventions. We had discussions about scientific or social matters in large circles or small friendly groups. Edith was our authority because of her infallible logic and her great knowledge of literary and philosophical questions. During our vacations we used to go into the mountains, full of the joy of life and adventure.

When, later, she went to Göttingen to study history and philosophy, she made many friends there, too, who remained her friends for life. But our old group was always the same for her and she was true to it.

After our State Examination in medicine my friend Hans Biberstein (now my husband) and I decided to visit Edith and Rese in Göttingen. It was an unforgettable time of lovely excursions and happy hours, while they tried to show us their beloved Göttingen and its beautiful surroundings at their best. We rounded it off with a glorious ramble through the Harz mountains.'

Edith threw herself into these pleasures and recreations with her whole soul ; in fact, with her fine intelligence she knew how to make them more intense. So she was a splendid companion, loyal, understanding, sympathetic, helpful to the point of self-sacrifice ; but nevertheless fundamentally detached. Edith Stein had only one love : knowledge. She had only one passion : books to deepen her knowledge. Her library had expanded so much in the course of years that, even after everything useless to the Carmel had been thrown out, she came to the convent with six huge cases of books as part of her dowry. But any such thought as this was still a long way off.

EDITH STEIN

The world war broke out. The lecture halls grew empty. Professors and students hurried to the colours. While Erna, who had begun her time as an assistant in Breslau early in 1914, merely went to another clinic, Edith felt herself compelled by sheer patriotism to discontinue her studies and volunteer for the Red Cross. After the required training she was sent to the contagious diseases ward of the war hospital in Mährisch-Weisskirchen. There, as everywhere, she threw herself into her work with her whole soul and her unique selflessness, and was loved by the sick and wounded as she had been by her fellow-students and teachers. In 1916 Edmund Husserl of Göttingen was called to a full Professorship at the University of Freiburg. He chose Edith Stein, his most discerning and therefore his favourite pupil, as his private assistant; she had taken her degree under him *summa cum laude*. Her doctor's thesis appeared in 1917; it dealt with the problem of empathy.

However, before following Husserl's invitation to Freiburg Edith Stein had another duty of a sadder nature to fulfil. Frau Reinach had invited her to Göttingen and requested Edith to arrange the philosophical papers left behind by her late husband. Edith was ready to do so immediately, but was really frightened of entering the house now that it had been robbed of Reinach's presence who had filled it with sunny warmth and overflowing kindness. Even more deeply she feared to find that Frau Reinach, whom she had only known as this fine person's radiantly happy wife, had become a broken, hopeless widow.

It turned out quite differently. What the atheist Edith Stein could only regard as a shattering blow of fate had been accepted by the Christian Frau Reinach as a part of her Master's Lay Cross. It was true that every fibre in her sensitive soul had been shaken by the sorrow, but this sorrow had at the same time laid bare the deepest sources of her nature, so that gratitude, the joy of sacrifice and ardent faith swelled up inside her as she drew the Cross closer to herself. The healing cross and its secret blessing had transfigured the sorrowful features of this admirable woman.

Edith never spoke to her about it, but the impression left on her by this experience could never be effaced. " It was then that I first encountered the Cross and the divine strength which it inspires in those who bear it. For the first time I saw before my very eyes the Church, born of Christ's redemptive suffering, victorious over the sting of death. It was the moment in which my unbelief was shattered, Judaism paled, and Christ streamed out upon me : Christ in the mystery of the Cross." Sister Benedicta revealed all this to a priest shortly before her death, ending with these words : " Therefore at my clothing I could express no other desire than that of being called in the Order, ' of the Cross '."

It is very surprising that the course of Edith Stein's later life did not lead her into the Protestant Church to which Frau Reinach and Edith's friend, Conrad Martius, both belonged. It almost seems as though she contemplated this course until a second experience in Bergzabern provoked a clear religious decision.

But for the moment, once she had performed this labour of love for her revered teacher, Edith went to Freiburg for Husserl's seminar, where her first job was to sort out Husserl's manuscripts and put them in order, which involved an almost superhuman effort. As is well known, Husserl's practice was to think stenographically, i.e. to write down his trains of thought in his own shorthand. With the result that tens of thousands of shorthand manuscripts lay waiting for the young assistant to transcribe and interpret, and to introduce some sort of arrangement into them. Heidegger and Koyré were both there to help her, but according to Frau Reinach, no one knew so well as Edith how to find her way quickly around these mountains of manuscripts and, with the expert's sure eye, dig out the hidden treasures. She found things there which Husserl had once laboured at and then long since forgotten, but whose importance she at once recognized ; away she went with them to the master, laid them on his desk and " ordered " him to work on them again. With her peculiar receptivity and her capacity for adapting herself to intellectual climates she soon realized that the philosophy students in Freiburg needed a different schooling from those in Göttingen, where Husserl's phenomenological method had become part of the tradition. It had never occurred to Husserl to smooth his new students' entry into his world of thought. But Edith appreciated the difficulties and started introductory courses which would permit their members to follow the lectures more easily and grasp them better, which accounts for an anecdote, passed on by Frau Reinach, and nicely illustrating Edith's affectionate wit. Someone asked Edith Stein, " I hear that you are running a philosophical preparatory seminar in Freiburg ? " to which she replied, " No, I'm running a philosophical kindergarten."

As well as her strenuous service as an Assistant Edith Stein managed to find time for her own work. In these years she composed her " Contributions to philosophical foundations for Philosophy and the Humanities ". It was a delight for her crystal-clear and penetrating intellect to glide amidst the deep and subtle reflexions of phenomenology. Her mind was at home there, as if in its proper element. The springs of this world's wisdom were opened up to her and she drank of them in full measure. Did this still her thirst for truth ? Perhaps it only became more tormenting through the knowledge that even philosophy is in no position to give unassailable answers to the ultimate questions.

In order to make up in part for the two years when her studies had been interrupted, Edith denied herself the joy of going home for her vacations in 1917 and 1918. But she was amply compensated by the visit of her sister Erna and Rese Gottmann. They went together on expeditions in the glorious Black Forest. A friend who took part in these rambles says :

' Though the war was weighing heavily on us all, and short rations might have had a bad effect on our temper, we were for the most part extremely happy. Sometimes we were at Husserl's lecture in the morning and then spent the night in the mountains. Once we were taken in by a farmer on the Feldberg, and it made a deep impression on us when this

Catholic householder said his prayers with his men in the morning and shook hands with each of them before they went out to the wood-cutting.

Living at close quarters with Edith, I often admired the way she was always cheerful—remaining unruffled when annoying things happened, and not getting annoyed, for instance, when we overslept and missed a beautiful sunrise ; or once on a walk along the Bodensee, when we went over the Hohenstiel, and on Insel Reichenau we were terribly hungry, because we couldn't buy anything on our ration cards. Edith took great pleasure in the splendours of nature. She was absolutely enraptured by the masses of flowers on the Belchen and the many-coloured butterflies. On the Blauen she was delighted because even at night from her bed she could look over the valley of the Rhine to the lights of Basel in the distance and the shimmering stars overhead. Unfortunately we could not go up the Turm, because of war-time restrictions.'

*   *   *   *

Within her own family Edith was equally generous with her love and warmth. A visit from her was an event, especially for the growing crowd of nephews and nieces. For them Aunt Edith was the essence of all that was kind and good. No one was so expert at inventing fascinating games, no one could tell a story so excitingly or, when necessary, intervene so effectively between them and their stern old grandmother.

Dr. Biennias tells of what happened when she went to visit Edith at the Stein home. With joyous shouts of " Auntie, Auntie," one of her little nephews was running down to the bottom of the stairs where Edith was waiting for him with arms outstretched. Then she led him to the newly arrived visitor, introduced him to her with every formality, all with an affectionate motherliness that Dr. Biennias had never suspected in her fellow-student.

At the end of the war, Erna Stein became engaged to her fellow-student, Dr. Biberstein, and Edith, of course, came to

Breslau for the celebrations. At the engagement party one of Aunt Edith's small nephews asked her gravely whether she would become engaged to him ? Then, he added quickly, they would share everything they had. His aunt understood at once, took her suitor on her knee and gave him the piece of cake to which she had just been helped. He ate it up with enjoyment, but when he had finished he was smitten with doubt. Hadn't he said they would *share* everything ? But he soon made himself easy, saying, " Well, we weren't really engaged." However, from then on he regarded his Aunt Edith as his fiancée, until his father undeceived him.

One of the other young nephews became ill. Aunt Edith was sitting in his room doing some writing when his mother came in to see whether he needed anything, to which she received the unexpected reply, " I don't need Mother or any nurses. Aunt Edith's enough for me."

When Erna got married in the summer of 1920 Edith composed poems for all her nephews and nieces, reviving all the gay memories of their childhood and youth.

These small details, often provided by Edith herself, show how deeply united she was with her family. Of her brothers and sisters, Paul had gone into a bank, Arno into his mother's business. Though both had long been fathers of families, their strong old mother, in true Old Testament fashion, subjected all her children, both sons and daughters, to her parental sway. None of them would think of doing anything important or abandoning anything without asking and receiving their mother's opinion. Apart from Edith only the eldest daughter, Else, lived away from Breslau. Edith tells us that of all her pretty sisters Else was the real beauty. She lived with her husband, Dr. Gordon, in Hamburg, where she was never properly acclimatized, but suffered from home-sickness for her dearly beloved mother. Frieda was also married, but did not find the happiness she had hoped for with her husband, Herr Tworoga. She left him after a year and returned to her mother's house with her child Erika. Rosa had no wish to get married. She stayed with her mother and in her own quiet, assiduous, willing fashion relieved her of the cares of the household. But even in her old age Frau Stein remained actively at the head of her flourishing business. Even at eighty she still kept all the business correspondence under her control. Her children and grand-children looked up to her with reverent awe.

It must have been a most strong and tender affection which united such a mother and such a daughter. And did Frau Stein, with her long experience and penetrating knowledge of human beings, see nothing of the change which was slowly taking place in her child's soul? Was there nothing in the philosophical studies of her " Fräulein Doktor " which showed her the way the wind was blowing?

V

THE CONVERT

AT this time, Edith's friend, Frau Hedwig Conrad-Martius, suggested that she should write an essay (" Plant-soul—animal-soul—human soul ") which was to cause a sensation among her colleagues. The whole work was an ascent, an acknowledgment of God, which seemed to show that she was already converted. Such was the opinion of her friends, but Edith was not convinced. Did she ever pray for the grace of faith ? She herself said later, " My longing for truth was a prayer in itself."

Her work and study with Hedwig Conrad-Martius and her husband had developed a real friendship between them, which often led Edith to make longer or shorter visits to Bergzabern, where her friends were running a large fruit-farm. Edith, who never shrank from practical work, found the fruit-picking, packing and grading a valuable mental relaxation. She threw herself into whatever was going on. During the day they worked ; in the evening they talked philosophy.

It happened, however, that during one of these holiday-visits both husband and wife had to go away. Before their departure Frau Conrad-Martius took her friend over to the book-case and told her to take her pick. They were all at her disposal. Edith herself tells us : " I picked at random and took out a large volume. It bore the title *The Life of St. Teresa of Avila, written by herself.* I began to read, was at once captivated, and did not stop till I reached the end. As I closed the book, I said, ' That is the truth '."

Day was breaking. Edith hardly noticed it. God's hand was upon her and she did not turn from Him. In the morning

she went into the town to buy two things : a Catholic cate-
chism and a missal. She studied them until she had mastered
their contents. Then for the first time she went into a Catholic
Church, the Parish Church at Bergzabern, to hear Mass.
" Nothing was strange to me," said Edith later. " Thanks to
my previous study, I understood even the smallest ceremonies.
The priest, a saintly-looking old man, went to the altar and
offered the holy sacrifice reverently and devoutly. After Mass
I waited till he had made his thanksgiving. I followed him to
the presbytery and asked him without more ado for Baptism.
He looked astonished and answered that one had to be prepared
before being received into the Church. ' How long have you
been receiving instruction and who has been giving it ? ' The
only reply I could make was, ' Please, your Reverence, test my
knowledge.' "

This was the start of a theological discussion ranging over
the entire doctrine of the Catholic Church. Edith never failed
in her answers. The priest, astonished by what he saw of the
workings of divine grace in Edith's heart, could not refuse her
Baptism. The formalities were arranged between them. Who
would be her sponsor ? Edith asked her friend Hedwig
Conrad-Martius to do her this service. They fixed her
Baptism for New Year's Day, 1922. The joyful catechumen
kept vigil during the preceding night and in the early hours of
the New Year the miracle of Baptism was performed in her.
As a thanksgiving she chose the name of Teresa. On the same
day she received the Sacrament of the altar, which from now on
was to be her daily food. Now she was a Christian, a child of
Mother Church.

And her mother according to the flesh ? The joy of conversion had not blinded Edith to the heart-break she would
cause. She went cold with fear whenever she thought of how
she must reveal her new life to the woman she loved so much—
a new life which threatened to swallow up everything bright
and warm and joyous in her previous existence. And it was
she, she herself, who had opened up this gulf. But there was
no help. Edith did not choose to escape by a written explana-

tion. Kneeling before her mother, looking her in the face, she said gently but firmly : " Mother, I am a Catholic." And the woman who had mastered her difficult lot with truly biblical heroism, and had by her own labour won security for herself and her children, felt the strength go out of her ; she wept. This was something Edith had not expected. Never had she seen her mother in tears. She had nerved herself for insult and abuse, she had even reckoned with the possibility of being cast out of the family ; she knew the righteous anger of which her mother was capable. Yet this strong woman wept ! Edith wept with her. These two great souls, knowing that they were intimately bound together by flesh and blood, yet recognizing in this moment that their paths had irreconcilably parted, rose up, each in the strength of her faith, to lay before God on the altar of her heart the victim demanded by His immutable laws.

A member of the family states :

'We were all dumbfounded by the news and did not know whether to be more astonished at Edith or at our mother's behaviour. Edith's step was incomprehensible to us all. We knew Catholicism only as it was to be found in the lowest social class in our East-Schleswig home, and thought Catholicism merely consisted in grovelling on one's knees and kissing the priest's toe. We simply could not conceive how our Edith's lofty spirit could demean itself to this superstitious sect.'

But a Catholic acquaintance of the Steins gives a further explanation, saying :

'I am convinced that the change which had taken place in Edith, and which lit up her whole being with supernatural radiance, disarmed Frau Stein. As a God-fearing woman, she sensed, without realizing it, the holiness radiating from her daughter, and though her suffering was excruciating she clearly recognized her helplessness before the mystery of grace. We could all see at a glance that Edith had become another person, though she clung to her people with as much love as before and did everything possible to prevent any alteration in their relationships.'

She stayed in Breslau six months for this reason. As before she went with her mother to the synagogue. On the Day of Atonement, which the old lady spent as usual in the synagogue without taking either food or drink, Edith even kept this strict fast with her. Her mother gazed with astonishment on her (as she thought) perverse daughter. To an intimate friend she confided, " I have never seen such prayer as Edith's, and the strangest thing is that she could pray with us out of her own book, and found it all there!" Edith had in fact brought her Breviary with her and prayed the Psalms with them. And when the Rabbi in ringing tones read out the words " Hear, O Israel, thy God is *one* !" her mother in her distress and love clasped her child and whispered, " Do you hear ? Thy God is but one !"

Poor mother ! She saw that her efforts were useless and yet could not desist from them. One day, when she came home from the town, she said sadly to Edith, " Well, I have chosen my burial-place !" These words were her last appeal to the tenderness of her child's heart. But against all these trials Edith stood unshaken as a courageous soldier of Christ.

On Candlemas Day 1922 she had received the Sacrament of Confirmation in the great Cathedral at Speyer. There she got to know Canon Schwind, who introduced her to his family and treated her like a father. Canon Schwind, a fervent and learned priest, was her director during these first years after her conversion. God had appointed him to guide the convert's fiery zeal into the paths of prudence, and to warn her against unconsidered excesses. It was necessary. The divine riches which the Church poured over her often carried her away with the serene rapture of the Holy Ghost.

She no longer felt at ease in Freiburg. Her innermost desire impelled her to the final surrender of a life devoted to God.

EDITH STEIN

But Canon Schwind, her spiritual adviser, would not hear of her entering an Order. However, he gladly offered to find her a peaceful occupation which would allow her to live in conventual surroundings, where she could apply herself undisturbed to her studies and at the same time deepen her spiritual life. This he found for her in the Dominican convent school of St. Magdalena in Speyer.

VI

"FRÄULEIN DOKTOR"

FROM over the enclosure door, as she crossed the threshold of the old convent building, she was saluted by the single word " Veritas ", the Dominican motto. Among the kind sisters in their timeless white habits she seemed to have been transported into a world that was not of this earth. Her soul breathed deep in the atmosphere of recollection and silence now all around her. This was the right framework for the new life which she had resolved to begin. It was to be divided between God and the duties she now undertook towards her pupils. But she had in mind a work to occupy her free time which was to bring immeasurable profit to her soul, now at last really hungering after eternal life : the study of St. Thomas Aquinas.

She came to an arrangement with the Dominican Mother Prioress by which she would have a quiet room and the ordinary convent food. The sisters themselves regarded her as an angel sent to their rescue in their hour of need :

' We had just opened the new daughter-house in Mannheim, the first one to have senior schools. These were to open immediately after Easter, 1923. The Principal of the teacher's course was transferred there. We could find no suitable substitute to take the German classes which she had taught. Along came Fräulein Stein. She took over the German classes in the teacher's course and in the Girls' School, and guided her pupils calmly and safely through their examinations. Her educational work was very fruitful ; she quickly won the hearts of her pupils. To all of us she was a shining example whose effect we still feel to-day. In humility and simplicity, almost unheard and unnoticed, she went quietly about her duties, always serenely friendly and accessible to anyone who wanted her help. And not a few did. She took an interest, too, in the convent's rising generation, and gave the young Sisters and Postulants private lessons to prepare them for their examinations. And then she was always busy with her intellectual work. God alone can know to how many people she gave her help, advice and direction, how often she came as an angel of charity to the relief of spiritual and corporal need. The pressure on her was often great. Her correspondence was very extensive. But she always had time for others. She was acting on a principle which she once expressed thus in a letter : " As to one's relationship with people : our neighbour's spiritual need transcends *every* commandment. Everything else we do is a means to that end. But love is the end itself, for God is love." The Fräulein Doktor kept entirely to the daily routine and way of life of the nuns. She had her place in the choir of the convent's church, which she occupied often and for long periods at a time. She had a good eye for opportunities of giving welcome assistance where it had not even been asked. On great feasts, for instance, when the nuns were all much in demand, she used to go into the kitchen to help the maids with washing up the dishes. So the years went by, every day filled to the very brim.'

The philosopher, then, had become a teacher. But a teacher in the widest sense of the word. Her ideal was that the children should receive from their convent education the strength to live their lives in the spirit of Christ. She wrote about this to a nun :

' The most important thing is that the teachers should really have Christ's spirit in themselves and really embody it in their lives. But it is also necessary for them to know the life into which the children are going. Otherwise there is a great danger that the girls will say to themselves : " The Sisters have no idea of what the world is like, they couldn't prepare us for the problems which we now have to solve "—and that then the whole thing will be thrown overboard as useless. You have the personal advantage that you did not enter too early and were in the Youth Movement. This means that approaches are open to you which others miss. But also one must keep one's feelings lively. The younger generation of to-day has passed through so many crises that they cannot understand us any more. But we must try to understand them, and then perhaps we shall be able to help them a little.'

As to what she meant by helping, an example will show how wisely she was able to give encouragement without in any way compromising the truth. She writes to a student :

' The most helpful thing, in the present problem, will be if I tell you frankly what I think of your abilities. You are not outstandingly gifted like your sisters. And of course it is a little oppressive to have such people always at your elbow. But you have a vigorous reasoning power, to which, in prin- ciple, everything is open. Only you work slowly and have difficulty in expressing yourself, so that you will never achieve brilliant successes—especially in examinations. But you will always produce something useful. You need not measure what you understand by what you are able to say. What you have taken in does take root, and is fruitful both for yourself and others, even if you can put none of it into words. But you will gradually learn to express yourself more easily. If we put ourselves entirely in God's hands, we may have confidence that He can make something of us. It is for Him to pass judgement. We do not need to examine and weigh ourselves. And do believe that those people whom you " would like to know", who seem to you so much nearer the ideal of a Christian, seen from within, are just as wretched, just as unsure of themselves as you.'

Just as she knew how to encourage the timid she had the

happy knack of suggesting valuable lessons to the youthfully self-confident. One of her pupils says, " I already had my final school examination behind me, I was very sure of myself and had a great opinion of my own ability. For the oral examination in German a small, quiet young woman came in, made me read out a set text and then began a searching examination on it of a kind which I had never experienced. I failed completely to meet it and grew very silent. My feeling as I came out was ' You've never met anything as clever as *that* before.' "

She must have been most deeply loved by her pupils. Let us listen to one more of her " children " :

' Unfortunately, I was only at St. Magdalena's for one year. We were the seventeen-year-olds, and the Fräulein Doktor taught us German. She really gave us everything. We were still very young, but none of us has forgotten the charm of her personality. We saw her every day at Mass in her place in choir, and we began to get an inkling of what it means to bring faith and conduct into perfect harmony. To us at that critical age she provided a pattern simply by her bearing. I would not be able to repeat a single thing she said, not so much because they have not stayed in my memory as because she was a still and silent person who led us only by what she *was*. And how she came down to our level in class so as to introduce us to everything involved in the study of German. " First weigh, then dare " ; " Character is destiny " ; " I am not a book to be read and understood, I am a man with all his contradictions "—these were the essay-subjects she gave us and illumined for us from the vantage-point at which she stood. In her criticisms she was a perfect combination of kindness and fairness. We never saw her other than calm, gentle and quiet. That is how she always came into the classroom, and how she bore herself every week, during a recreation-hour which otherwise we spent with the Sisters. She wanted to be with her pupils during their free time, too—though she had to take this hour from her own free time which she must have needed to rest herself. And how cheerfully she would then give in entirely to whatever games we wanted to play ! Silly games of forfeits, such as we at our age loved. I can still see the sweet, courteous, motherly smile on her face as she joined in our childish pleasure. But no one was disobedient, even in thought, when she was there. It was she who, in her generosity, won for us strictly-controlled girls our first visit to the theatre. It was Shakespeare's *Hamlet*. We saw the play through her eyes, for she had thrown open the great English dramatist's world to us. Her heart stood wide open for everything noble and beautiful to take its place beside her union with God. That is how she stands before us still.'

And another :

'I saw Fräulein Dr. Stein for the first time in March 1926. She tested me in grammar for the training-college entrance-examination. She asked me if I was more familiar with the Roman script than the Gothic. However, I was not happy with my grammar at all, because it was already nine years since I had left the elementary school. I did my test very badly, but she remained absolutely calm and friendly all the same. She made a very deep impression upon me ; her appearance was refined, delicate and womanly. Not until some weeks later did I learn more about her life, from the pupils in the top-class. Everyone loved her and considered her the best and cleverest teacher in the school, as well as the fairest. One of the older pupils put it to me in this way : " You can't tell any longer what kind of temperament she has, because she has become perfectly balanced." Actually she had an excitable temperament, because on one occasion—about four years later, I imagine—she left our class before the end of the period because we were unable to construe a phrase. We were left utterly dismayed. Nor could she understand why we were so unversed in the Old Testament, for we had only been given the extracts in the Eck-Bible. She herself had the whole of the scriptures at her finger-tips, and every day used to say the office. As we knew, she came into our Church through studying the works of St. Teresa, for whom her admiration and devotion were plainly visible. I was often amazed at the profound humility of her fine mind, and even more at her unruffled friendliness and modesty towards everyone. Before I had moved up into her class I fell ill and was in bed near her room ; and although only the nursing Sister was supposed to visit me, Fräulein Doktor came to give me Mescheer's St. Aloysius and Eichendorff's immortal *Taugenichts* to read. On one outing I had the good luck to be sitting next to her ; she peeled an orange and offered me a half with the utmost kindness. Apart from a card which she wrote to me later, these were the only occasions when I had personal dealings with her.

There was something about Fräulein Doktor that made her difficult to approach, she was too distant—perhaps too intelligent and intense, which made us all rather shy of her. Yet I trusted her completely as my teacher ; in my school-work, so long as only she saw it, I had no hesitation in setting down my innermost feelings and personal viewpoints. I felt very deeply : here you could say everything, be open and truthful about everything without being misunderstood. When correcting our essays she was extremely painstaking as well as strict ; her comments were very learned and interesting, and went into great detail without ever becoming pedantic, for she never hurt anyone or squashed them. Those periods with Dr. Stein are amongst the dearest memories of my stay in the training college ; my life was full of sorrow at that time and her periods were like rays of light in the darkness. And when I had to leave for a new post what I missed most were my periods with her.

Fräulein Doktor was a personality, a human being in the fullest sense, with no narrowness or pretence. Her natural, social and religious endowments had all been integrated in complete harmony.

May she, who has completed her course, pray for us, that

we may live as she did and labour for our unhappy Fatherland, which she loved truly with all her heart.'

The last witness to be called is a young teacher from Speyer :

'I saw the Fräulein Doktor for the first time from my class-room window as she went across the court into the seminar with a pile of books under her arm. I was so struck by her personality—though I did not know in the least who she was—that I have never forgotten that first impression. Later on I entered St. Magdalena's and therefore had the chance of going to the lectures which she gave to the Sisters. Later still I got to know her personally and spent many happy hours with her, as she gave me Latin lessons and some instruction in English and French. When it was fine we used to meet in the convent garden—a flag at her window, which I could see from the noviciate corridor, let me know that she was waiting for me out of doors. With very few words—just by her personality and everything which emanated from her—she set me on my way, not only in my studies but in my whole moral life. With her you felt that you were in an atmosphere of every-thing noble, pure and sublime which simply carried you up with it.

To see her praying in church, where she often knelt motion-less for hours at a time, besides the times of the services, was an impressive sermon. And with it all she was so open and so simple. There were always great goings-on in her room before Christmas. There was a surprise for everyone in any way connected with her, all beautifully wrapped up. And what big parcels found their way secretly to the poor in the town ! I do not know how she got hold of the addresses for it. It was the Sister who looked after her room who told me about it. Before the Feast of Christ the King was kept for the first time, she translated the new Office and read it out to the assembled nuns. That was a glorious and unforgettable hour.

She visited me once in Würzburg. We used to go together to Matins at the Carmel nearby. When I could no longer kneel and had to sit down, she knelt through the whole long office without flinching.[1] '

Edith Stein had retired, then, from public life into the quietness of a provincial town and the limitations of a round of every-day duties. Was that what God wanted of her? Looking back on these days in 1928, she wrote :

' During the time immediately before my conversion, and for a long while after it, I thought that leading a religious life meant giving up every earthly thing and living only in the thought of divine things. I gradually learnt to see that in this world something different is required of us, and that even in the contemplative life the connexion with the world is not to be severed. It was through St. Thomas that it first dawned on me that it was possible to pursue learning in the service of God, and not until then could I bring myself to go on again seriously with intellectual work. I think, even, that the deeper anyone is drawn into God, the more he must go out of himself in this sense, i.e., out into the world, to carry the divine life into it.'

Working with St. Thomas, then, according to her own words, built a road for her back to philosophical work. She found herself resolving the tension between the intellectual world of Thomism and the intellectual world which had hitherto formed her thinking. This tension produced an essay in Husserl's Year Book : " Husserl's Phenomenology and the Philosophy of St. Thomas Aquinas. Dedicated to Edmund Husserl in Commemoration of his Seventieth Birthday " (Verlag Niemeyer, Halle, 1929).

As a return gift Husserl sent her his *Formal and Transcendental Logic* in the summer holidays of 1929. But on account

[1] Edith Stein asked to be admitted to the Carmel *Janua Coeli* in Würzburg but was refused.

of her own work she was not able to settle down to study it before the spring of 1930, by which time she had already visited Husserl personally. It was the first time since her conversion ; in between lay the significant changes of the last eight years. She herself writes of this first re-encounter with her revered master :

'I was able to speak to him openly, without the least restraint. His wife was also present, and whenever she expressed her incomprehension he would reply so graciously and understandingly that I scarcely needed to add anything. Yet I believe that one must beware of illusions. It is good that we should be able to discuss ultimate questions with him so freely ; but it heightens his own responsibility as well as our responsibility for him. Prayer and sacrifice are much more important than anything that we can say to him, and they are— as I have no doubt—very necessary. There is a lot of difference between being selected as an instrument and being in a state of grace. It is not our business to judge, and we must always trust in God's unfathomable mercy, but this should not lead us to gloss over last things. After every encounter in which I realize my inability to influence others directly, I become more intensely conscious of the urgent need for a personal *holocaustum*. The decision is pointed ever more sharply to, *hic Rhodus, hic salta*. It may seem very much as though our present way of life is inadequate—what do we ultimately know about this ? Except that we are here at this moment so that . . . ? ? ? ? '

But the world had not forgotten her. The Catholic world, in particular, had begun to notice this young convert and her published writings.[1] She was urged on all sides to undertake lectures on educational, philosophical and religious subjects. Her lecture in Lüdwigshafen on " The proper dignity of woman and its importance in the life of the nation " laid the

---

[1] To be found in Edmund Husserl's Year Books for Philosophy and Phenomenological Research.

foundation for her fame as a speaker. In Heidelberg she delivered a lecture (very well received) on a theme from St. Thomas. She was invited to Freiburg, Munich, Cologne, Zürich, Vienna and Prague. Her greatest success was at the meeting of the Akademikerverband in Salzburg in 1932, where she spoke so convincingly about woman's vocation that this evening was the climax of the whole congress. She made two friends on this occasion who remained faithful to her even unto death : Dr. Waitz, Prince-Bishop of Salzburg, and Professor Peter Wust. The extraordinary modesty of her bearing was an occasion of astonishment as soon as she appeared, and the organizers of these lecture-meetings even considered it neces- sary to announce that the audience must not be misled by the youthful appearance of the lecturer, who was in fact thirty-six years of age. Indeed, the carriage of her slim figure, the soft colouring of her fine face, her thick hair gathered simply into a knot on her neck, and, above all, the light in her dark eyes would have done credit to a twenty-year-old. Nothing in her features betrayed her Jewish origin. She dressed to suit the occasion, but always with simplicity. So she would stand at the rostrum, quietly confident, her voice clear and easily audible, using no gestures, no special effects, as though delivering an academic lecture. Sometimes her success was overwhelming and the publicity that surrounded her almost dangerous. But while everyone was still speaking of her and the newspapers publishing her speeches, she would be back at Speyer, sitting over her pupils' exercise-books, as though nothing had happened. The centre of her life was in God, and could not be disturbed by human praise or blame. Those who spoke to her felt that she would dedicate herself entirely to Him.

Since her conversion the monastic life had been the silent desire of her heart. But on every occasion that she raised the matter in her confidential talks with Canon Schwind he advised her that the time was not yet ripe. She believed him, and left her direction in his hands. What a hard blow it must have been for her childlike trustful heart when one mellow autumn evening the news ran like wildfire through Speyer that Canon Schwind, the Vicar General, was dead. It was a Saturday, the 17th September 1927. That evening, as usual, the Vicar General had set off for the Cathedral to hear confessions. In the confessional he had had a stroke which caused his sudden death. How deep her affection and gratitude towards him had grown comes out in the obituary notice which Edith Stein published in the Innsbruck Clergy Review.

' Our reverend father, Canon Schwind, whom the Eternal High Priest has taken to himself after 51 years of richly blessed service in the priesthood, always had great faith in the powerful inspiration which souls derive from reading vivid descriptions of saintly lives . . . though even when the work was not describing a saint, so long as it lit up the secret riches and profound temptations of human beings, his experience and love of mankind enabled him to draw out its treasures. He and I used to find relaxation sometimes in reading together during our scanty leisure time, and the last book we were going through was Grisar's *Life of Luther*.

He was always glad whenever he came across some fresh observation to fill in his picture of " Dr. Martinus ". He looked upon this book as a masterpiece precisely because it contained a wealth of apparently trifling, yet concrete facts which brought Luther vividly before one's eyes.

More than once Cardinal Newman has emphasized that it is relatively easy for us to develop one aspect of our Christian life, strictness, or gentleness, seriousness or cheerfulness. But truly Christian perfection is only attained when these contrasted virtues are exercised in unison. Canon Schwind satisfied this condition in full measure. I have heard it said that he had a reputation for being just—but strict, a judgment that immediately astonishes anyone who knew him well. Yet if one reflects for a moment one can understand it. From youth onwards the guiding-thread of his life was the strict fulfilment of duty ; he had the very highest conception of the priesthood and never spared himself in his faithfulness to that ideal. No doubt he fulfilled his office as Vicar General with this ideal in mind, for he certainly never deviated one hair's breadth from his principles ; and it is quite likely that anyone with different opinions would consider his attitude unbending and strict. But, equally certainly, whenever he had to hurt anyone by a word of blame or by refusing them something, it was only after he had tormented his own gentle heart over it. He was never happier than when he could conscientiously follow the promptings of his kind heart, as anyone knows who went to him with some request. And how he gave you his undivided attention, listening to every word that you said ! If it was a question of making the right decision in a difficult situation a picture would immediately spring before his mind's eye of the person involved, whom he had never seen ; and his advice nearly always hit the nail on the head. If there seemed any chance that he might help in the matter he would do so without being asked. Nor did he expect to be thanked ; and if one ever ventured to do so, the reply would come " I am doing no more than my duty and, as far as I can see, not even that." And he was ready to help everyone, without exception, including people unknown to him personally, whose need or distress he had heard of at second hand.

In his spiritual direction he was calm, firm and prudent. He relied upon his deep knowledge of human beings and his years of apostolic experience, yet his penetration remained gentle through utter reverence before the workings of God's grace in the soul. Whenever he found a soul responsive to God's demands he would show boundless trust, leaving it alone and refusing to interfere. In such cases he would even encourage proposals which from outside must have seemed audacious and questionable. He possessed an unshakable confidence in the ways of divine Providence and the power of prayer ; therefore in situations where every human suggestion was inadequate he could always strengthen souls, bringing peace and consolation.

His own soul was securely rooted in eternity ; it seemed

that he scarcely knew how to view things other than *sub specie aeternitatis*, which endowed his personality with a deep and saintly gravity. You could see this from his tall dignified figure and the recollection in his impressive face when you met him in the street or visited his study. Yet as soon as he recognized anyone a warm, cheerful smile would light up his serious features. And his child-like gaiety used to sparkle whenever he was entertaining guests at his table ; with infectious spontaneity he would tell stories about his student-days as if they had happened only yesterday ; and how intensely absorbed he would listen whenever some widely travelled, intelligent man was describing the ebb and flow of events in the wide world. Many a Sunday, if he had no calls of duty, he was still to be found chatting over the tea-things when the bell rang for dinner.

Strict and kind, serious and gay, dignified and humble, his soul brought these many contrasting shades of character into harmony because they reflected his pure love for God. To be a servant of God ; that expressed his purpose in life, the nobility and responsibility of which he was always conscious. He prayed his office joyfully and devoutly, never curtailing it no matter how busy he was. Also he used to introduce lay folk to the office when he found them in love with the beauty of the liturgy and longing, like him, to share more intimately in the life of the Church. Daily meditations upon divine truth and good spiritual reading contributed indispensable nourishment for his interior life ; this nourishment he gladly shared with others, and his well-stocked library was open to all who could use it. No other book was so dear to him (apart from the Scriptures and the Breviary) as the *Imitation of Christ*.

With the death of Canon Schwind a good and faithful servant has entered into the joy of his Lord. In the *Kirchenverordnungsblatt* a tribute from his Bishop has already appeared, full of gratitude for the departed Canon's services. The Theological Faculty and the seminary in Innsbruck may well be proud to count this noble soul and model priest amongst their former pupils (1873–75). May he be a model for the younger generation, and for all of us a faithful intercessor with the Father. " *In pace Christi vivat.*" '

But God did not leave Edith Stein without a director for long.

VII

BEURON

THE development of the liturgical movement had brought the Abbey of Beuron to her notice; following a suggestion from her friend Father Erich Przywara, S.J., she had gone there for Holy Week and Easter, in 1928. With all the capacity of her sensitive nature she had contemplated and lived through the marvellous mysteries of the Passion and Resurrection of Our Lord. She was given great graces about which she would never speak. She gave thanks to God with the decision to go every year for Easter to this hallowed spot, so long as she was able. Beuron became her spiritual home.

At her first visit she asked for a short interview with Abbot Raphael Walzer. This meeting proved to be of decisive significance. In the young Abbot, who with his monastic *hilaritas*, was the embodiment of the joy of the religious life, Edith saw the ideal type of Benedictine monasticism. He recognized her for " one of the greatest women of our time ", and later wrote this testimony of her : " I have seldom met a soul which united so many excellent qualities ; and she was simplicity and naturalness personified. She was completely a woman, gentle and even maternal, without ever wanting to ' mother ' anyone. Gifted with mystical graces, in the true sense of the word, she never gave any sign of affectation or a sense of superiority. She was simple with simple people, learned with the learned yet without presumption, an enquirer with enquirers, and I would almost like to add, a sinner with sinners."

This is a judgment of the greatest value, because Edith

allowed no other priest to see so deeply into her interior life, nor confided her aspirations to any other with the same child-like openness as to Abbot Raphael. She thought of herself as his daughter, and would often say jokingly that she would have liked best to become a Benedictine. Abbot Walzer, for his part, would assure her that he already had in mind where he would send her in that event. Seriously, however, the Lord Abbot set himself firmly against his spiritual daughter's constantly renewed longing for the monastic life. As he saw it, her task was to use the rich talents the Lord had given her in the commerce of life, making them fruitful for the salvation of many. So he spurred her on to refuse none of the opportunities for this which might be offered. Lectures, publications, commitments, journeys, and work multiplied accordingly, and one wonders how this woman, devoting a great part of her day and night to prayer—she recited the Office daily from the time of her conversion — could carry out such a programme.

She herself gives the answer :

' I use no special means to increase my working time. I do as much as I can. What that is plainly increases with the number of things to be done. When there is nothing urgent on hand, the limit comes much sooner. Heaven surely understands economy. That things do not in practice run smoothly according to the laws of reason is due to the fact that we are not pure spirits. There is no sense in rebelling against it, it is merely necessary that one should in fact have a silent corner in which to converse with God as if nothing else existed—every day. The early morning seems to me to be given for this, before the day's work begins. Further, that one should there accept one's special mission, this too preferably each day, and not choose it. Finally, that one should see one's self entirely as a tool, and those powers especially with which one chiefly has to work as something which we do not use ourselves, but which God uses in us.'

BEURON

The Abbey of Beuron was for Edith Stein the " silent corner " where her soul could draw breath. It was there that the substance of her being came most clearly into the light. Without exaggeration, Father Damasus Zähringer describes this essential character of her life as *ecclesia orans*. He writes :

' When I saw her for the first time in a corner of the entrance to Beuron, her appearance and attitude made an impression on me which I can only compare with that of the pictures of the *ecclesia orans* in the oldest ecclesiastical art of the Catacombs. Apart from the arms uplifted in prayer, everything about her was reminiscent of that Christian archetype. And this was no mere chance fancy. She was in truth a type of that *ecclesia*, standing in the world of time and yet apart from it, and knowing nothing else, in the depths of her union with Christ, but the Lord's words : " For them do I sanctify myself ; that they also may be sanctified in truth ".'

Ecclesia orans. The classic phrase is indeed the most concise way of expressing the essence of Edith Stein. She was the embodiment of the Church's prayer. No happier theme could have been offered her, to touch the deepest springs of her heart, than that set her by the Academic Union of St. Boniface : The Prayer of the Church. In 1936 she contributed an essay under that title to a symposium on " The Lifestream of the Church " (Bonifatius-Verlag, Paderborn). The thoughts she there expresses are the precious fruits of her own enlightened devotion.

Edith experienced the rise of that most welcome and quickly-growing movement, the liturgical revival. But she was quick to recognize the danger of an over-emphasis on the community-idea and a consequent onesidedness in the life of prayer. She considered it an error to describe interior prayer, without set traditional forms, as " subjective piety " in opposition to the " objective prayer " of the Church's liturgy. She thus touched on a hotly-disputed question, then seriously agitating souls and troubling religious communities. The swelling flood of liturgical enthusiasm was threatening to sweep away respect for silent interior prayer. In the essay we are considering, Sister Benedicta faces this question and writes with the wise assurance of practical experience :

' In every prayer something takes place in the Church, and it is the Church herself who prays in it, for it is the Holy Spirit living in her Who in each individual soul " asketh for us with unspeakable groanings ". It is precisely this that is " true " prayer : for " no man can say : the Lord Jesus, but by the Holy Ghost ". What could be the prayer of the Church if not the surrender of God's great lovers to Him, Who is Love ?

Boundless loving surrender to God, and God's response, full and lasting union, this is the highest elevation of the heart to which we can attain, the highest degree of prayer. The souls who have reached it are truly the heart of the Church.'

She seems here to open the carefully-guarded door to the holiness of her soul and to let us glimpse a little of her intimacy with God, kindled to a flame of love by the Holy Ghost in the *opus Dei* and in contemplation. Many people who were not very close to her were surprised when Edith Stein chose to enter the contemplative order of Carmel rather than a liturgical order. But anyone who reads her article on the Prayer of the Church will unhesitatingly include her among the great men and women of prayer from whom she there quotes, and will realize that this soul, inclined to contemplation by nature and grace, by inclination and vocation, could only become a Carmelite.

True, she was as yet far from this goal. Any temporary stay in the cloister was all the more a joy to her, especially in her beloved Beuron.

" She could pray for hours before the picture of Our Lady of Sorrows ", writes a Swiss lady. " I could never understand it, for medieval and Beuron-style art had no attraction for me. But now I have come to think that Edith Stein not only prayed to have sufferings, but also had intimations that she was to travel the road of suffering."

In support of this opinion let us quote the poem which was found amongst Sister Benedicta's posthumous papers.

Good Friday 1938.

JUXTA CRUCEM TECUM STARE

To-day I have stood with you beneath the Cross
And felt more certainly than ever before,
That you became our Mother beneath the Cross.
How faithfully an earthly mother strives
To fulfil her dying son's last wish.
But you were the handmaid of the Lord,
Subduing wholly your own life and being
To the life and being of God incarnate.
You have taken your own to your heart
And with your heart bleeding from bitter sorrow
Have purchased for each one of us new life.
You know us all, our wounds and our defacement,
But you know also the heavenly radiance
In which your son's love eternally bathes us.
And so you carefully direct our footsteps.
You find no pain too great to bring us to our goal,
So those whom you have chosen for companions,
To stand beside you at the eternal throne,
Must stand beside you here beneath the Cross
And with hearts bleeding from bitter sorrow
Purchase heavenly radiance for the precious souls
With whom the Son of God entrusted you.

Maria Schäfer describes in a letter her memories of the lovely days of Holy Week and Easter which she and Edith Stein spent together at Beuron.

'I can only say " together " in the sense that we were in immediate proximity to each other and took part in the services together. Apart from this the holy events of these days passed in absolute solitude. Edith Stein was always the first to appear in choir, usually before four in the morning. She spoke hardly at all. But her greetings and good wishes on Easter morning, radiant and full of warmth, made you feel how deeply she must have descended into the dereliction and sufferings of the God-Man, so as to shine with such Easter brightness. She seemed during these days to live more than usually in the spirit ; she seemed even more pale and delicate-looking than usual ; her eyes and features betrayed something of her *compassio*. To me it was, so to speak, a criterion of her very holiness that there were sometimes people, and devout people, who did not restrain their criticisms even in face of her unassuming ways. " Must Dr. Stein always have the first place in church and hold on to it so obstinately ? " Or people would take her choice of dishes at table for part of a pose, think that she used to leave the table early, and maintain strict silence, out of pride. They had, of course, no inkling that this future Carmelite was already guiding her life in the world by the principles of Carmel. And these people had no final knowledge of the reality which is sung in the words of the psalm : *Quam dilecta tarbernacula tua Domine virtutum : concupiscit et deficit anima mea in atria Domini.'*

Yes, her soul longed for a hidden life in a cell in the house of the Lord. But Abbot Walzer would not hear of it. On the contrary, he persuaded her at last to give up her retirement in St. Magdalena's.

Edith Stein herself had already considered this possibility, as she explains in a letter of the 10th December 1930 :

' Perhaps I shall give up the school, Salzburg drew amazing crowds. I have to go off giving addresses here, there and everywhere. And in between, piles of essays . . . what will come of it I don't yet know. I have put off thinking about it until Christmas because it is pointless and only wastes time.'

BEURON

Christmas took her to Beuron to be present for the baptism of a young Jewess, a special joy because " I was in a small way instrumental in it as a *causa secunda* ". After an interview with the Lord Abbot she realized that she could not combine her lectures with school-teaching. Shortly after leaving Beuron she confided her decision to the Reverend Mother of St. Magdalena, " and she gave me permission to leave, thoroughly sympathizing with my viewpoint ". It was kept secret until the end of term, " and so everyone was very dismayed when I suddenly said goodbye to them on the last day. The few who were in the know had shown their sisterly affection by helping me with all my packing so that I was able to escape to Beuron immediately school ended."

From Beuron she wrote to a friend :

' I left Speyer on March 27th [1931]. St. Thomas is no longer satisfied with my spare time, he claims me entirely. On Easter Tuesday I have to go to Munich for a conference of young teachers from all over Bavaria. From there I am going straight on to Breslau, to get on in complete quiet with some work which I have begun. It is certainly a very good thing that in this way I can be at home for some time longer. My sister seems to have particular need of me just now.'

VIII

THE "WAY OF KNOWLEDGE"

THE work of which Edith Stein was here speaking was her translation of St. Thomas's *Quaestiones disputatae de veritate*, which came out in two volumes in 1931 and 1932.[1] Martin Grabmann wrote a preface to give the book a send-off. A translation of this kind could only be achieved by someone who was " at once at home in the world of scholastic thought and understood the language of contemporary philosophy ". Edith Stein had both qualifications, having " taken up the study of scholasticism after being immersed in the currents of contemporary philosophy. So equipped she has undertaken the translation of the *Quaestiones disputatae de veritate* and made this basic work of Aquinas available for the first time in German. Without obscuring the character of Thomistic terminology she has clothed Thomism in modern speech and translated its arguments into current German." And Father Erich Przywara wrote of it :

'The astonishing thing about this work is the fact that for the first time it strikes the perfect balance : on the one hand, here is German through which shines Aquinas' plain Latin with almost uninterrupted brightness ; on the other, everything, not only in the abundant annotations but in the manner of the translation itself, has become living modern philosophy. It is St. Thomas and nothing but St. Thomas throughout ; but he is brought face to face with Husserl, Scheler and Heidegger. Phenomenologist terminology, which Edith Stein commands as a philosopher in her own right, has nowhere

[1] Recently reprinted by the *Wissenschaftliche Buchgemeinde*, Tübingen.

replaced Aquinas' own language, but the transition from one
to the other can now be made smoothly. This is surely the
most significant feature of this important work : that in the
German footnotes the basis is laid for an exposition of
Thomism in German, i.e., in terms of living, present-day
philosophy. Edith Stein, in her comparative treatment of
St. Thomas and Husserl, has written something in the nature
of a programme. It would be a blessing for German Catholic
philosophy if she could gain an intelligent hearing for it at the
opportune moment.'

Such were the judgments made in 1931.

The name of Edith Stein was becoming well known.
Therefore friendly parties suggested that she should try to be
accepted as a lecturer at Freiburg University. She had
mentioned this suggestion when she was talking to the Lord
Abbot in Beuron during the Christmas holidays, because she
did not wish to take it up without his approval. Back in
Speyer once more she had written immediately to Prof. Finke
asking whether she might have an interview with him in
Freiburg on the 24/25th January to discuss the matter. For a
time there was no answer. " So far I have had no answer ",
she wrote on the 19th January. " Obviously I won't come
without some acknowledgment from him. If there is no point
in applying—and I am assured by reliable people that there is
none—then I understand why he would rather not tell me
personally. Clearly he does not know that it is a matter of
indifference to me personally, and I shall be neither disturbed
nor disappointed if nothing comes of it." Eventually Prof.
Finke referred her to Heidegger, whom she visited in Freiburg
on the date arranged. The account of it, written on the 26th
January, runs :

'As soon as I rang on the door-bell at No. 47 Rötebuckweg
there was a clatter down the stairs indicating that someone had
been posted there. It was their eldest kiddie, who had
obviously been instructed to receive me ; he did so with

consummate politeness. This was a friendly start. Heidegger was not in the least surprised at my request, saying that he personally had nothing against it and did not doubt my competence. But he could not guarantee anything until he knew whether the government would give him a grant for me. From which I gathered he thought I wanted to work under him ; and I immediately began to puzzle out how I could disillusion him. But he himself saved the situation—if I intended to take a Catholic line, then it would prove quite impracticable to work with him. Furthermore other people would find it easier to secure a grant ; there was not half so much chance of the government's refusing Honecker, because so far he had no one with him. I was very surprised when I found myself standing in the street.

Honecker was at first non-committal. In the end he explained that he would raise the matter at the faculty-meeting, on condition, however, that it would not mean the exclusion of his own candidate. The next time he went to Karlsruhe he would also enquire about the grant. The Husserls were very excited and glad to see me. The result was that I did not catch my train until half past six. At a pinch I could have caught an earlier one, but that would have meant rushing away immediately after lunch, which would not have been nice for the old couple. So they were able to take a rest after lunch— I was made to lie down on a sofa—and then we were able to chat in peace. Frau Husserl took me to the tram.'

With her lectureship in mind Edith Stein had taken advantage of the remaining six weeks before leaving Speyer in order to organize the philosophical work that she had slowly been putting together. It had already assumed the proportions of a bulky manuscript when a fresh possibility presented itself. This was due to two people, Professor Dr. Steffes, the head of the theological faculty in Münster and Principal of the German Institute of Educational Theory, and Maria Schmitz, President of the German Association of Catholic Teachers. They were trying to persuade Edith to move to Münster and become a tutor in the Institute, where she would give lectures and supervise the course on women's vocation. With her usual calmness Edith Stein just let things take their course, and carried on with her work undisturbed. She writes from Breslau : " I should like to have my work finished before coming to Freiburg. And when that will be I do not know. Should I receive a definite invitation first from the Institute I might abandon the lectureship at Freiburg altogether. Once I had begun the work it became more urgent than any purpose which it might eventually serve. God knows what He wants of me, and I have no need to worry about it." (28 IV. 31.)

Suddenly another quite different possibility was opened up in Breslau itself. We hear about it in a letter of Edith's on the 28th June 1931.

' My brother-in-law (Dr. Biberstein) meets one or two Catholic theologians in the lecturer's common-room. One of them—Koch—has often enquired about his sister-in-law (especially since Salzburg).

Recently he was talking about the very favourable opinions he had heard about me (i.e. about my " Thomas ") in Rome ; he would be glad to get to know me, and wondered whether I would like to hold a lectureship here. Then I asked my mother whether it would be all right to her if I were to carry on my Catholic teaching publicly in this place ; and, to my surprise, she says that it is all the same to her so long as I stay here. On Tuesday Prof. Koch was invited to my in-laws along with me. He is very anxious for me to teach phenomenology here (i.e. my modified version), and has since started to win round the head of the Catholic philosophy department. Tomorrow I am supposed to meet Baur over coffee. But I am letting matters take their course and waiting to see what comes of it. It makes no difference to my work wherever it is used. It has already become a monstrous size and shows scarcely any sign of coming to an end. I shall stick at it without interruption until the autumn, if possible. During October the Akademikerverband has arranged a lecture-tour for me through the Rhineland-Westphalian industrial region, with 14 places on the list so far. On the 22nd Nov. I am to give the address in honour of St. Elizabeth to the Heidelberg Catholics in their large city-hall. And in the second half of January I am booked to give two series of four lectures to the Catholic women in Zürich. I do not know where I shall spend the time in between, which depends rather upon the question of my lectureship.'

Prof. Koch has given us this reminiscence of their first meeting in Breslau :

'I was sitting with Dr. Biberstein, his wife, and her mother, Frau Stein. Then the door opened and Edith came in. I can remember very vividly the plain, bright blue dress she was wearing, and how I was struck by her simplicity. She had already made a name for herself but she showed no trace of posing. The eyes with which she surveyed the visitor had an extraordinary charm which I cannot forget. Nor can I forget something she said. It was her brief but exact description of Heidegger's philosophy as " the philosophy of a bad conscience ". The phrase says so much for her knowledge of humanity, and for her integrity when truth was in question.'

IX

THE "WAY OF LOVE"

BESIDES the great "work", as Edith Stein herself called it, of translating St. Thomas, God had called her back to Breslau for another formidable task. Edith referred to this in a sentence, quoted above, in a letter of March 28th, 1931, saying that her sister in particular seemed to need her presence at home.

In Speyer and Freiburg Edith Stein had already had opportunities of helping on their way young people who wanted to reach the Christian faith from Judaism. In fact she had dedicated herself to this task, with thorough-going devotion, inexhaustible patience and exquisite understanding. God blessed her zeal with abundant success. Many times she had the privilege of instructing catechumens and then acting as godmother when they were baptised : amongst others, Dr. Ruth Kantorowicz, Alice Reis, Hede Hess and her childhood friend, Katharina, later Dr. Ruben. The latter describes Edith's part in her conversion in the continuation of her narrative, quoted earlier in this book :

'I never lost interest in my childhood companion. I heard of her going over to Catholicism. That was amazing news. I knew that Frau Stein was anything but tolerant. I knew, moreover, how passionately attached Edith was to her mother, no less than her mother was to her. I knew, too, how indifferent Edith had been to religious matters. During the religious instruction class—which was, it is true, exceedingly bad—she even lost her desire to shine. How she must have changed! But I did not meet her again—not till 1931 or 1932;

it must have been early in the summer. I had heard that she was in Breslau to see her old mother. I myself made an effort to obtain light and faith. I rang her up. She was at once ready to come to me, and we met often, near where she lived, where one could take beautiful walks. Once, when I could not give her a definite time for an appointment, I suggested that I should come and fetch her. But she objected: " My mother knows that your husband has gone over to Catholicism. She has her own idea, of course, of what we talk about, and she would not want to see you."

Her mother was then already eighty. But it was amazing how she herself had changed. Where there had been ambition, there was now only tranquil detachment ; where there had been egoism, there was only understanding and kindness. She discussed things with me with endless patience, as well as consoling me in personal matters and discussing questions of faith, philosophy and everything that affected us. We came very close to each other. She was my godmother, too, and we parted from each other in deep and genuine love. To the last, up to the outbreak of war, she wrote us frequent and affectionate letters in South Africa and told us of the fullness and perfection of joy which she had found in Carmel.'

Dr. Albert Ruben, missionary doctor and District Surgeon in Tweespruit, South Africa, completes his wife's account :

' I met Edith Stein only a few times in all. The first was when I was just emerging from a severe crisis in my life. I had not, of course, entirely recovered my equilibrium. She sat opposite me in my wife's room, her slim figure almost lost to sight in the big armchair. I have never forgotten that picture. Why ? To put it shortly, I was completely defeated in the discussion ; for in her quiet fashion, never raising her voice even for a moment, with nothing affected in her perfect style of speaking, she presented me with one inexorable truth after another.

Once, I think in 1932, she visited us in the medical mis-

sionary institute in Würzburg. But all I know of this is that
Mgr. Becker, professor and director of the institute, a Salva-
torian, was deeply impressed by her. The last time I spoke
to her was in December 1933, through the grille of the Carmel
in Cologne. It was cold and she was wearing a thick coat.
I have forgotten the content of our conversation. In part, of
course, it revolved round our departure to the Mission. I
revered her greatly. I have in my Missal her definition of the
Church of Christ. I have never found a more beautiful one.
Her fate is an indication of how far removed men are from it.'

So God blessed her apostolic zeal. But in her own family,
where she so dearly longed for it and so unceasingly and
passionately prayed for it, she found little interest in Christ.
Only her thoughtful sister Rosa opened her heart to grace, and
would gladly have followed her younger sister's example.
But they could not inflict this fresh wound on their beloved
mother, now very old, and not yet recovered from the first
blow. Edith was usually away from home, but Rosa was
constantly with her mother, helping her. Living so completely together, conflicts would surely arise. So Rosa had
decided to delay her Baptism till after their mother's death.
This sacrifice to filial piety afforded her no escape from the
conflict in her heart, and it was Edith alone who could bring
harmony out of her painful doubts, torn as she was between
duty and love.

These years of 1930–31 made Rosa's position harder than
ever. " The situation in Breslau has now become terribly
delicate. For months my sister has been in deep distress.
Mother's niece, Erika, is living at home with us and by impos-
ing her increasingly strict Judaism upon the household she
has made life almost unbearable for Rosa. So far Rosa has
avoided arguing at all for mother's sake ; but she has now
let Erika into her secret and one cannot overlook the consequences this must produce. At the moment I see no other
help except prayer, but that is something for which I am now
rallying all my auxiliaries " (10 xii. 1931).

They were blessed hours for Rosa when her beloved sister spoke to her of Jesus, or prayed with her, or kept her mother company so that she could pay a secret visit to the church. And so the summer of 1931 passed happily, with Edith in Breslau except for a lecture-trip to Vienna, where she stayed with Dr. Rudolf Allers.

Towards the end of autumn she came back to Freiburg and stayed at St. Lioba, " happy to have found a home in the cloister once more and to be taking part in the monastic office, Here (Breslau) the silent liturgy is my lot. Whatever one needs is given in full measure ; at the same time it is when I am again sharing fully in the office that I realize how much I have been thinking of it. I knew that I should miss the cloister very much when I decided to leave Speyer, but I hadn't expected it to be so hard as it turned out in the first months. Though I have never regretted it for a minute, since I cannot doubt that this·is God's wish " (28 VI. 31).

Countess Tes von Bissingen tells of the impression that she left behind her in St. Lioba :

' She was so extraordinarily modest that one hardly noticed she was there. She never put herself forward, always stayed in the background. And yet from the first moment one felt as it were spell-bound by the great sanctity which emanated from her quiet person. There was never any drifting along with her—nothing but stern self-denial and striving towards God. But she exercised the greatest gentleness towards others —and the more wretched a poor creature was, the more touching would be her joy in seeking in such people the favourites of God, just where the rest of us really saw wretchedness and nothing else. By nature she took a very serious view of our obligations towards God. She could not conceive how it was that some of our party—I mean, during the winter in the little house of St. Lioba—only went to Vespers when they were sung, and otherwise took the time off. From the way she spoke one had the impression that she had lived just as seriously and ascetically before her conversion as after. I even think that her conversion had actually made her more gentle towards herself, since her inclination was to be too severe. This great sanctity of hers gave one a slight sense of shyness. A deep affection bound her to Beuron, but even more to Carmel, and she was obviously delighted when she met some- one who shared and understood her predilection.'

Maria Schäfer, who was staying at St. Lioba at the same time as Edith Stein, had the joy of reading the proofs of St. Thomas's *De Veritate* with her.

' We read them in her little room, just opposite my own, sitting side by side at her desk. She would go very gladly into the questions which occurred to me during the reading ; and how clear her answers were. An old carved crucifix which lay on the table kept catching my eye, or were they drawn to it rather by the loving glances which Edith Stein would give it from time to time ? Though her time was very full and she made a strict allocation of it, she always found an hour or two to talk to me about her small book *Ethos der Frauenberufe*, or we would read some poems from Przywara's *Karmel*, or discuss *Die Letzte am Schafott* or *Marie de la Trinité*. At that time I was deeply under the spell of her radiant, simple, com- pletely unassuming personality. For me she was the very type of the *vita contemplativa*. The Reverend Mother Prioress of St. Lioba once said that she would sometimes go to the chapel very early in the morning, but she was never the first, Edith Stein was always there before her. She would hide her knowledge and ability in simplicity. I was often touched by it ; I even had the impression that she chose her unassuming dress, her old-fashioned, much-mended linen in a spirit of holy poverty. Her work too went forward so quietly and unobtrusively ; I sometimes wondered how it was that she had so few of a learned person's customary paraphernalia around her.'

EDITH STEIN

During this winter, from the 18th to the 28th of January, she gave a series of lectures in Switzerland. After this she spoke at Septuagesima at the great *Kantons-Elizabethfeier* at Zürich. From this period dates the article *Ways to Interior Silence*, which has fortunately been preserved. It was written for the *Societas Religiosa*, a society of professional women, living according to a rule. Maria Buczkoska had asked her to write it. Similar articles had been appearing each month and were intended to stimulate their readers towards greater self-sacrifice in some particular direction. Maria Buczkoska had proposed the theme in connection with the lecture that Edith Stein gave at Bendorf in November, 1930. What she recommends in this article is obviously the result of years of faithful practice in self-denial.

WAYS TO INTERIOR SILENCE

' In a lecture attempting to draw a picture of woman's soul as it should be in accordance with her eternal vocation the following attributes were used : wide, silent, empty of self, warm, clear. The question arose of how these qualities are to be obtained.

It is not a question of a multiplicity of qualities to be separately mastered or laboriously acquired, but rather of a simple condition of the soul, of which these attributes express different aspects. We cannot achieve this condition by our own will, it must be a work of grace. What we can and must do is to open ourselves to grace. That means denying our own will entirely and surrendering only to the divine will, laying our whole soul, receptive and ready for re-shaping, in God's hands. One arrives at emptiness through silence, and at silence through emptiness. By nature the soul is occupied with many things ; so much so that one thing is always crowding on another in a constant state of movement, and often of tumult and uproar. When we wake in the morning, the duties and cares of the day at once begin to press on us (if

indeed they have not already driven away our night's rest).
The nagging questions begin : how is it all to be done in one
day ? When am I going to do this, that or the other ? How
am I to tackle this or that ? We feel inclined to rush out in a
panic and throw ourselves into it. Then it is that we must
get a grip on the reins and say " Gently now ! First of all,
none of all this must break in on me now. The first hour of
my morning belongs to God. Whatever work for the day He
gives me I will set about, and He will give me the power to
accomplish it. So I will go in unto the altar of God. It is
not myself and my tiny little affairs that matter here, but the
great sacrifice of atonement. I am permitted to take part in
it, to be washed clean and rejoiced, and to lay myself, with all
my actions and sufferings, beside the oblation upon the altar.
And when my Lord comes to me then in holy Communion, I
can ask Him " What do you want of me, Lord ? " (St. Teresa).
And after this silent converse whatever I see as my next task
I will set myself to do.

After the morning's celebration, when I enter upon my
working day, there will be a solemn stillness in me, and my
soul will be empty of what would have disturbed and burdened
it, being full instead of holy joy, courage and strength. It has
grown greater and wider, because it has gone out of itself into
the divine life. The love that the Lord has enkindled in me
burns tranquilly as a steady flame, compelling me to manifest
my love and kindle it in others. *Flammescat igne caritas
accendat ardor proximos.* And I clearly see the next stretch
of the road before me ; I do not see very far, but know that
when I have arrived where the horizon now closes down, a
new prospect will open before me.

Now the day's work begins : perhaps four or five hours in
the schoolroom. That means keeping our mind on the subject
—a different subject for each hour. In this period or that we
cannot achieve what we wanted—perhaps in none. There is
our own fatigue, there are unexpected interruptions, the
children's unsatisfactory behaviour, all sorts of annoying,
exasperating, worrying things. Or office-work : dealings

with unsympathetic superiors or colleagues, impossible demands, unjust reprimands, human failings, and every form of human need. Then it is midday. We come home exhausted and on edge, probably with fresh trials to face. Where now is the soul's morning freshness ? The inclination to storm and ferment is there again : irritation, anger, bitterness. And so much to be done before evening ! Mustn't we go on at once ? No, not until quietness has returned at least for a moment. Everyone must know, or get to know, where and how she can find peace. The best, if possible, is to shed all cares through spending another short period before the tabernacle. For someone who cannot manage that, who perhaps needs some physical relaxation as well, a short rest in her own room. And if it is not possible to achieve any sort of exterior quiet, if there is nowhere where we can withdraw, if unavoidable duties prohibit an hour's silence, then inwardly, at least, we must for a moment shut ourselves off from everything else and flee to God. He is really there, and can give us what we need in a single moment. Then, even though the rest of the day goes by in great weariness and toil, it will go by in peace. And when night comes and a backward glance shows that it has all been unfinished work, and much that we had planned remains undone, and so much of it makes us deeply ashamed and regretful, then we must take it all, just as it is, lay it in God's hands and leave it to Him. Then we can rest in Him, really rest, and begin the new day like a new life.

This is only a slight sketch of how the day should be arranged so as to make room for God's grace. Each individual will know best how to apply it to the circumstances of her own life. Thus we should go on to show how Sunday must be a great doorway letting the life of heaven into everyday life and giving strength for the work of the whole week ; and how the great feasts, festal seasons and fasts, lived in the spirit of the Church, help the soul to ripen year by year towards the eternal sabbath rest.

It will be an essential task for each individual to consider how she must arrange her daily and yearly life, in accordance with her own talents and circumstances, to make ready the way for God. The outward divisions of time will have to be different for each and in course of time be adapted to changed circumstances. But the spiritual situation likewise is different with different people. The means of establishing our link with the eternal, keeping it alive or re-infusing life into it— meditation, spiritual reading, taking part in the liturgy or popular devotions—are not all equally fruitful for all persons and at all times. Meditation, for instance, cannot be practised by all nor always in the same way. It is important to find out what is effective at each particular time and to make use of it.

E. S.

If we meditate upon the road God's mother followed from Candlemas to Good Friday, we shall find roads through her to interior silence.'

Now and again criticisms were levelled at her lectures, on the ground that she overstressed the supernatural. " But if I did not speak about that, I should never mount another rostrum," came the retort. " Fundamentally what I have to put across is a quite small, simple truth : how to start living as a handmaid of the Lord. So if people then demand something else of me, intellectual themes which do not interest me, for instance, then I can only accept them as a way of working round to my *Ceterum censio*. Perhaps that is a censurable procedure, and perhaps I should have thought more about whether it is justifiable, but this whole spate of lecturing just burst upon me unexpectedly. In any case I must thrash the question out soon. In Salzburg my subject now is to be ' Woman's Vocation', although ' The Christian's Vocation ' was the title originally suggested ; and I only agreed because that was occupying my mind at the time. Then the people in Salzburg maintained that something specifically for women was indispensable, and so I gave way. Hildebrand has undertaken the other one " (28 VI. 31).

X

MÜNSTER AND THE *MARIANUM*

THIS last stay at St. Lioba also meant good-bye to Freiburg. Various colleges had offered Edith Stein tutorial positions. She chose the German Institute for Educational Theory at Münster, where she went in the spring of 1932, after spending Easter at Beuron. She took up residence in the Collegium Marianum, basing her way of life, as always, on simplicity. Her name went like wild-fire through Münster, arousing curiosity particularly amongst the numerous students, clerical and lay, who lived in the Collegium Marianum. Her appearance at lunch on the first day was awaited with keen anticipation, after it had been announced that Dr. Stein would have her meals in common with the students, and not alone in her room. When she did arrive, excitement changed to astonishment. A little insignificant-looking woman came in, her dress almost exaggeratedly simple, with nothing whatever remarkable in her appearance. Nevertheless, even this first encounter made a deep impression. We learn this from Dr. Schweitzer, who was then studying in Münich:

'Her very being radiated perfectly disciplined energy. Her every act revealed an interior disposition such as one only finds in those rare people who live a rich spiritual life, moulded by intellectual discipline and held in perfect control. The charming, modest way in which she returned our greeting bore witness to a state of soul where humility and dignity were combined with a humanity which would display itself in some gesture or another whenever one met her.'

Another student writes :

' Edith Stein had a large and beautiful room, provided for her by the Sisters of Notre Dame who were in charge of the Marianum. But the students were none the less astonished at a tutor in an academic institution with such modest requirements. By the standards of that time it was extremely unassuming to be content with a single bed-sitting room.'

Another tells us :

My friend Helene (now a Carmelite) and I had our little rooms just facing hers. Until late at night we used to see the light on her desk, which stood in the window. But next day she would be first in the Chapel, before any of the nuns, as they themselves told us. She seldom went out of the house, and was hardly ever even in the garden. Her life was all prayer and work. She thought little of her own writings. John, the handy man of the house, had one time made a little rock-garden in the courtyard with flowers in bloom. She said : " How quickly he has made that lovely thing, and how little we achieve with our work."

Normally we only saw each other at meals. Even at that time she used not to eat meat. We used to guess why not—whether it was because of a digestive complaint or out of asceticism, and we never found out. She ate very little altogether, which astonished us, considering the intensity of her intellectual work. She was a wonderfully harmonious person, always gentle, kind and so unpretentious.'

Apparently Edith Stein was, during her short stay in Münster, an object of pious curiosity to the nuns sent from various Orders to study there. It was known when she got up and went to bed. " The Fräulein Doktor got up long before the rising-bell." " When I put out my light late last night, there was still a light in Edith Stein's room." She was observed at prayer and at work, in general company and in private conversation :

' In spite of her frail constitution Edith Stein kept a strict fast even though engaged in strenuous intellectual work. She already practised monastic asceticism. If she could arrange it so that she could hear three Masses in succession, she could be seen throughout them all kneeling reverently upright, never leaning, never sitting. And at every Mass she followed every prayer of the priest with the greatest devotion.

During the day, too, she would visit the Saviour in the Eucharist.

She affectionately devoted her free time to the young students. They loved to listen to her lectures, and willingly accepted the encouragement and advice she gave them for living exemplary Catholic lives. She saw this work for young people as a God-given task, and sacrificed to it her longing to devote herself entirely to God in the religious life. She was always ready to give her time to the men-students, too, for answering questions about religion or their academic work. She was an example to us all of sheer, fine humanity and deep Christianity. She understood so charmingly how to hide her enormous knowledge under her equally great, always helpful modesty.'

The same student continues :

' We liked to be with her. She was interested in all our affairs, our studies, our students' union, and also in the political questions which we were than getting heated over. It was the time when National Socialism was spreading amongst students. We organised a student meeting against the A.N.S.T. (Union of National Socialist Students), at which Helene Weber spoke and some of the National Socialist students behaved very badly. Dr. Stein also came to this meeting and spoke in the discussion. What she had to say was essential, but it effected little outwardly. Her voice was low and almost inaudible in the big hall.

Her personality had a much stronger effect in a small group. She loved to join in our small parties and celebrations in the house and at the union. In the winter of 1932 we had a celebration for St. Nicholas. After St. Nicholas' visit, which one of us had performed, we sat down together in our common room in front of a plate and a glass of punch. She had put a picture of the Immaculate Conception from Beuron beside each plate. It was December 8th. We sang Advent songs, and she was just like one of us.

There are one or two other details which show what she was like. It was summer, and strawberry-time. At the midday meal we were talking of our homes, and I was strongly regretting that I could not be at home now, where there were lots of strawberries in the garden. Since students are notoriously short of cash, however, I had to do without such expensive fruit. In the afternoon there was a knock on the door of our room. I opened it expecting nothing in particular, and—there was Edith Stein with a basket of strawberries, which she handed to me with a smile, and vanished. Helene and I were really moved as we ate the expensive fruit sitting on the edge of the bed.

Another little incident. At the end of October 1932 there was a rather hard frost. Then the heating system in the Marianum broke down and had to be repaired. It took several days. We shivered with cold in our rooms. Edith Stein sat well wrapped up before her books and worked as usual. We asked her if she were not cold. Frozen blue, but smiling, she said, " So long as my head doesn't freeze up, it's all right ! "

In the summer of 1933 there were rather a lot of students living at the Marianum, about ten. Amongst them was one enthusiastic National Socialist, who praised Hitler's *Mein Kampf* at table as the greatest revelation of the world's history. Though Dr. Stein was very restrained in all her dealings with people, a certain antipathy was discernible in her attitude towards this student. Once during a meal the conversation turned on women smoking. The student in question smoked like a chimney. Edith Stein made some biting remark in this connection, which I am afraid I have forgotten. She liked a little playful malice, and once said, " Wit is malicious and malice is witty ". Later on I was sitting with her, and she suddenly said, " Was what I just said very sharp ? " To which I was able to assure her that it had given us all some satisfaction to see that young lady catch it for once.

Edith Stein was often merry and gay like a child, but mostly serious and thoughtful. Especially when the persecution of the Jews began, she got more and more grave when she thought of her family. You never heard her complain, but it was shattering to see her quiet face, drawn with pain. Already her features showed a glimmer of the mystery that was to be expressed in her religious name, " of the Cross ". Even to-day I can hear her saying, " All this will be avenged some day," and I do not doubt that she even then saw the bitter punishment in store for our poor people.'

It was a comfort to her sister Rosa that Edith was again able to spend her autumn holidays in Breslau, where they celebrated their mother's eightieth birthday.

' Usually she is very cheerful [writes Edith] though there is no denying the marks of age. But the atmosphere at home is very oppressive. My sister complains of the difficulty in living together with relatives whose outlook is so different. And obviously I cannot take her with me, as far as I can see. In present circumstances one has to be thankful that the Institute even remains open. I am having a hard enough fight to re-establish my position in scholarship—not through personal opposition, since everyone treats me kindly—but because I have been out of the university atmosphere for ten years and am fundamentally at odds with the rhythm of modern life. It is a great consolation to be gradually finding my feet amongst the tutors and students (and the slowness is

due to me, since I have so little spare time for it). Two
Catholic student organizations and the academic Elisabeth-
Konferenz instructed their representatives to call on me ; they
have asked me to visit them some time. I took charge of a
discussion for the first group one evening, a most lively discussion on woman's problems. I believe that in this way we shall
succeed in attracting university students to the Institute for
lectures, which would prove a gain for both parties.'

That was how she saw things at the beginning of June ;
looking back at the end of August her hopes are confirmed.

' The summer term in Münster proved very fruitful. Above
all my relationships with the students have grown remarkably
warm—and not only with my own students but with those
from the university, and with the nuns taking courses at the
Marianum. This winter I am counting on a good part of my
audience coming from these two groups and its no longer
being composed mainly of school-mistresses and pupil-
teachers.

24/25 July I took part in a fine conference of young women
at Augsburg : I spoke to a meeting of group-leaders on
" Woman's role in leading people into the Church. " '

On the 2nd of September she set off for a week with her
friend Koyré, " to learn a bit about Paris, and a lot about
scholasticism ". The Société Thomiste had invited her to
Juvisy on the 12th of September for a conference on
" Phenomenology and Thomism ". Professor Rosenmölh
writes :

' The idea was to have an exchange of opinions on phenomenology, on the impetus that had been given to philosophy
by Husserl, first when he was at Göttingen, then when he was
at Freiburg. Noel von Lowen took the chair. The foremost
philosophers of France, amongst others Maritain and Berdiaev,
were there. From Germany there were Father Mager, O.S.B.,

Father Daniel Feuling, O.S.B., von Rintelen of Münich, Professor Soelingen of Bonn, Edith Stein and myself. Father Feuling gave the lecture. The discussion was dominated entirely by Edith Stein. Certainly she had the best understanding of Husserl, having been for years his assistant in Freiburg, but she developed her thoughts with such clarity, in French when necessary, that she made an extraordinarily strong impression on this learned company of scholars.'

One of those taking part in the Congress, Father Daniel Feuling, has retained a clear recollection of Edith Stein from this meeting :

' Life has twice brought me into contact with Sister Benedicta. The first was a remarkable meeting. I came back one Monday morning from the Schwarzwald, where I had been discussing my forthcoming lecture on phenomenology with Martin Heidegger. We had talked of Edith Stein, whom I did not yet know personally, though her name was well known to me. I was having considerable linguistic difficulties over my lecture. Both Husserl, the founder of phenomenology and formerly Edith Stein's master, and more especially Heidegger, wrote in a highly individual idiom, and it was not easy to render the German expressions intelligibly in French. When I spoke about this to Heidegger he told me that the Russian Professor Koyré, who had been one of Husserl's assistants along with Heidegger and Edith Stein, had edited some of his (Heidegger's) works in French.

As Heidegger had not got these books with him in the mountains, he suggested I might go to see Koyré in Paris, and find out how he had done the translation. But I did not know how I was going to do this, since I was not going to stay in Paris, but some distance away, with the Dominicans at Juvisy, where the congress was to be held. With this problem in my mind I came back to Neuberg Abbey.

That Monday afternoon I had something to do at the Monastery gate. While I was there the Brother Porter handed me a visiting card. He thought it was something special which might concern me. To my surprise, I read " Dr. Edith Stein ". Of course, I asked at once " Is she here ? I must speak to her ! " She was there, come out from Heidelberg with her friend Dr. Hedwig Conrad-Martius to see a friend, Father Peter Jans. Dr. Hedwig Conrad-Martius had been ill in Heidelberg, and Edith Stein had come to visit her. We were all delighted, for, as a philosopher in Glasgow once said to me, " Philosophers are all brethren ". And we talked for a good while on matters of common interest. I soon asked whether she knew where in Paris I could find Koyré, and repeated what Heidegger had told me about his translations. To which Edith Stein replied, " I am going to Paris on Wednesday to stay with Professor Koyré." And she promised to bring the things out to Juvisy. So one afternoon as I was crossing the great courtyard of the Dominican Priory I saw a lady coming towards me. It was Edith Stein who had come out by train to bring me what I wanted. On the Sunday I was able to compare my translations with Koyré's.

On Monday, the day of the congress, I met and talked to Edith Stein again. Koyré had come with her, and on Tuesday afternoon I went to have a philosophical discussion with them both. We sat together for hours. Then Koyré took us up to the Sacré Cœur, Montmartre, where we prayed for a time. On the way the two of them spoke together of various things, especially of Jewish philosophers—Husserl, too, was of Jewish race, and Henri Bergson and Meyerson in Paris ; " he is another of ours " was the constantly recurring phrase. It amused me a little to hear the way Koyré and Edith Stein, speaking of Jews and Jewish matters, would say simply " we ". I had a vivid impression of that blood-brotherhood which was so strong in Edith, as formerly in St. Paul, who spoke with such pride and emphasis his, *Hebraei sunt–et ego*. Then I was a little naughty, and asked with a serious air, " And where are you banishing *me* ? " They looked at me in great concern, and asked " Are you one of us, too ? " until I assured them of the contrary.

Towards evening Professor Koyré took us to another part of Paris to see the philosopher Meyerson. There we had more discussions over our cups of tea. Edith Stein had to bear the brunt of this hour's talk and give the answers ; I was so exhausted by the strain of all this discussion that by this time in the evening I couldn't put my thoughts together any more. Later still that night we had a meal together. Then we separated, and I went back, very late, to Juvisy.'

During her time at Münster Dr. Edith Stein was called upon just as frequently as ever to give addresses and conferences. Here is an account of one such event, as reported by herself in early October 1932.

' The Committee of the Catholic Women's League had arranged a conference on " The spiritual attitude of the younger generation ". As a basis for discussion Professor Aloys Dempf from Bonn delivered an address on the Saturday evening. He is a native of Upper Bavaria. a first-rate man, very mature and perfectly straightforward. He acted as one of the advance-guard in the youth movement before the war, and along with Professor Hermann Platz-Bonn and Heinrich Brüning belonged to the first liturgical group in Germany. All of which helped to enliven the occasion. Of the leading Rheinland ladies present I had already met many at previous conferences ; and I soon found myself on common ground with others, whose personal acquaintance I had not made previously. Amongst these the most notable was Annie Bender.

As always, such discussions tend to underline differences of opinion, but even those ladies who opposed me so vigorously at the time I was in Bendorf have now adopted a friendly attitude. But one has to move cautiously because they are all strong-willed individuals who throw their whole personalities into their particular jobs, and I have begun to realize the disturbing effects that I myself inevitably produce on people immersed in the world. For I have begun to notice

how the world has become completely alien to me, how far
I stand outside it, and how difficult it is to make contact
again. In fact, I don't think it can be done much longer'
(2 X. 32).

Did her audiences also appreciate how much it cost her to
" stand outside ", as she expresses it ? Let us listen to the
words of one member of her audience :

' In my last term at Münster I attended Edith Stein's lectures
on " The structure of the human person " at the German
Institute for Educational Theory. Her memory is still fresh
in my mind, for I was deeply impressed by her simplicity and
modesty. She used to speak slowly and calmly, without
gestures but with great clarity and intensity. She was said to
be " the most uncompromising representative amongst the
tutors of the strictly Catholic standpoint," and everyone who
heard her endorsed this judgment. Frequently I came across
her in the College chapel sunk deep in prayer. It was a moving
experience to see her there, so completely absorbed in God
that nothing could disturb or distract her. But when one
went to have a word with her she was unassuming and always
ready to help.'

Again, one of her colleagues who met Edith rather more
frequently because she had charge of the Institute Library,
writes :

' She stood head and shoulders above the other tutors on
account of her intense thought, her broad culture, her masterly
exposition and her capacity for recollection amidst many
distractions ; in fact, to compare her with all the rest of us
who were employed there one would have to use some entirely
different standard of measurement. Even at that time her
essential saintliness displayed itself. I am quite convinced that
she was fully aware of her neighbours' many human weak-
nesses, yet she never accused anyone, but went so steadily and

graciously along her way that we, with our worldly notions, often did not understand her humility.'

Nor was it only her humility which struck one—her love of poverty also was enough to astonish anyone who prizes the virtue of poverty. One Sister from the Marianum writes :

'It was during the very cold winter of 1932–33. One day we were discussing the poverty-stricken condition of a certain hamlet I knew, whose inhabitants still continued to go regularly to Mass despite the Church being so distant and the weather so bitter. Not long afterwards Fräulein Doktor came up to me, her arms full of thick clothing and undergarments, and asked me to send them to the needy folk I had been speaking about. When I protested that she should think a little about protecting herself from the cold, she replied that she could easily spare these things, and that I should send them on, which I did.'

During this Advent Edith Stein prepared for Christmas even more thoroughly and fervently than usual. In response to an invitation from the Reverend Mother of the Ursulines in Dorsten she kept the feast in the silence of their convent. Mother Petra tells us :

'On Christmas Eve she joined with us in singing Matins ; then we went to rest for an hour until midnight. When I returned to the Church I found her still kneeling motionless in the same position as we had left her ; she then sang the Office of Lauds with us. When I asked her later whether she had not been weary, her eyes lit up and she replied : " How could one grow weary on this night ? " '

In the course of the following months the National Socialists strengthened their hold over the German people and began to show their hand. Even Edith Stein was affected by the laws excluding non-Aryans from public office. She was abruptly suspended from teaching at the very moment when she was preparing an extensive reform of higher grade teaching which had been most promising. Although the Berlin authorities had co-operated with her in these plans they were abandoned as soon as she was suspended. Though full of sorrow at the suffering which was being imposed on her Jewish brethren she accepted her own fate with complete composure. Her work as a tutor in the German Institute for Educational Theory at Münster came to an end on the 25th February 1933, the day she gave her last lecture.

XI

THE ROAD TO CARMEL[1]

Fourth Sunday in Advent,
18th December 1938.

PERHAPS I shall leave this house soon after Christmas. The circumstances which have compelled us to arrange my transfer to Echt are strongly reminiscent of the conditions at the time I entered. There is no doubt an inner link between them.

When the Third Reich was set up at the beginning of 1933, I had been for about a year a lecturer at the German Institute for Educational Theory in Münster. I lived in the Collegium Marianum with a large number of nuns of various Orders who were there to study and a small group of other students, all of us well taken care of by the Sisters of Notre Dame.

One evening in Lent I came back late from a meeting of the Catholic Akademikerverband. I do not know whether it was that I had forgotten my key or that there was a key in the lock on the inside, but in any case I could not get in. I rang and knocked to try to get someone to come to a window, but without success. The students living in the rooms over-looking the street had gone on holiday. A gentleman passing by asked if he could be of assistance. As I turned to him he bowed and said, " Dr. Stein—I have only this moment recognized you." He was a Catholic teacher who took part in a course at the Institute. He excused himself for a moment to explain things to his wife, who, with another lady, had already gone by. He said a few words to her and then came

---

[1] Edith Stein's own account of her entry into the Carmel of Cologne.

back to me. " My wife gladly invites you to spend the night with us." It was a good solution and I gratefully accepted. They took me to an unpretentious bourgeois house. We sat down in the sitting room. My kind hostess put a bowl of fruit on the table and then went to get a room ready for me. Her husband began a conversation, and told me what American newspapers were publishing about the atrocities being committed against the Jews. They were unconfirmed reports which I will not repeat. I am only concerned with the impression made upon me that evening. I had indeed already heard of severe measures being taken against the Jews. But now on a sudden it was luminously clear to me that once again God's hand lay heavy on His people, and that the destiny of this people was my own. I did not let the man sitting opposite me see what was going on inside me. It was plain that he knew nothing of my origin. I usually explain the position on such occasions, but this time I did not. It seemed to me that it would be a violation of the law of hospitality to spoil his night's rest by telling him such a thing.

On Thursday in Passion Week I went to Beuron. Every year since 1928 I had kept Holy Week and Easter with them there, and given myself a quiet time of recollection. This time I had a special reason for wanting to go. I had been constantly thinking during the last few weeks whether there was not something I could do in the Jewish question. I had finally conceived the plan of going to Rome and asking the Holy Father in private audience to issue an Encyclical. But I did not want to take such a step on my own initiative. I had taken the three vows privately years before. I had found my monastic home, so to speak, in Beuron, and so could regard Abbot Raphael as my father in religion and bring all questions of importance to him for decision. It was not, however, certain that I should see him. At the beginning of January he had gone on a journey to Japan. But I knew that he would do all he could to be home for Holy Week.

Although taking an outward step of this sort was in accordance with my nature, I felt that it was not yet " the real thing ".

But neither did I know in what the real thing consisted. I broke my journey at Cologne from Thursday afternoon till Friday morning. I had a catechumen there to whom I had to devote some of my time whenever I had an opportunity. I wrote to her to find out where we could go to the Holy Hour that evening. It was the eve of the First Friday in April, and in that Holy Year 1933 Our Lord's sufferings were everywhere being commemorated with special solemnity. At eight that evening we found ourselves at the Holy Hour in the Carmel of Cologne-Lindenthal. A priest (Domvikar Wüsten, as I learnt later) gave an address and announced that this service would be held every Thursday from then on. He spoke beautifully and movingly, but something else deeper than his words was occupying me. I spoke to our Saviour and told Him that I knew that it was His Cross which was now being laid on the Jewish people. Most of them did not understand it ; but those who did understand must accept it willingly in the name of all. I wanted to do that, let Him only show me how. When the service was over I had an interior conviction that I had been heard. But in what the bearing of the Cross was to consist I did not yet know.

I went on to Beuron next morning. Changing at Immendingen in the evening I met Father Aloys Mager. We travelled the last part of the journey together. Soon after we had exchanged greetings he told me, as the most important piece of Beuron news : " Father Abbot arrived back safely from Japan this morning." So that was all right.

From my enquiries in Rome I learned that, owing to the great pressure of business, I had no chance of a private audience. Only a " special audience " (that is, in a small group) could be arranged for me. This would not serve my purpose, so I gave up the idea of the journey and submitted my plea in writing. I know that my letter was handed, sealed, to the Holy Father [1] ; and some time afterwards I received his

[1] It was transmitted to the Holy See by the Lord Abbot of Beuron, with a letter of his own warmly recommending the writer and stressing the menace of National Socialism to Christianity. This was in April, 1933, before the signing of the new Concordat.

blessing for myself and my family. There was no further result. But I have often wondered since whether my letter may sometimes have come into his mind. For what I predicted about the future of Catholics in Germany was fulfilled step by step in the following years.

Before leaving Beuron I asked Father Abbot what I ought to do if I had to give up my work in Münster. He found it quite impossible to believe that this could happen. On the journey to Münster I read a newspaper report of a big National Socialist teacher's conference in which denominational organizations had also had to take part. It was clear to me that in educational matters least of all would there be toleration of influences opposed to the régime. The Institute at which I worked was purely Catholic, founded—and maintained—by the Catholic teachers' union. So its days were doubtless numbered. I must reckon immediately on my short career as a tutor coming to an end.

I arrived back in Münster on April 19th, and next day I went to the Institute. The Director was on holiday in Greece. The manager, a Catholic teacher, took me into his office and told me his tale of woe. For weeks he had been having most disturbing interviews and was already quite worn out. " Just think, Doctor, there has been someone here already saying that no doubt Dr. Stein will not be giving lectures any more ? " It might be best, he said, if I gave up lecturing for this summer and worked quietly in the Marianum. The situation should be clarified by the autumn, the Institute would perhaps be taken over by the Church, there would then be nothing to prevent my working with it. I took the news very calmly, without accepting the consolation. " If I can't go on here," I said, " there is nothing possible for me any more in Germany at all." The manager expressed his surprise that I should see so clearly although I lived in such retirement and took no interest in the affairs of the world.

I was almost relieved to find myself now involved in the common fate of my people, but I had of course to consider what I was to do. I asked the president of the Catholic

women teachers' union for her opinion. It was at her suggestion that I had come to Münster. She advised me to stay in
Münster for the summer at least and to go on with some work
I had begun. The union would take care of my maintenance,
since the result of my work would in any case be useful to it.
If it were not possible to resume my activities at the Institute
I could later look round for possibilities abroad. In point of
fact I soon received an offer from South America. But by the
time that came I had already been shown quite a different road.

About ten days after I returned from Beuron the thought
came to me : is it not time at last to enter Carmel ? For
nearly twelve years Carmel had been my goal ; since the
summer of 1921 when the *Life* of our holy mother St. Teresa
had fallen into my hands and brought to an end my long search
for the true faith. When on New Year's Day, 1922, I received
Holy Baptism I thought that this was but a preparation for
entering the Order. But when a few months later I stood
before my mother for the first time since my Baptism, it was
clear to me that she was not yet ready for this second blow.
She would not die, but it would fill her with a bitterness for
which I could not be answerable. I must wait in patience.
My spiritual directors also confirmed this decision. Waiting
had lately become very hard. I had become a stranger in the
world. Before I took the Münster post and after my first term
there I had begged to be allowed to enter the Order. I was
refused, out of consideration for my mother and also of the
influence which I had exercised for some years on Catholic life.
I had submitted. But now these barriers had broken down.
My influence was at an end, and would my mother not rather
think of me in a convent in Germany than in a school in South
America ? On the 30th April—Good Shepherd Sunday—the
Church of St. Ludger was celebrating his feast with thirteen
hours of prayer. I went there late in the afternoon, and said
to myself : I will not leave until I see clearly whether I may
now enter Carmel. As the final blessing was given, I received
the Good Shepherd's consent.

I wrote the same evening to Father Abbot. But he was in

Rome, and I did not wish to send my letter across the frontier. It had to wait on my desk until I could send it to Beuron. It was the middle of May by the time I had permission to take the first preliminary steps. I did so without delay. Through my catechumen in Cologne I asked for an interview with Frau Dr. Cosack. We had met in Aachen in October 1932. She had introduced herself to me because she knew that I was close in spirit to Carmel, and she told me that she was closely connected with the Order, and especially with the Carmel at Cologne. I wanted now to find out from her what was to be done. She sent me word that she could give me some time the following Sunday—Rogation Sunday—or on the Feast of the Ascension.

I got this news by the morning post on Saturday. At midday I went to Cologne. I telephoned Frau Dr. Cosack and made an appointment to go for a walk with her next morning. Neither she nor my catechumen knew yet why I had come. The latter went with me to Mass at the Carmel. On the way back she said, " Edith, while I was kneeling beside you, the thought came to me : She isn't wanting now to enter Carmel ? " I did not want to keep my secret from her any longer. She promised to keep it to herself. A little later Frau Dr. Cosack arrived. As soon as we had set out together on the road to the Stadtwald, I told her what I wanted. I immediately added the things that were against it : my age (42), my Jewish origin, my lack of funds. She thought all this of no great importance. She even held out the hope that I would be accepted here in Cologne, because a new foundation was being made in Silesia which would leave some vacancies. A new foundation at the gates of my own city, Breslau ! It seemed a fresh sign from Heaven.

I told Frau Dr. Cosack about my past development, so that she could form her own opinion of my Carmelite vocation. She herself then suggested that we should pay a visit to the Cologne Carmel. She was particularly intimate with Sister Marianne (Countess Praschma), who was to go to Silesia for the new foundation. She wanted to talk to her first. While she was in the parlour I knelt in the chapel, close to the altar of the little St. Teresa. There came over me the peace of one who has reached her goal.

The conversation lasted a long time. When Frau Dr. Cosack finally called me she said confidently " I think it will be all right." She had talked first with Sister Marianne, then with Mother Prioress (then Mother Josepha of the Most Blessed Sacrament), and prepared the ground for me. But the convent's daily round left no more time now for the parlour. I was to come back after Vespers. I was back in the Chapel long before Vespers, and joined in with the prayers. Then followed May devotions behind the grille. It was about half past three when I was at last called to the parlour. Mother Josepha and our dear Mother (Teresia Renata de Spiritu Sancto, then sub-prioress and novice-mistress) were at the grille. Once more I gave an account of my journey : how the thought of Carmel had never left me ; I had been teaching for eight years with the Dominicans at Speyer, was most intimately united with the whole community, and yet could not enter there ; Beuron I thought of as the fore-court of Heaven, but I never thought of becoming a Benedictine ; it always seemed to me that our Lord was keeping something for me in Carmel which I could find only there. This made an impression. Mother Teresia doubted only whether they could accept the responsibility of taking someone out of the world who had still much that she could accomplish outside.[1] Finally I was told that I should come back when Father Provincial was there ; he was expected shortly.

That evening I went back to Münster. I had got further than I had expected at my arrival. But there was a long wait for Father Provincial. During the days of Pentecost I spent most of my time in the Cathedral of Münster. The Holy Ghost gave me courage to write to Mother Josepha and ask urgently for an answer, since in my uncertain situation I had

[1] A remark intended to remind the postulant that she could not count on being able to continue her intellectual work in Carmel. To this she gave the beautiful answer : " It is not human activity that can help us but the Passion of Christ. It is a share in that that I desire."

to be clear about what I could count on. I was at once summoned to Cologne. The Superior of the Convent would see me, they would not wait for Father Provincial any longer. This time, too, I was to be presented to the Chapter nuns, who had to vote on my admission. I was once again in Cologne from Saturday afternoon till Sunday evening (the 18th and 19th of June, I think), and talked to Mother Josepha, Mother Teresia and Sister Marianne before I visited the Monsignor, and I was also able to meet my friend.

On the way to see Dr. Lenné I was caught in a thunderstorm and arrived wet through. I had to wait for an hour before he appeared. When we had exchanged greetings he passed his hand over his forehead and said " Now, what was it that you wanted ? I have quite forgotten." I replied that I was a postulant for Carmel and had been sent to see him. He was now *au fait*, and stopped addressing me as " du ". It was clear to me afterwards that he had done this to try me. I had swallowed it without turning a hair. He made me say over again everything that he already knew, told me what objections he would bring forward against me, but gave me the comforting assurance that the Sisters did not usually let his objections stand in the way and that he was accustomed to give way to them. He then dismissed me with his blessing.

After Vespers the Chapter nuns came in a body to the grille. Our dear senior, little Sister Teresia, came up close to it so as to be able to see and hear. Sister Aloysia, the liturgical enthusiast, wanted to hear about Beuron ; that was something I had to offer. Finally I had to sing a little song. I had already been told about this the day of my former visit, but I had taken it for a joke. I sang " Segne, Du Maria ", rather shyly and softly. Afterwards I said that it had been harder than speaking before an audience of a thousand people. I heard later that the Sisters did not understand this, because they knew nothing of my lecturing activities. After the Sisters had gone Mother Josepha said that the voting could not take place until the following morning. So for this evening I had to go away without a decision.

Sister Marianne, with whom I finally spoke alone, held out the prospect of having the verdict by telegram. Next day, in fact, the telegram came : " Glad agreement. Greetings. Carmel." I read it and went into the Chapel to make my thanksgiving.

We had already discussed what was to follow. By the 15th July I would have settled everything in Münster, and on the 16th I would keep the feast of the Queen of Carmel with them in Cologne. I was to live for a month as a guest in the outer part of the house, go home for a visit in the middle of August, and on our dear Mother's· feast, October 15th, I should be received into the enclosure. There was the further prospect of my being transferred later to the Silesian Carmel.

Six big cases of books preceded me to Cologne. I wrote that I supposed no Carmelite had ever brought such a dowry before ! Sister Ursula took care of them, and gave herself immense trouble trying to keep Theology, Philosophy, Philology, etc., as the cases were marked, separate from each other while unpacking them. But they all got mixed up in the end !

Only a few people in Münster knew where I was going. I wanted to keep it as quiet as possible until my family had been told. The Sister Superior at the Marianum was one of the few who knew. I had confided it to her after the telegram came. She had been much concerned about me, and was now very happy. Shortly before my departure there was a farewell evening in the music room. The students had put their hearts into preparing it, and the nuns also took part. I said a few words of thanks, and told them that when they heard later where I was they would share my gladness.

The Sisters of the House gave me a Cross with relics which the late Bishop Johannes von Poppenburg had given them. The Sister Superior brought it to me on a silver plate covered with roses. Five students and the librarian from the Institute saw me off at the station. I had great bouquets of roses to bring to the Queen of Carmel for her feast. Less than a year and a half before I had come to Münster as a stranger. Apart from my official activities I had lived in cloistered retirement. Nevertheless I was now leaving behind a large circle of people bound to me in love and loyalty. I have always held the lovely old town and all the country round Münster in affectionate and grateful remembrance.

I had written home that I had been accepted by some Sisters in Cologne and would be going there for good in October. They took it for a new appointment and congratulated me.

My month outside the enclosure was a very happy time. I followed the daily programme, working except during the hours of prayer, and coming often to the parlour. Any questions that arose I submitted to Mother Josepha ; her decision was always the same as I would have reached myself, and this agreement of minds made me very happy. My catechumen was often with me. She wanted to be baptized before my departure, so that I could be her godmother. On August 1st Monsignor Lenné baptized her in the Cathedral Chapter House, and next morning she made her first Communion in the Convent Chapel. Her husband came to both ceremonies, but he could not make up his mind to follow her. On August 10th, at Trier, I met Father Abbot, and received his blessing for my difficult journey to Breslau. I saw the Seamless Robe, and prayed for strength, and I knelt for a long while before the beautiful miraculous statue in St. Matthias. I was welcomed for the night at the Carmel in Cordel, where our dear Mother Teresia Renata had been novice-mistress for nine years before she was recalled to Cologne as subprioress. On August 14th my godchild took me to Maria Laach for the feast of the Assumption. From there I went on to Breslau.

My sister Rosa was waiting for me at the station. Since she had for a long time belonged to the Church at heart and was completely at one with me, I told her at once what I was doing. She showed no surprise, but I saw that the thought of it had never occurred even to her. The others asked me no questions at all for two or three weeks. Only my nephew Wolfgang (then twenty-one years old) asked as soon as he came to visit me what I was going to do in Cologne.   I told him the truth, and begged him to keep it to himself.

The events of the day were causing my mother great suffering.   She was continually being aroused to fresh indignation that " there could be such wicked people ".   On top of this came a personal loss which went very deep.   My sister Erna was taking over the practice of our friend Lilli Berg, who was going with her family to Palestine.   The Bibersteins had to move into the Bergs' house in the south of the town and leave our home.   Erna and her two children were my mother's consolation and joy.   Not to have them living around her would prove a bitter loss.   But despite all these cares pressing upon her, she came to life again when I arrived.   Her cheerfulness and her sense of humour reasserted themselves. When she came home from the office, she liked to bring her knitting and sit down beside my desk and talk about all her domestic and business worries.   I got her to tell me all her memories, too, as material for a history of our family which I began to write.   It was evident that being together like this was doing her good.   But all the time I had to think " If you but knew ! "

It was a great comfort to me that Sister Marianne, with her cousin, Sister Elizabeth,[1] were in Breslau getting the new foundation ready.   They had gone from Cologne to Breslau before I did.   Sister Marianne had come to see my mother and give her greetings from me.   While I was absent she came twice more to our house and was very charming to my mother. When I went to visit her at the Ursulines in the Ritterplatz where she was staying I was able to speak freely of what was on my mind.   I, for my part, was allowed to share in all the joys and tribulations of the foundation, and was able on one occasion to go with the two Sisters to see the site in Pawelwitz (now Wendelborn).

I helped Erna a great deal during her removal.   Going on a tram to their new home she finally asked what was to happen in Cologne.   When I gave her my reply she became very pale

[1] Countess Stolberg, d. 1948.

and tears came into her eyes. " It is a terrible world," she said. " What makes a person happy seems to others the worst thing that could happen to them." She made no attempt to hold me back. A few days later she gave me a message from her husband, saying that if I had arrived at this decision through worrying about how I could manage to live, I must know that I could live with them so long as they had anything themselves. (My brother-in-law in Hamburg had said the same.) Erna added that she had to pass this on to me : she knew quite well that as far as I was concerned such motives did not come into the question.

On the first Sunday in September I was alone at home with my mother. She was sitting at the window with her knitting and I was beside her. Suddenly the long-expected question came : " What are you going to do with the Sisters in Cologne ? " " Live with them." Then came a desperate effort to deter me. My mother did not stop working. Her wool got into a tangle ; she tried with trembling hands to unravel it, and I helped her, while we carried on our discussion.

There was no more peace from now on. A cloud hung over the whole house. From time to time my mother made a new attempt to shake me. ' This again would be followed by silent despair. My niece Erika, the most convinced Jewess in the family, also thought it her duty to work on me. My brothers and sisters did not try, because they considered it hopeless. It got even worse when my sister Else came from Hamburg for mother's birthday. Though my mother usually controlled herself when with me, she became extremely over-wrought when talking to Else. My sister recounted all these outbreaks to me, because she thought that I did not know my mother's state of mind.

The family was also burdened with great economic worry. For a long time the business had been going very badly. And now half our house, where the Bibersteins had been living, stood empty. People came every day to view the house, but nothing ever came of it. Among the most eager applicants was a Protestant parish. When two of the pastors came for a second visit, my mother asked me to go into the empty part of the house with them, because she was already very tired. I progressed so far with these two gentlemen that we drew up all the conditions. I submitted them to my mother, and then wrote on her instructions to the Head Pastor, to ask him for a written acceptance, which was given. All the same, shortly before my departure the arrangement threatened to break down. I wanted to relieve my mother of this worry at least, and I went to see the clergyman where he was staying. It seemed that there was nothing further to be done. But as I tried to take my leave he said, " Now, you are looking really sad. I am sorry." I told him that my mother had so many troubles to bear at present. He asked sympathetically what sort of troubles they were. I told him briefly of my conversion and my intention of entering a convent. It made a great impression. " You shall know, before you go there, that you have won a heart here." He called his wife in, and after a short discussion they decided to call another meeting of the Parish committee and put the case before them once more. And before my departure the Head Pastor and his colleague came to our house to conclude the agreement. As he went out he said to me in a low voice " God keep you."

Sister Marianne had one more private talk with my mother. Little came of it. Sister Marianne could not allow herself (as my mother hoped) to deter me from going. And no other consolation was of any avail. Neither Sister, on the other hand, dared to encourage and strengthen me in my resolution. The decision was so difficult that no one could say with certainty whether this road or that was the right one. Good reasons could be advanced for either. I had to take the step entirely in the darkness of faith. I often thought during those weeks " Which of us will break, my mother or myself ? " But we both held till the last day.

Shortly before I went I had my teeth seen to. While I was sitting in the dentist's waiting-room, the door opened and my niece Susel came in. She flushed with delight. Our appointments had been made for the same time without our knowing it. We went into the surgery together, and then she went home with me. She clutched my arm and I took her sunburnt hand in mine. Susel was then twelve, but very mature and thoughtful for her age. I had never been allowed to talk to the children about the change in my belief. But Erna had now told them everything ; I was very grateful to her. I asked the child to go to see her grandmother often after I had gone. She promised. " Why are you doing this now ? " she asked. I could detect in her question the kind of parental conversations she had been overhearing. I gave her my reasons as I would to an adult. She listened thoughtfully and understood.

Two days before I left, her father (Hans Biberstein) visited me. He felt impelled to tell me his objections, though he expected no result. What I was planning seemed to him to draw a yet sharper line between me and the Jewish people—at this moment when it was being so oppressed. He could not understand that from my point of view it seemed quite different.

The last day I spent at home was October 12th, my birthday. It was at the same time a Jewish festival, the end of the Feast of Tabernacles. My mother went to the service at the Synagogue of the Rabbinical Seminary. I went with her, because we wanted to spend this day completely together as far as was possible. Erika's favourite teacher, a distinguished scholar, gave a fine sermon. On the way there in the tram we had not spoken much. So as to give some small comfort I had said that the first period was only a trial. But that was no help. " If you undertake a trial period, I know that you will go through with it." Now my mother wanted to walk home. About three quarters of an hour, and she was eighty-four ! But I had to consent, for I could see that she wanted very much to talk with me undisturbed.

" It was a beautiful sermon, wasn't it ? "

" Yes."

" Then it is possible for a Jew to be pious ? "

" Certainly—if one has not learnt anything more."

Then came the despairing reply :

" Why have you learnt more ? I don't want to say anything against him. He may have been a very good man. But why did he make himself God ? "

After lunch she went to the office, so that my sister Frieda should not be alone during my brother's lunch hour. But she told me she would come back very soon, and did so (entirely for my sake. Otherwise she was always in the office all day). During the afternoon and evening we had many guests—my brothers and sisters, all their children, my own friends. That was a good thing, because it acted as a distraction. But it was hard when, one after another, they said good-bye and went away. In the end my mother and I were alone in the room ; my sisters were still clearing away and washing up. Then she hid her face in her hands and began to weep. I stood behind her chair and laid her silvery grey head on my breast. We stayed so for a long while, until she let me persuade her to go to bed. I took her upstairs and helped her to undress, for the first time in my life. Then I stayed sitting on her bed until she herself sent me to get some sleep. I think neither of us had any rest that night.

My train went about eight in the morning. Else and Rosa wanted to go with me to the station. Erna had also wanted to come, but I asked her instead to come to the house early and stay with my mother. I knew that she more than anyone else would be able to calm her. We two youngest girls had always preserved our childish tenderness in our relations with our mother. The others were shy of showing it, though their love was certainly not less.

At half past five I went out as always to the first Mass at St. Michael's Church. Then we were all together for breakfast. Erna came about seven. My mother tried to take something, but soon she pushed away her cup and began to weep as on the evening before. I went to her again and held her in my arms until it was time to go. Then I signed to Erna to take my place. I put on my hat and coat in the next room. Then came the parting. My mother embraced me and kissed me very tenderly. Erika thanked me for all my help (I had worked with her over her teacher's examinations, and while I was packing she had come to me with her questions). Afterwards she said, " The Eternal be with you." As I embraced Erna my mother wept aloud. I went out quickly. Rosa and Else followed me. When the tram came past our house there was no one at the window, as there always used to be, to wave good-bye again.

At the station we had to wait a little for the train to come in. Else clung to me tightly. When I had secured a seat, and was looking down at my sisters, I was struck by the difference between them. Rosa was as calm as if she were going with me into the peace of the cloister. But Else in her suffering suddenly looked like an old woman.

At last the train began to move. The two of them waved for as long as there was anything to see. Finally they disappeared. I could retreat to my place in the compartment. So what I had hardly dared to hope for was now real. There could be no violent access of joy. All that lay behind me was too terrible for that. But I was in deep peace—in the haven of the Divine Will.

It was late in the evening when I got to Cologne. My godchild had begged that I should spend the night with them once more. I was not to be received into the enclosure till after Vespers next day. I told the convent by telephone next morning of my arrival, and was able to come to the grille to be welcomed. We were back soon after lunch, and in the Chapel for Vespers : the First Vespers of our holy Mother. As I was kneeling there before it began, I heard someone whispering at the sacristy turn, " Is Edith there ? " Then some huge white chrysanthemums were brought out. Some teachers from the Palatinate had sent them by way of greetings, and I was to see them before they were made part of the altar decorations.

After Vespers we had to go and have coffee together. Then a lady came who introduced herself as the sister of our dear Mother Teresia Renata. She asked which of us was the postulant, as she wanted to give her some encouragement. But that was not necessary. This patroness and my godchild went with me to the enclosure door. It opened at last, and in deep peace I stepped across the threshold into the House of the Lord.

PART II
CARMEL

I

THE SCHOOL OF HUMILITY

"IT always seemed to me that our Lord was keeping something for me in Carmel which I could find only there."

In these words this outstanding philosopher and famous lecturer, already revered as a saint by many people, recognized that something more was required before her life could be consummated in happiness. What was it? And what is meant by Carmel, where she hoped to receive this treasured gift which our Lo.[1] had been storing for her?

Carmel presents a mystery which cannot be taken in at a glance. Even those intimately acquainted, like Edith, with Carmelite spirituality through reading the works of its great exponents can scarcely avoid shrinking when for the first time they begin to breathe the dry air of Carmel. They soon have a sense that they have been set in a trackless desert, a waterless land which only slowly surrenders its secrets.

Carmel may be summed up in the two words, " all " and " nothing ", the two poles about which Carmelite life revolves. The hidden force of this paradox startles outsiders when they encounter it for the first time ; they react like a person suddenly seeing an abyss on either side of him. Yet, for those called to it, the nothingness of this solitude opens up limitless horizons, and there is music in its silent meditation. Outward poverty and freedom from external needs are not the essentials. What matters is conscious striving after voluntary emptiness in thought and will, in one's reason and faculties, for then God's presence can come pouring in without hindrance until the soul is filled to overflowing.

The solitude of Carmel is filled by God, in face of Whom

every desire is quenched and every voice sinks into silence, in that stillness empty of everything save God. God alone is all in all. It is an emptiness overflowing with His life.

Edith Stein was a Carmelite in spirit whilst still in the world. Nevertheless the claims of the world made it difficult for her to be completely detached. Her status in learned society, the demands made upon her by her everyday duties, and her connections with so many circles of brilliant people, all contributed to this difficulty. But now our Lord had called her into His loneliness, where with Mary at the foot of the Cross she would find the better part that no man could take away from her.

Only in Carmel, moreover, was she to find something else which our Lord had been saving for her. As we can infer from her own account, she had been favoured with a vision in which God had shown her His Cross as the Cross under which her own people were suffering. At the same time He had requested her to take her allotted share in this Cross, as the innocent Lamb of God had taken it upon Himself in the name of all, for them and for their salvation. Edith had courageously responded by declaring herself ready for this sacrifice, but she wrote, " In what the bearing of the Cross was to consist I did not yet know." But God had elected her to share in the sacrifice of the Lamb and had foreseen the way in which she would be conformed to the Son of God, even to dying a violent death for the sake of the people. Carmel was the way, for its essence is a radical purging of the soul through contemplation, leading it to a nothingness where the soul is opened to the inflowing of love.

The first step towards this conformity was to lay aside all dignities, and to be humbled. Edith's entry into Carmel was a descent from the summit of a famous career into the depths of insignificance. Perhaps she herself did not regard it in the way we do, but it is true that when she crossed the threshold of Carmel and left the world she also abandoned everything in it for which she was respected and reduced herself to the level of everyday mankind. She was received into the Cologne

Carmel as just another postulant.   Most of the sisters have not
even heard of her.   None of them was aware of her great
reputation ; very few would have been able to follow her if
she had tried to introduce them into her own intellectual
world.   But no one thought about this—least of all Edith
herself.   Everyone assumed, quite naturally, that she should
undertake the thousand and one little tasks which a postulant
has to get used to from the beginning.   And it was a moving
experience to watch the child-like way in which Edith struggled
to fall in with the regulations of the house at every point,
promptly responding to all requests and trying to accustom
herself to this new mode of life.

It did not come easily, even with the best will in the world.
" Does she sew nicely ? "   The searching question came from
one of the older sisters, and it helps one to appreciate the
standard of values applied to the new postulant.   Unfortunately Edith sewed very badly ; worse, it was positively
painful watching her trying to do housework, at which she
was so clumsy and unskilled.   But she always bore with good
humour the humiliations arising out of these deficiencies, no
matter how they affected her inwardly.   Later she wrote to
one of her pupils who had followed her into Carmel and was
experiencing the same difficulties with housework ; and in the
letter she said how well she understood her feelings, because
she had always been in the same position.   Never was there
anyone so left-handed in a kitchen.   But she added that it all
formed part of the school of humility and was good for someone who had been excessively praised all her life.   In Carmel
no one thought for a moment of revering this new postulant,
though she had made herself loved by her disarming friendliness ; and Edith saw to it that no one noticed how she out-
stripped them all intellectually.

A few days after she had entered she wrote to her colleague
Dr. Brunnengräber, " Now I am in the place where I have
belonged for many years, so far be it from me to reproach those
who have cleared the way for me."   And to a nun in an active
Order, " We also are *in via*, for Carmel is a high mountain

which one has to ascend from below. But it is bounteous grace to follow this path. And please believe that I am continually remembering in my prayers those who would gladly be in my place. Please help me to be worthy of living at the heart of the Church's holiness, and to offer myself for those whose lot lies in the world."

From the time when St. Teresa reformed the Order and very wisely limited the numbers in each convent on the ground that the medieval communities had been too large, every Carmelite convent has formed an intimate little family of twenty-one members. Eighteen of these are choir-sisters and three of them lay-sisters, though a fourth lay-sister is allowed if one of them is ill or too old. The maximum number was reached when Edith Stein entered, and she could only be accepted because another foundation was being planned in Breslau, to which three of the sisters from the Cologne Carmel departed in the summer of 1933.

In 1894 the Carmelites, who had been driven out of their convent at St. Gereon by the Kulturkampf, returned to Cologne. They were unable to re-acquire their old house, however, because in the meantime it had been turned over to some charitable institution ; and so they built a modest little church and tiny convent in a Cologne suburb, at Lindenthal, Dürenerstrasse, 89. Attached to it was a lovely but equally small garden. When Edith entered this foundation it had been standing for about forty years ; in 1944 it was completely destroyed by air-raids. In charge of the convent at this time, in 1933, was Mother Josepha of the Blessed Sacrament, the Mother Prioress, while the sub-prioress, Sister Teresia of the Holy Ghost, was also novice-mistress.

The novitiate then numbered two novices, who had already made their first profession, and one lay-postulant, all nearly twenty years younger than Edith. This was another circumstance which made demands upon the humility, adaptability and constant self-control of the mature woman who had to live with them. Still no one could have guessed that it was

proving a source of trouble or strain to her. She blended into
the prevalent mood during their recreation and lent her
sympathy to all the sorrows and joys of her young companions. In return she shared with them her own interests,
telling them about what was happening to her own family.
She was a first-rate story teller and could turn even the most
trivial incident into a thrilling adventure. She delighted
everyone with the witty remarks she would throw out in
conversation.

Besides this attractive and companionable side of her
character she had a great inclination towards the seclusion
which is the true life of Carmel. When she came to her cell
for the first time her joy was unmistakable. A happy smile
flickered across her face at the sight of the poverty of the
room in which she was to live. It was about ten feet square,
the walls whitewashed, the window looking straight out into
the peaceful convent garden ; on the walls a plain wooden
cross without the figure of our Lord, an equally plain holy-
water stoup, and unframed pictures of Carmelite saints. On
the floor was an earthenware water-jug standing in a basin,
on the little table a work box, and in front of the table a low
narrow bench. Her resting-place was in a corner ; on a
slightly raised board, a straw mattress on which were a pillow
and a few rough, woollen blankets, hidden by the brown
woollen coverlet draped over them. Such is the equipment
of a Carmelite cell, that secret battle-ground where the nun
struggles daily against her self-love until her nature is wedded
to grace and she is free to serve Him who created her for
Himself.

It is possible that even Edith's heart began to beat faster and
louder when for the first time she encountered this harsh and
unconditional poverty in all its nakedness. But this was the
Cross she had longed for, which only Carmel could give to her.
Outward poverty is no more than a symbol for the complete
stripping of one's self, giving all to God and holding nothing
back. It expresses a life based upon utter faith, guided by the
ray of darkness which draws one ever closer to the presence

of God. Is such a life of prayer and penance gloomy and boring ? Edith could easily have quelled such a suspicion—and not with words alone ! Her very being and her every act gave it the lie. It was sheer joy to observe her growing younger and more radiant after her first weeks in the enclosure. One might have imagined that Edith herself had forgotten her past, her abilities and her learning, and had retained just one desire, to be a child amongst other children. Excessive intellectual work, fasting, irregular hours of sleep, all these mortifications which she had laid upon herself were abandoned in the name of obedience. To eat sufficiently, to sleep contentedly and to be thoroughly joyous ; these are the three recognized signs of a true Carmelite vocation according to our holy Mother, St. Teresa. Edith never found it any trouble to display all these three qualities, and especially the decisive one, joyfulness. It was appropriate that we should celebrate the joyful feast of Christmas so soon after she joined the Order.

Christmas in Carmel ! One might say : heaven on earth ! Edith was now to celebrate it with us, the one night of the year when the great silence in Carmel is lifted, when all the rooms and corridors, the stairs and every part of the cloister echo with music and jubilation, when every nook and corner contains its own little crib, each one lovelier than the last. This holy night when, instead of being wakened by a hard clapper, one wakes to the sound of silver bells and the singing of carols, so that it seems as if one had really been sleeping in Bethlehem and was hurrying into the ante-choir to be there before the shepherds. Dressed in their white habits the sisters stand waiting for the bells to ring for the third time, the sign for them to move into the choir, now blazing with light. Matins are never sung more beautifully than during this sacred night before the Blessed Sacrament exposed on the altar. Soft noises can be heard through the wide-open grille in spite of the curtains over it ; indicating that the little chapel is filling with people. Now it is almost midnight. The jubilant sounds of the *Te deum laudamus* fade away and the sisters retire to the ante-choir to receive their lighted candles. There in front of the altar, laid upon a silk cushion, is the Christ-child. Carefully the Mother Prioress lifts it and holds it up to the community who now begin to move back into the choir amidst a peal of bells, the youngest sister at the head of the procession.   Complete silence reigns throughout the chapel ; everyone is listening to the sisters singing : " Bethlehem, dost thou hear thy Saviour ? Let Him in . . . "   The sisters themselves stand on either side of the choir whilst the Mother Prioress carries the Christ-child to the grotto and lays Him in the crib.   And now it strikes twelve.   The organ thunders, the priests approach the altar, and the choir intones the eternally beautiful *Dominus dixit ad me : filius meus es tu* . . .   What the sisters have symbolically represented by their play in the choir is now going to take place in reality.   The Christ-child is coming into the world, descending onto the altar, finding a resting-place in our hearts.   *Ave Jesu!*   The priest is giving the Christmas blessing.   The servers are coming away from the altar.   There follows a second, then a third Mass.   Now the congregation takes up the melody and bursts forth into the old, familiar Christmas carols, so dear to the music-loving people of Cologne.   To hear them once is to remember them always.   After the last *Amen* the chapel slowly empties.

There is a stir again in the choir ; the sisters are intoning Lauds.   The Brides of Christ hardly wait for the liturgy to come to an end before they sing aloud their hearts' love in their German mother-tongue, accompanying themselves on the flute and the lute.   Who thinks of sleep ? or of bodily refreshment ? Until finally the Mother Prioress singing the invitation " Oh, children, come . . . ", gives the sign to disperse.

Edith Stein was at home in the conventual family from the beginning.   She used to laugh and joke like a child with the other sisters till the tears ran down her cheeks.   She used to declare that she had never laughed so much in all her life as during recreation in Carmel.   Everyone was at their ease with her.   Soon after she herself had entered the Cologne Carmel

she was given the wonderful experience of bringing in one of
her young friends through her own example.   This is what
she wrote about it : " When we now stand facing each other
in choir or pass close to one another in procession I am struck
more than ever by the wonderful ways of God.   Our seclusion
from each other affords us the stillness and beauty of an
Advent.   How much one longs to send some of our riches to
those in the world.   I believe that it would do them untold
good to learn more of the peace in Carmel " (11 XII. 33).

An even deeper impression emerges from a letter of about
the same date.

' My deepest thanks for your greetings on the anniversary of
my Baptism which of course I have celebrated this year as
never before.   The fact that you have not received any word
from me in Carmel and that I could not send you any visible
token even at Christmas should not make you imagine that I
do not have permission to write.   In fact I am allowed very
wide freedom in maintaining my old contacts.   But each day
is so ordered that one has to concentrate upon doing whatever
happens to be most urgent.   I need your prayers for my
mother as much as ever, since she is not one whit more
reconciled to the situation than before.   Meanwhile our little
Carmel in Breslau-Pawelwitz continues to flourish.   Recently
I heard from my sister Rosa that she had just paid her first visit
to this little convent, and she will be very happy to slip away
there whenever she can, but she finds it rather difficult to
manage.   The two children (Susel and Ernst Biberstein) know
quite well where their aunt is going.   Apparently Susel is
greatly impressed because she writes to me more often than
she used to.   She is serious beyond her years, having matured
very rapidly through hearing so much political talk and
through having to suffer, as she has, at school.   My brother-
in-law cannot make up his mind to let the children change their
school, but my sister said in her last letter that they want to
send Susel at any rate to a Catholic Girls' High School, where

Jewish children are rather better treated. As yet nothing has been said to the child herself. Naturally my mind often turns towards those in the world outside ; it must be a great strain to teach these days. As I stand in our peaceful choir I cannot thank God enough for having lifted me out of the whirlwind and set me in this profound peace, which I have done nothing to deserve. I have never celebrated Advent and Christmas as I did this year.'

In this way Edith's six months of probation passed quickly. On the 15th of February, 1934, following the custom of the Order, she knelt before the assembled community and asked to receive the habit of Our Blessed Lady of Mount Carmel ; she was granted her request on the 15th of April. During the two months that she was preparing for her clothing she grew in love and gratitude towards her superiors and her sisters. It was not easy for her to grasp that, as the " bride-to-be ", she should be the object of so much attention and solicitude on the part of her sisters. Everyone was busy helping her to prepare for her clothing as it drew nearer. Besides the bridal-dress all the clothes she would need in the convent had to be made—a long white tunic of wool, a pair of rope sandals, a rosary with big beads and a coarse brown handkerchief. She had to go from one work-room to another to try on first one thing and then another ; and though nothing more was done for her than for anyone else, she accepted each service as though it were a special token of love for herself.

II

THE NOVICIATE

EDITH had announced the wonderful event to her family. When she had presented herself at the Carmel in the previous summer, as soon as the conversation turned towards her mother she had asked for just one privilege : that she might write her a weekly letter. This had been her life-long practice, and if letters had suddenly stopped arriving her aged mother would have been cut to the quick. The Mother Prioress gladly granted the postulant her request in view of her unusual family circumstances, and even in Carmel Edith continued to write her regular weekly letter to her mother. But her mother, who had previously replied just as regularly, now ceased writing to her ; Frau Stein could not bring herself to send letters to her daughter in a convent. Rosa therefore undertook to act as intermediary, and to keep them in contact with each other. On hearing the news of the forthcoming clothing she eagerly enquired whether she herself could contribute anything to her sister's marriage-feast. When Edith asked her for the bridal dress Rosa sent some white silk material, which is still in the Carmel, having since been made into a Mass-vestment.

On the 15th of April, 1934, Good Shepherd Sunday, Edith Stein was clothed in the habit of Our Blessed Lady of Mount Carmel and received a name which she herself had suggested, Teresia Benedicta a Cruce. It was a feast such as the Cologne Carmel had never seen. The generous bouquets of flowers given by many friends and acquaintances lent the little church a most marvellous beauty. Everyone had expected a lot of people to be present at the ceremony, but no one had anticipated the great throng which did come. It was an overwhelming testimony to the high esteem and love which Edith had enjoyed in the world. And yet she did not allow this demonstration of universal admiration to disturb her soul even for a minute. An hour before the ceremony began she left the enclosure " as a Bride adorned for her Husband " to receive the guests of honour in the guest-room. These included the Lord Abbot of Beuron, who was to celebrate the Pontifical Mass, the Father Provincial of the Carmelites, Fr. Theodore a St. Francisco from Regensburg, who was to perform the clothing, Professors Dr. Dempf, Dr. Danders, Peter Wust, Dr. Rosenmöller, Dr. Brunnengräber and many more. Naturally her godmother, Frau Dr. Conrad-Martius, was there also, as well as many representatives of the Catholic Women's League, Frau Dr. Gerda Krabbel, Annie Bender, Dr. Cosack, and many of her old school-friends and pupils from Freiburg, Speyer and Münster. Representatives from many different religious orders had also come. It made no difference whether they knew each other or not, they all pressed around her with their good wishes. For each one of them she had a friendly word, but the ringing of bells for the ceremony to begin must have come as a relief to her. At the head of the procession of clergy coming out from the sacristy, and dressed in his robes of office, was the Lord Abbot who received Edith at the Church door and led her towards the altar. There she knelt at the prie-Dieu to follow the liturgy of the Mass, which was rendered even more beautiful by the singing of a choir of Third Order Dominicans.

After the High Mass the celebrant delivered an address which must have severely tried the humility of our unassuming Bride of Christ. Then her Carmelite superior, Fr. Theodore, moved towards her, and there followed a dialogue which has remained unchanged for centuries, in which the postulant bears witness in clear, unambiguous words, before Holy Church and the whole world, to the strength and freedom of her love, which has drawn her to remain enclosed for ever behind the convent walls. " What do you ask for ? " Calmly, and distinctly audible to everyone present, came the answer from Edith's lips, " The mercy of God, the poverty of the Order and the company of the sisters." " Are you resolved to persevere in the Order until death ? " " Thus do I hope and desire, through the mercy of God and the prayers of the sisters." With the closing blessing, " May the Lord divest thee of the old man together with his works " her superior left her side.

Edith Stein rose, took the lighted candle in her hand and approached the convent door as it opened before her. Awaiting her in the cloisters were the veiled nuns standing in two ranks, each of them holding a lighted candle. Stepping forward, one of the sisters held up the crucifix ; Edith sank on her knees before it and kissed it. She crossed the threshold and the door closed behind her.

While the congregation now pressed towards the wide-open grille and the sisters threaded their way through the cloisters singing *O gloriosa Domina*, Edith Stein rid herself of her worldly adornment. Over her shoulders was laid the penitential hair-cloth. the bridal veil and myrtle-wreath gave place to the Carmelite veil, and helping hands changed her pretty shoes for a pair of coarse sandals. When the procession drew into the choir at the last verse of the hymn the transformation was complete, and she and Mother Prioress came in together, the last pair in the procession.

The novice knelt on the carpet before the grille ; lying on a footstool nearby was the rest of her Carmelite habit. " May the Lord clothe you with the new man who is created in the justice and holiness of the truth." The Mother Prioress, standing on the novice's left, took the leather girdle, handed one end of it to the novice-mistress standing on the right, and together they fastened it round her waist. " When thou wast younger," said the Provincial, reminding her of her complete obedience, " thou didst gird thy self and didst walk where thou wouldst : but when thou shalt be old, another shall gird thee : In the name of the Father, and of the Son, and of the Holy Ghost." Taking the blessed scapular the Reverend Mother, together with the novice-mistress, laid it on the shoulders of the kneeling novice. " Receive the sweet yoke of Christ and His burden which is light : In the name of the Father, and of the Son and of the Holy Ghost " ; the words were the Provincial's, praying for her to embrace voluntary chastity : " Those who follow the Lamb without stain shall walk with Him in white garments. Therefore let thy vesture be ever unspotted in token of purity of heart."

The clothing was now over. Whilst everyone knelt and the Provincial intoned the hymn *Veni Creator Spiritus*, the new Carmelite prostrated herself on the floor in the form of a Cross, the sign of the mystical death her nature must die ; she remained thus until the novice-mistress gave her the sign, her call to the higher life of grace.

The new sister was led by the novice-mistress to the Mother Prioress to kiss her hands as a pledge of her grateful submission, after which she embraced all the other sisters while the cantors joyfully sang, " Behold how good and how pleasant it is for sisters to dwell together in unity ". Slowly the choir emptied. Those outside the grille continued looking and listening until at last they moved out again into their everyday life ; they had said good-bye to one who had won the pearl of great price by surrendering herself freely to the truth. Some days later the following article by Professor Peter Wust was published in the *Kölnische Volkszeitung* :

From Husserl to Carmel

' In the little chapel of the Carmelite convent at Cologne on Sunday the 15th of April, a circle of people, mainly intellectuals, assembled to celebrate together an occasion of more than everyday significance.

A bride was led to the altar whose life might be taken as a symbol of the intellectual movements of the last decade. For it was no earthly bridegroom to whom she united herself in marriage. She wore a wreath and veil, it is true, and carried a lighted candle in her hand, when we greeted her before she proceeded to the Altar. But at the end of the ceremony we took our leave of a nun dressed in the Carmelite habit. And no longer did the newly-clothed novice bear the name by which we had known her and admired her in the world, the philosopher, the disciple of Husserl ; she now bore the name of Sister Teresia Benedicta.

It is many years since her career brought her into contact with the founder of phenomenology. For a time she worked as assistant to Husserl. She was thus enabled to develop a profound understanding of his philosophical works, which since the appearance of *Logische Untersuchungen* have provoked a revolution in current philosophical thought. From the very beginning there must have been some hidden impulse movitating this philosophical movement, a longing to regain objectivity, to reach for the sacredness of being, for the purity and chastity of things, for " the thing itself ". Because, although the father of this whole school, Husserl himself, has never been able to free himself completely from the disease of subjectivism, many of his pupils have remained true to its original impulse, they have developed in themselves an " openness " towards things, towards the actual facts, towards being itself, acquiring that habit which marks off the truly Catholic man, the habit of allowing things to act as the measure for the mind which knows them. One recalls how Max Scheler one day recognized that his phenomenology must lead him directly to the objectivity of Catholic thought and how, for a while, though only for a while, this same thought helped to balance a thinker who was always so inclined to follow his emotions. Unfortunately he was swept once more into the relativistic undercurrent of the age, taking him further and further away from the direction which had once looked so hopeful and promising.

Edith Stein, on the other hand, for she is the pupil of Husserl's to whom we referred, and who is now the Carmelite Sister Benedicta, had the good fortune to keep to the path she had entered upon. Like Scheler and others her first step was to be received into the peace of *Una Sancta* ; but for her this was not the end. At first she remained true to philosophy, and especially to that philosophical movement to which she had been introduced by her master, Husserl. But it soon became obvious that she attached extraordinary importance to the elements of objectivity latent in phenomenology. Shut off from all the clatter of the contemporary world she plunged herself into the ontological thought of Aquinas by translating his comprehensive work, the *Quæstiones disputatæ de Veritate*. In this translation she stressed Aquinas' ontology in such a way as to leave the impression that she was holding up his work to contemporary phenomenologists as a kind of mirror in which they would see how far removed their own subjectivism was from the pure objectivity of this great medieval phenomenologist.

Clearly Husserl's pupil was deeply influenced in her out-look and her language by translating the work of a thinker so intoxicated with " being ". So deeply, indeed, that not only did her own person become ever calmer, simpler and more child-like, but one day she even awakened to the mystical inspiration which reveals itself in Aquinas' every thought. She went on, guided further and further into the reality of being, into the reality of the supernatural as it is described by those great figures, St. John of the Cross and St. Teresa of Avila, the classical exponents of the mystical, contemplative life.

At this clothing ceremony the spectator was inevitably filled with wonder as he followed each individual stage of the liturgical journey to the final, moving scene, when the new novice embraced her sisters one after the other during the singing of the *Veni Creator Spiritus*. Now a member of the community, Sister Benedicta, sealed with the seal of divine truth, withdrew with them towards the choir—towards the choir, away from the world.

One picture, however, seems to stick in my own mind more than any other, because it wonderfully expresses the symbolism of that whole feast. The guests had nearly all said good-bye to Sister Benedicta in the convent parlour. On one side of the grille stood the newly-clothed Carmelite and on the other Hedwig Conrad-Martius, the noted phenomenologist. What a curious play of circumstances it seemed that two of Husserl's outstanding pupils should now stand looking at one another for a moment under such unusual conditions. The one had applied the basic principles of phenomenology to plumb the depths of metaphysics far more surely than her master himself had done ; but the other, seeking for the very ground of being, had been drawn to the mysticism of Carmel. That same morning a telegram had been received at the Cologne Carmel ; it was from Husserl, sending his best wishes to Edith.

For a long time they stood before the grille of the enclosure going over the years in their minds, pondering on the symbolism of the long journey which this novice had made from Husserl to Thomas, and through Thomas to the present moment. Then the strict rule of the cloister interrupted their thoughts ; the last good-bye was said, and we went our ways —back into the world—back out of the world.'

Lord Abbot Raphael Walzer, when asked to explain more about Sister Benedicta's choice of a vocation, wrote the following lines :

' It is certainly right that I should be called upon to record my memories of her, at least of her later years. Yet I cannot help saying how hard I find it to provide answers to questions about her. For one thing, it is not really in accordance with her retiring character to be publishing the deepest secrets of her heart. In addition, as far as anything written is concerned, we have almost nothing in the way of letters or remains. Again, her interior life was so simple and free from problems that, from all my conversations with her, nothing remains in my memory but the picture of a soul of perfect clarity and maturity. *Fuit et quietus.* Tranquillity and balance, as we sing of them in the Hymn for Confessors in the monastic breviary, were in her the pitch of all her other qualities. Nevertheless, in spite of all the difficulties, I think that in what follows I shall be able to throw some light on certain aspects of her character.

When Edith Stein first came to Beuron, she was already no beginner. She brought so much treasure with her that, while she at once found her true home in the monastic atmosphere of this quiet spot on the banks of the Danube, she needed to make no adjustment, nor to learn anything essentially new. It was a kind of harvest of what others had sowed and she herself had cultivated in a most fruitful soil. In any account of her life this may be brought out as one of the most surely attested facts about her, without any fear of exaggerating the truth. But what was the special attraction for her of Beuron and the *opus Dei*? Certainly not the length of the services. She seems, it is true, to have had unlimited powers of endurance. She would spend, for instance, the whole of Good Friday from early morning till late at night in the Abbey Church. She was like her strict, ascetic Jewish mother in not seeing in this any special " performance ". Any form of pious " performance " was as alien to her as personal comfort or selfish desire for interior joys and graces. She neither had nor sought after any extraordinary exaltation or delight. Neither her intellect nor her senses lent themselves to any such thing. She simply wanted to be there, to be with God, and to have the great mysteries there before her, which she could not have either in the open country outside the enclosure or in her quiet cell. I do not think that she made much use in her meditation and prayer of written texts, nor that she went in for biblical exegesis nor thought out intellectual discourses, to which the world was always summoning her back. Certainly innumerable thoughts would mount and descend in her mind, as if on a Jacob's ladder thronged with heavenly messengers, and fervent aspirations would awake in her fresh fields of vision. But, like her external, almost rigid attitude, her interior spirit remained in tranquillity, blissfully gazing and rejoicing before God. Ever thankful for the grace of conversion, and happily at home with her Mother the Church, she recognized in the monastic choir, to which her liturgical and dogmatic knowledge enabled her to unite herself fully, the great praying Church. As Edith saw in Christ the Divine Head of the Mystical Body in uninterrupted prayer before the Father, so for her the supernatural life consisted first and foremost in the official prayer of the Church, in the carrying out of the apostolic injunction, " Pray without ceasing ". She took this command at its deepest level, so that no service was too long for her, no effort too great nor merely to be seen as a mortification : to her faith it was self-evident that one should plunge into and be submerged by the *laus perennis*. The strict, solemn liturgical form was certainly everything to her, and in a certain sense indispensable. And yet, when she finally entered Carmel, she did not find it difficult to give up the Benedictine way of belonging to the *Ecclesia orans*. I did not try to suggest that she should enter one of the Benedictine Abbeys dependent on Beuron. Humanly speaking, she would have made a splendid daughter of St. Benedict. It gave her pleasure to choose, as her second name in religion, the name of the Patriarch. Souls like hers, who have grasped the spirit of the whole, can afford to deepen and develop this same spirit in more specialized forms of religious life.

The mere beauty of the strict liturgy had no power to move her mind and heart. It is certainly true that form took a prominent position in her speech, in her vision, and in her creative work. In her dress and her whole appearance she gave an impression of wishing to please by her simplicity ; the very shape of her regular, oval face expressed a feeling for harmony and true art ; surely she found a rare satisfaction in the official prayers and rites of the Church. But nothing human could shake her from it ; not the in some ways unfortunate shape of the Abbey Church, for instance, nor other imperfections, which certainly did not escape her, with her wide command of culture and information. Her thought and prayer never suffered from the merely æsthetic, from art for art's sake. We hardly ever spoke of the questions then being discussed everywhere which were the product of the æstheticist approach. These problems held no interest for Edith. She kept away from them and did not occupy herself with criticizing or combating them. On this count too she had no difficulty in deciding on Carmel. No one saw more clearly than she that as well as having to adjust herself to the poverty and simplicity emphasized there, she would also encounter much that would irritate her own cultured taste. Yet she said nothing of this to the man to whom she spontaneously confided all her secrets. I had no need to prepare her for it, in the manner of the Novice Master of the fifty-eighth chapter of the Rule, telling the beginner of all the difficulties and annoyances, so as to test his vocation. She simply ran to Carmel like a child into its mother's arms, blithe and singing, without later regretting this almost blind eagerness even for a moment : somewhat as St. Benedict describes this going : " Now we must run, and do all that will have worth for eternity ". I can moreover expressly state that Edith most certainly did not choose Carmel out of ascetic rigorism on account of its liturgically less attractive constitution, so as to mortify herself with, humanly speaking, more difficult circumstances—an idea which some might attempt to attribute to her. No, she did not spend much time considering her choice. Carmel had for long been her love and her dream. Once the situation in the Third Reich made it impossible for me to deter her any longer from entering, she simply wished to realize this dream. She heard the voice of the All High, followed it, and did not ask for long where the road led.

It seemed almost a duty to prepare the future Carmelite for one final difficulty which she might encounter. But I soon saw how little it troubled her. Even here everything seemed quite self-evident to her. There was no need to come back to it again. Edith, if anyone, could justly and in the true sense of the word be called an intellectual, though she herself would have counted it presumption and spiritual pride to place herself in that class. Now the great St. Teresa recognizes only one class of sisters, usually not more than twenty-one of them living together in religious equality. Edith certainly did not seek the little convent in Cologne in the hope of finding there an academically-trained superior or a circle of similarly-gifted sisters. So far as I know, she was the only intellectual among them. Whether they would allow her to go on with intellectual activities, or even encourage them or make them a matter of obedience—over such questions she did not bother her head or try to obtain any kind of assurance. None of her learned friends could, either directly or indirectly, obtain any information on this matter from Husserl's assistant and the former lecturer of the German Institute of Educational Theory in Münster. She was ready to disappear into the Order. Not the shadow of a doubt darkened her intention. It is not difficult to appreciate what this alone must have meant for a mind that so hungered after knowledge. In fact it did seem to me that community life in a strictly enclosed convent, very small and situated in the middle of a town, in what seemed practically to amount to a community of lay-sisters, was too great a venture even for a heroically-inclined soul like Edith Stein. I was completely mistaken. When, after her clothing, I was able to see and speak to her alone—for the last time—I asked her for a quite definite and undiplomatic answer to the question of how she had taken to her sisters in the community and the new spiritual direction. I got what I might expect—that she was completely at home in heart and mind—an answer spoken with all the vehemence of her naturally fiery temperament. And one was not even tempted to suppose this an extraordinary miracle of grace. It all seemed to be the result of a natural development within the ripening of her supernatural life.

So too her love of the Cross and longing for martyrdom do not seem to me to have been a conscious attitude of soul likely to express itself in aspirations and prayer-intentions, but rather as a deeply rooted readiness to follow Our Lord wherever He might go. I do not think she deliberately neglected to make the effort to flee in time to Switzerland and so escape a fearful death. She would have accepted this way out in simple obedience. But on the other hand she did not trouble herself with the carrying out of this plan, sustained always by a holy indifference and abandonment to the Divine Will.'

In Freiburg " the dear old master ", Husserl, was waiting for news about Edith Stein's clothing, which he had been unable, to attend. On the 3rd of May he had an account of it read to him by Sister Adelgunis, O.S.B., also one of his pupils, who had received a description of the feast in a letter from their friend Maria Merz. Husserl listened to it all most intently ; occasionally he would interrupt her to ask some question about the Church's institutions and customs. It afforded him real pleasure that Edith was esteemed in the Church and in the Order ; he gave the impression of an anxious and yet proud father whose daughter (he used to call her his best pupil) is marrying into a new family. With fatherly pride he exclaimed: " I do not believe that the Church has any neoscholastic of Edith Stein's quality. Thank God that she will be able to keep up her learning in the Cologne Carmel." Subsequently he expressed his sorrow at not having travelled to Cologne ; as he said affectionately, " And I should have been the bride's father ", or again, after reflecting a while, " Your personal reactions can still be good, even when your opinions have diverged, like Edith's ". " She has come to understand clearly the intellectual world of the scholastics—'how do you explain that there is no trace of this in St. Teresa ? " And after hearing the reply, " Every true scholastic will become a mystic, and every true mystic a scholastic. It is remarkable— Edith stands on a summit, so to speak, and sees the furthest and broadest horizons with amazing clarity and detachment, yet there is another side, for at the same time she sees into herself with equal penetration. Everything in her is utterly genuine, otherwise I should say that this step was romanticism. But—deep down in Jews is radicalism and love faithful unto martyrdom." Pictures of St. Teresa were produced to show him the Carmelite habit, and he accepted a photo of the clothing as a keepsake.

To terminate this feast of Edith's clothing the Father Provincial held his visitation of the Cologne Carmel. In his conversation with Sister Benedicta he made long and detailed enquiries about her activities previous to her entry, and showed keen interest in her philosophical work. One of the things which Sister Benedicta brought with her when she left the world was an incomplete work entitled *Potentiality and Act*, which, in her own opinion, needed completely re-casting to bring it into line with her recently acquired knowledge. Therefore Father Provincial laid it down that Sister Benedicta should be relieved of all other duties so as to have enough time for this work. It was not long before requests for her to write articles and books began to be received both from inside and outside Carmel. A sister was being clothed and was taking the veil, for instance, so Sister Benedicta translated the customary prayers of the ceremony and prepared a version for printing, one page in Latin the other in German. This booklet was followed by a character-sketch of St. Teresa of Avila, which can truly be described as a gem precisely because it was so tiny whilst at the same time presenting all the essential features of the saint and her work. Kanisiusverlag published it in 1934. Teresia Margareta Redi, a young Carmelite saint canonized that same year, formed the subject of a second and similar character-sketch which Rita-Verlag, Würzburg, published. The academic Bonifatius-Einigung asked her for a contribution on the prayer of the Church for their anthology, *Ich lebe und ihr lebet* (I live and you live). In Fr. Eugen Lenses' book *Die in deinem Hause wohnen* (Who dwell in Thy house) appeared her biography of Katherina Esser, a native of Cologne, who in face of unspeakable odds managed to found the Cologne Carmel in 1848, the first contemplative convent established in Germany since the secularization. All this work was crammed into her very rare periods of leisure. Most of her energy was devoted to the difficult task of preparing the Index for her translation of St. Thomas, which was eventually brought out in 1935 by Borgmeyer after months of weary proof-correcting. Sister Benedicta herself writes : " It took a great deal of patience to get it into a satisfactory form ." At the same time she was carrying on with the history of her family which she had begun in the world ; she received permission to do so because it acted as a relief from the intellectual strain of her learned work. And so Sister Benedicta followed in the footsteps of her predecessors who, in their hermitages on Mount Carmel, had worked and prayed in order, as Jacques de Vitry (*circa* 1190) puts it, " to live as bees of the Lord, preparing a honey whose sweetness is wholly spiritual ".

Sister Benedicta also had learned how to imitate the industry of the bees, using every single minute of the day which was given to her. No matter how desirable or necessary it might have seemed for her to have long periods to spend on her creative work, her love of the Rule led her to adhere strictly to the convent's daily routine. One can imagine how hard it must have been for her when one remembers that the severest penance in Carmel comes through having to be constantly changing one's occupation. You have scarcely become warmed up to one occupation when you have to break off suddenly and get used to another. Two hours of continuous work, the most she ever enjoyed, were no time at all for someone with her tremendous power of concentration. But she gladly submitted to this custom of the Order, because she saw in it the wisdom of St. Teresa, who did not want her daughter's hearts and minds to be attached to any particular occupation.

As a Carmelite Sister Benedicta did not close her heart to all those whom she had loved in the world, and whom she had only left in order to conform to the will of Jesus. This does not mean that she used to look for her friends and relatives to visit her : she knew well enough that the noise of the world and all its bustle must be silenced at the threshold of the *hortus conclusus*, where the Beloved rests who can only be received by the calm and recollected soul. But she was too good a daughter of St. Teresa not to follow the saint's example, who never ceased all her life to share in her family's joys and sorrows, and whose heart the more overflowed with love for them the more it was detached from earthly ties. Edith used to watch over her friends' lives with affectionate concern and to greet her visitors with a supernaturally natural warmth.

' Most of the Sisters regard it as a penance [she wrote shortly before her clothing] to be called into the parlour. Certainly it is like passing into a strange world, and one is happy to escape again to the peace of the Choir, and to lay before the tabernacle the petitions one has received. But I receive this gift of peace as a completely unmerited grace, which is not meant for one person alone. And when someone comes to us all broken and in turmoil, but takes away some peace and consolation, that makes me very happy. Of course it is impossible to bear in mind all the detailed intentions that I receive from different quarters ; the most one can do is to live the life one has chosen ever more faithfully and purely, to offer it as an acceptable sacrifice for all those to whom one is bound. A constantly fresh incentive for this is provided by the confidence placed in us and the frighteningly high opinion of our life which is current in the world ' (11.1.34).

In the first year only her old friends used to come, especially her god-child Hede, with her husband Dr. Spiegel, because her godmother's teaching always proved a source of strength for her newly found faith. A frequent visitor was Peter Wust, Professor at Münster University, who used to protest constantly that the greatness of Sister Benedicta made him realize the insignificance of his own self-taught philosophy. Other visitors who kept her abreast of the most important contemporary issues were Fr. Petrus Jans, O.S.B. and Fr. Erich Przywara, S.J., neither of whom had been able to come to her clothing. Gertrud von le Fort came once in order to discuss her book *Die ewige Frau* (Eternal woman) ; she had just begun to work on it at the time, and she now assures us that it was Sister Benedicta who inspired that section of her book which describes the meaning of the veil; facing her on her desk as she was writing it stood a picture of Sister Benedicta in her bridal dress. Referring to this visit somewhat later Sister Benedicta wrote:

'When Gertrud von le Fort visited us in November I realized more clearly than ever how terribly trying this delicate creature must find it to be so much in the public eye, and to be always travelling about. And I began to wonder whether the results in any way corresponded to the sacrifice. When I asked her if the lecture that evening had made a good impression she simply said "Yes". Gertrud von le Fort is also going to visit my acquaintances in Breslau, and in December "Nonni" (the famous Icelandic story-teller, Fr. Svenson, S.J.) was here, and promised to visit my relatives whenever he is in Breslau' (7.III.35)

Through the medium of such messengers she tried to keep in touch with her family whom she had left for love of them. Although her mother still did not know that she had now taken the Carmelite habit her sisters had all sent their greetings for the occasion. It grieved Rosa that she had not been able to witness the feast, particularly after she heard the enthusiastic descriptions of it which some of those present had sent to her. Month after month she set her hopes on visiting Cologne but she could not have left her mother for so long without causing suspicion. So Sister Benedicta contented herself with writing to her mother week in and week out, but never receiving an answer.

The year's novitiate which she had to serve as the ultimate test of her vocation before going on to take her vows came to an end.

On the 11th of February she wrote to her late spiritual director's nephew, Dean Schwind:

'Please remember me particularly during the coming months.

I hope to take my first vows in April. As to your question about how I have settled down to this lovely life, I cannot help smiling a little. For most of my life I have been far lonelier than I am here. I miss nothing that is outside and have everything that I missed when I was outside, so that I am utterly thankful for the wholly unmerited grace of my vocation.'

Just as the subsequent development of all human beings is closely linked with the habits they are taught in the nursery, so the first years of formation in the monastic life, i.e. the noviciate, to a large extent determines and reflects the measure of their subsequent striving for perfection. Day after day Sister Benedicta plunged ever more deeply into the spirit of the Order in accordance with that counsel of the Foundress, which bids her daughters seek nothing but God alone and to give themselves unreservedly to His will.

What a high conception of the religious life Sister Benedicta cherished while still in the world is indicated by the following lines, taken from an address to some nuns.

' The motive, principle and aim of the religious life is to forget oneself entirely in an utterly loving surrender to God, allowing one's own life to end and leaving room for God's life.

The more completely this is realized, ever the more richly is the soul endowed with divine life. But divine life is love, overflowing, unforced, self-giving love ; love which humbles itself compassionately for each creature in need ; a warm, nourishing love which protects, instructs and forms us ; love which mourns with those who mourn, rejoices with the joyful, and puts itself at the service of every creature so that each creature becomes what the Father wishes it to be—in a word : the love of the divine heart. . . .

To surrender oneself lovingly to another being, to become wholly the property of another and to possess this other wholly—this is the deepest longing of a woman's heart, and accounts for that specifically womanly quality of concentrating on persons and seeing them whole. When a woman makes this surrender to another creature she is underestimating her worth, enslaving herself and making demands which no creature can fulfil. Only God can receive us wholly, so that He fills our whole being and yet loses nothing of Himself. That is why the aim of the religious life, complete surrender, is also the one adequate fulfilment of a woman's longings. . . .'

All her sisters were so edified through living with her that there was not the slightest hesitation about her profession, which was fixed for the 21st of April, Easter Day. Sister Benedicta's happiness and gratitude knew no limits. By nature she was very modest and recollected, but during this Lenten season God seemed to draw her more than ever into herself. On the evening of the 10th of April she began her retreat. She adopted an even stricter seclusion from her sisters and an even greater silence. This was her desert, or rather her oasis in the desert, of whose overflowing bliss St. Jerome speaks : " O desert, adorned with the flowers of Christ ! Desert where grow the mystical stones of the Apocalypse, from which the city of the great king is to be built. Holy solitude, wherein to enjoy the intimacy of God ! Friend, what are you doing in the world who are greater than the world ? Why do you remain captive beneath the dark shadows of the houses ? Why do you remain imprisoned in the golden bird-cage that is the city ? Though I know not how, believe me when I say that I see the light more clearly here. Freed 'from the burden of the body, the soul takes flight towards heaven." [1] She had every reason to share the abundant joy of her sister in the Order, blessed Magdalena del Pazzi, who kissed the high convent walls which enclosed herself and her Beloved, allowing her to enjoy here below a foretaste of the eternal wedding-feast by a union with her Bridegroom which was none the less real for being purely spiritual.

The graces of a profession-day are kept as a secret by the King and His elected Bride. Consequently St. Teresa, in a clause of her constitutions for which her daughters are ever

[1] Letter to Heliodor.

grateful, laid it down that nuns should make their profession in chapter without the presence of prelates or priests, so that this act may be treated as an intimate family-feast. This Carmelite custom means that no acquaintances of the sister being professed are invited on that day. On this day of her marriage the sister declares her absolute and undivided love for her Lord who has raised her to be His Bride on the heights of Carmel.

In the early hours of the morning, whilst the earth was still covered in darkness, the Easter bells began to ring out in Carmel breaking the silence they had kept during the sorrowful season of Lent. The community formed a triumphant procession as they entered the choir, which was all gaily decorated for the occasion, the first spring flowers on all sides and everywhere the sweet scent of myrtle. As the tabernacle was opened the *Surrexit Dominus vere, Alleluia!* rang out. At her place in choir Sister Benedicta was standing amidst the row of novices. How did she find it so easy to pray Matins in the penitential monotone of the Carmelites when she was so accustomed to celebrating the Easter liturgy with all the splendour of monastic ritual in Beuron? Gradually day dawned. With joyful hearts the community raised their lighted candles to greet their Mother and Queen, the glory of Carmel, to thank Jesus for His conquest of death and the devil : *Regina cœli lœtare, Alleluia!* The procession of light was set in motion ; the cantors began to intone *Aurora cœlum purpurat.* As the red light of morning began to stream through the high cloister-windows the procession went from station to station until it eventually came to the beautifully wrought tomb. From there they filed back into the choir and assumed their places. The succeeding ceremony, the taking of vows, was performed with moving simplicity. Mother Prioress had taken up her position on the Gospel side of the choir ; Edith knelt before her, folded her hands, and raised them for her superior to clasp whilst she herself began to recite her short but tremendous promise :

" I, Sister Teresia Benedicta of the Cross, make profession

of my temporary vows for three years. I promise obedience, chastity and poverty to our Lord God, to the ever Blessed Virgin of Mount Carmel and to you, Mother Prioress, as well as to your successors, in accordance with the original rule and constitutions of the Order of Discalced Carmelites."

" Offer a sacrifice of praise to the Lord " came the Prioress' command ; the voices of the sisters took it up with the cry : " and fulfil your vows to the Almighty."

" I will fulfil my vows to the Lord in the sight of his people, and in the mansions of the Lord ! " came the calm, firm, answer from Sister Benedicta. A wreath of white roses was handed to Reverend Mother who crowned her with it. Again the bells sounded the *Te Deum* whilst Sister Benedicta prostrated herself before the altar in the form of the Cross, her consecration complete. It was about six o'clock in the morning. After the Office Holy Mass was offered for the intention of Christ's new Bride who was also the first to receive the Lord's Body, taking precedence even over the Mother Prioress. After Mass, however, she had to wait a whole day before being allowed to communicate her joy to her sisters.

A few months previously a young Cologne girl had entered the novitiate at Lindenthal. She had taken all the day's happenings to heart, and now she clung to Sister Benedicta like a small child and asked, " How does Your Charity [1] feel ? " The answer, given as only Sister Benedicta's own voice could give it, left an indelible impression on her soul : " Like the Bride of the Lamb ! "

Describing her feelings after visiting Sister Benedicta some days later, the wife of a local schoolmaster writes :

' I shall never forget her radiant countenance and her youthfulness during the week she was professed. It seemed as though she had become twenty years younger and I was deeply impressed by her happiness. She must have received great graces from God—like the saints.

[1] The form of address from one Carmelite to another.

But I must also let you know what she said to me as she was sitting opposite me with her veil drawn aside. During our conversation I happened to remark that she would be out of harm's way here in Carmel. To this she quickly replied : " No. I don't think so. I am sure that they will come and search me out here. In any case I should not count upon being left here in peace." It was clear enough to her that she had been called to suffer for her people so that many might be saved.'

III

THE BRIDE OF CHRIST

SOME time after she had taken her vows Sister Benedicta decided that she ought to give her mother in Breslau a full account of it all. Her mother's obstinate silence had never prevented her from sending off her weekly letter, and her novice-mistress never missed the opportunity of adding a few lines of her own. It would be impossible to describe Sister Benedicta's intense joy when she opened her letter from Rosa one day and found in it her mother's best wishes. Even greater was her surprise when she learned that one fine autumn day the old lady had gone off alone without saying a word to anyone to pay a visit to the new Carmel in Breslau-Pawelwitz. Was she hoping to hear or see something of the strange life into which her daughter had plunged? In any case, from now on every letter from Breslau brought with it a few lines from her mother, and one fine day she went so far as to include " Sister Therese " in her good wishes—and continued to do so. This was a great comfort to Sister Benedicta, who had borne all her grief without flinching and without ever allowing it to disturb her constant warmth and friendliness.

A lady who knew her well writes in reference to this period, " Later I was able to visit Sister Benedicta more often in Carmel and each time I noticed how gay and happy she was, much gayer and brighter than when I knew her in the world."

The new year of 1936 brought with it a change in the Cologne Carmel. Mother Josepha wished to be relieved of her office of Prioress which she had held for twelve years. At the election on the 8th of January the former novice-mistress, Sister Teresia Renata, was elected Prioress, and Sister Aloisa of the Blessed Sacrament was made Sub-Prioress. However, Mother Josepha was given charge of the novices and so continued to look after Sister Benedicta. The change made no difference to Sister Benedicta, who held both her superiors in equal affection. Meanwhile she herself had become the senior novice. Her two predecessors had transferred to the community after making their solemn vows ; this left three choir-postulants and one novice under her wing. She displayed wonderful understanding and sympathy in helping these young souls to make their first steps in the Ascent of Mount Carmel. It frequently happens that souls who flee from the world with violent enthusiasm find that the effort has worn them out, and they break up once they are behind the " strait gate " for which they were aiming. They begin to suffer from that interior anguish which St. Thérèse of the Child Jesus wrote about after her own long experience of it. " I kept asking myself if it was not killing me ! What a time ! What a deathly torment ! One has to live through it if one is to comprehend it." Such sufferings are quite sufficient to shake the composure of anyone finding themselves so suddenly transplanted into the desert. At the beginning, therefore, many postulants seem like a convalescent who, if she has not just eluded death itself, has at least been threatened by serious disease. This courageous child has broken through the net and liberated herself from the snares of the world ; and now she stands there, empty and weary ; only yesterday she seemed to hold the riches of the earth in her hands, to-day she has scarcely the strength to fold them and lift them in prayer to the Lord of Hosts Who is the strength of the weak.

It is of course the novice Mistress's task to inspire souls with steadfastness and courage on the road of self-denial, but how these young souls, as yet so inexperienced in the spiritual life, were comforted and helped by the example and advice of their fellow-novice ! They needed no telling that she had found her peace and happiness in God, that her own heart and the rule formed a single unity, and that one could have placed in her mouth the words of St. Thérèse : " I set myself the single aim of becoming more and more united to God, knowing quite well that everything else would then be given to me." Nothing gladdened Sister Benedicta's heart more than to guide others towards the happiness which God had granted to her.

She also did everything in her power to have her godchild, Dr. Ruth Kantorowicz, taken into the Carmel, but her superiors refused to allow it in view of the unfavourable times. Along with many other events this disappointment was a reminder that the storm raging outside could even break into the silence of the Cologne Carmel. Sister Benedicta never deluded herself about what consequences were to be expected from the growing anti-semitism. She had already made several contributions to the journal *Die Christliche Frau* (Christian Woman), and one of her essays on St. Thomas was due to appear in December 1935. The proofs arrived, but no review copy was sent. Her friends wished to go into the matter but she herself guessed what it implied and wrote :

' My deepest thanks, but please don't take it any further. After I had sent off a second article to Aachen I suddenly saw that neither this one nor the other would appear. The editors must have realized that the journal would be suspect if they accepted my co-operation, but they had not the courage to write and tell me. All this became clear to me when I learned that I was no longer eligible to vote. So far I have not had any confirmation of this, but it will soon arrive. Please do not disturb yourself about it any more. For a long time I have been prepared for much worse things.'

And in the same letter :

I return your Easter greetings with all my heart. I am

overjoyed each day when I recall how long Easter lasts, and that we can draw to ourselves ever more of its inexhaustible richness. It is the time in the Carmelite year when we are brought closest to heaven. The trees and bushes in our garden are now blossoming, and they seem intimately bound up with the grace-filled days of my religious life ' (19 IV.36).

Some weeks later, just before Whitsuntide, alarming news was brought from Breslau. For the first time in her life Frau Stein was ill. Sister Benedicta immediately feared the worst and said : " Now she will not see her eighty-eighth birthday." She asked the sisters for their prayers. Was she still hoping that her mother would be converted ?

In Breslau everything possible was done to alleviate the patient's suffering, and, in fact, Frau Stein recovered sufficiently to send her last good wishes to her child in Carmel. But towards the end of July her suffering increased and it became obvious that she was incurable. The doctor had detected a swelling on her stomach which he presumed to be a cancer.

Inwardly Sister Benedicta must have suffered a great deal, but outwardly she was unchanged. In a letter which she wrote about this time she says : " These summer months have been hard upon my mother and all those at home, and for me as well."

The year drew on to the Feast of the Exaltation of the Holy Cross, the 14th of September, a very important day in Carmel, since it marks the beginning of the great fast which lasts until the day of Our Lord's Resurrection. Also the whole Order renews its vows in accordance with St. Teresa's instructions, and this was the third time that Sister Benedicta had taken part in the ceremony, held in the silent hour before dawn. Afterwards she said to one of her sisters who was specially intimate with her, " As I was standing in my place in choir waiting to renew my vows my mother was beside me. I felt her presence quite distinctly." On that same day a telegram came from Breslau with the news that Frau Stein had died—at the very time when her daughter was renewing her vows. These circumstances greatly consoled Sister Benedicta, who bore up nobly even when the first waves of sorrow were sweeping over her. All the same she did not allow herself any illusions. In the letters of condolence which she received it was frequently suggested that Frau Stein had been converted to Catholicism before she died. Her reply is to be found in a letter dated the 4th of October, 1936.

' The announcement of my mother's conversion is a completely unfounded rumour. Who began it, I don't know. My mother remained steadfast in her own beliefs until the very end. But since her firm faith and trust in God remained unshaken from her earliest childhood to her eighty-seventh year and was her last support in her hard struggle with death, I am confident that she has found a most merciful Judge, and that she is now my most faithful helper on my own journey towards my homeland.'

Frieda and Rosa were now alone. In their mother's will they were asked to maintain the house at 38 Michaelistrasse as a permanent home for the rest of the family. Already, however, Sister Benedicta guessed that the circumstances of the time would soon make this impossible. Furthermore, she was longing to speak with Rosa once again—just as Rosa herself felt that she could not go on any longer without seeing her sister. As soon, then, as everything to do with the inheritance had been put in order Rosa began arranging to come to the Rhineland. She was expected in Cologne on the 15th of December, as this would enable her to spend Christmas in Carmel. But a quite unexpected episode happened beforehand.

It was on the 14th of December at about seven o'clock in the evening. The Carmel lay wrapped in the darkness of winter ; and the lights were shining in only one room, the community room, towards which everyone who had finished her evening duties was hurrying to join in recreation. Owing to shortage of coal the novices' room was not heated and the " little ones " had to come with their Mother, the novice-mistress, to the " big ones ".

The Sub-Prioress was missing from the circle because, as part of her ten-day private retreat, she was just then praying the stations of the Cross, moving from one station to the next in the dark cloister. Suddenly she heard someone coughing lightly, which is the way Carmelites attract each other's attention during the time of strict silence. " Who is there ? " she called into the darkness. There was no reply. But the same sound, now like someone in pain, seemed to come from the direction of the stairs. Quickly she went across to the switch and turned on the lights. A few quick strides and she was up on the landing where she found Sister Benedicta lying on the floor. She had been feeling for the switch on the wrong side of the door, had stepped too near the stairs and fallen down. She was carried to her cell in great pain and the community's doctor was called in. Dr. Eugen Hopmann was soon on the spot, and after examining her foot, which was apparently fractured, ordered the patient to be taken to the Trinitarian hospital to have her leg X-rayed and set. This was done as soon as we had received permission for her to leave the enclosure. Everyone in Carmel was most concerned about Rosa, who was due to arrive next day and would be disappointed at not finding her sister, until it suddenly struck them how much better it was that Rosa should visit her in hospital when they would not have to talk through a double grille.

The same evening the result of the X-ray was received from the hospital : her left hand and left foot were both broken.

Rosa Stein arrived in Cologne the next day. It was easy to see whose sister she was because she had the same beautiful features as Sister Benedicta, but, even more noticeably, the same calm gaze in her soft eyes and the same modesty of speech and behaviour. Every day she used to visit her sister from whom she received instruction, because the week leading up to Christmas was to serve as her last preparation for her

Baptism. Christmas Eve was the date fixed ; Canon von
Aacken was to administer the sacrament of her rebirth in Christ
at the lovely church of Hohenlind. The arrangement of these
details was undertaken by Heinrich Spaemann, the sculptress
Hildegard Domizlaff and Frau Hantelmann, who were all
converts themselves. Everything was in order except that
no one knew where to get a white dress for the candidate.
Eventually someone thought of Sister Benedicta's white
Carmelite cloak, and Rosa was overjoyed at the suggestion
that she should use it. As it happened Sister Benedicta herself
had recovered well enough to leave the hospital on the 24th
of December, strapped in a plaster-of-paris cast ; and since
Doctor Hopmann said that it would be all right to make a
slight detour to Hohenlind on the way to Lindenthal she was
given the wonderful Christmas present of attending her sister's
Baptism. At four o'clock the sacrament was administered,
and a few hours later Rosa Stein received the Body of our Lord
for the first time. None of the faithful who came to church
that night was aware that Rosa was making her first Communion, but around the crib of the newly born Saviour they
noticed brilliant baptismal candles, the silent witnesses to the
hidden ways of God.

To celebrate her sister's re-birth by water and of the Spirit
Sister Benedicta composed the following lines, speaking in
the person of Rosa herself.

HOLY NIGHT

IN REMEMBRANCE OF CHRISTMAS EVE, 1936

My Lord and God,
You have guided me on a long, dark road,
Stony and hard.
How often the strength has gone from me,
And I almost hoped never to see the light.
Yet when my heart sickened in the depths of sorrow
A star rose before me, gentle and clear.
Steadily it guided me—and I followed.

Stumbling at first, but ever more surely.
Until at last I stood before the door of the Church.
It was opened—I prayed to enter—
And from the lips of your priest I received your blessing.
Within shone row upon row of stars
Red Christmas stars,[1] showing me the way to you.
They led me forward.
The secret of my heart, which for so long I had to hide,
I now proclaim aloud
I believe, I confess !
The priest takes me with him up the altar steps,
I bow my head—
And the holy water cleanses my soul.
Is it possible, Lord, to be born again
After leaving a mother's womb ?
It is You who said it and You I believe.
The burden and sorrow of a life-time fell from me.
Standing up I received the white cloak
That was laid on my shoulders,
The shining symbol of purity !
I carried a candle in my hand,
Its flame announcing the glow of your holiness within
    me.
Now my heart has become a crib
Waiting for your Son.
Though not for long !
Mary, my Mother and your Mother,
Has given me her name
And at midnight gives me her newly born Child
To lay in my heart.
No human heart could ever conceive
What you are preparing for those who love you.
Now I possess you and will never leave you.
For wherever the road of life leads me, you are beside me,
Nothing can ever divide me from your love.

[1] The Church of Hohenlind was brightly decorated with flowers known as
" Christmas Stars ".

THE BRIDE OF CHRIST

And what happy days of festivity God now granted to the two sisters, and to the whole Carmelite community who were their sisters in charity. It was not until New Year's Eve that the convert travelled back to Breslau where she was to receive the sacrament of Confirmation at Pentecost, 1937, in the crypt of the Kreuzkirche.

Looking back on these events Sister Benedicta wrote :

' Rosa is living peacefully with the family again, though inwardly she is very lonely. This makes her all the more determined to be spiritually united with those who are separated from her in the body. This spiritual gulf between herself and her surroundings is proving a strain on her. But we must be very thankful that they are all living together in peace. And it is wonderful to see how she derives all her strength from sharing in the life of the Church. In her heart she is here with us always, and we on our part are doing whatever we can to make her realize that she is one of us.

Whilst she was here the community treated her just like one of our own little family, which pleased her beyond words—more so perhaps because in the outside world you are all in continual danger and never know whom you can trust ' (7 v.37).

Even before the end of 1936 Sister Benedicta had completed her set task, the revision of her comprehensive philosophical dissertation, *Potentiality and Act* (1931). The result was a thick manuscript of 1,368 sides. The work ranks as an important contribution to contemporary discussions on ontology, because it skilfully relates the phenomenological way of looking at things with the Thomistic teaching about things themselves. Her title for it was : *Finite and Eternal Being, a survey of the philosophia perennis*.

By *philosophia perennis* she did not mean any particular scholastic system, but unwearied investigations which men pursue in search of true being. Describing how the book came about, she writes :

EDITH STEIN

' This book has been written by a learner for her fellow-learners.   Its author, in an age when others ventured to call themselves teachers, found herself compelled to begin at the beginning.   She received her formation in Husserl's school, and wrote several works along phenomenological lines.   These essays appeared in Husserl's *Jahrbuch*, and so her name became known at the very time that she had abandoned philosophical work, when she had not the remotest intention of publicizing her thoughts.   She had been led to Christ and his Church and was wholly occupied in realizing the practical consequences of this step.   As a teacher in the Dominican nuns' training-college at Speyer she learnt to be thoroughly at home in the Catholic world.   Inevitably, however, the desire to examine the philosophical implications of this world was aroused.   Almost inevitably she went first to the writings of St. Thomas Aquinas, and it was through translating his *Quæstiones de veritate* that the province of philosophy was once more opened to her.

St. Thomas found a reverent and willing pupil—but her mind was by no means *tabula rasa* ; it had already received a sharp, unmistakable impression.   The two philosophical worlds seemed to run together and demand to be related to each other.   The first response to this demand was the small contribution to the Husserl *Festschrift* : " Husserl's philosophy and the philosophy of St. Thomas Aquinas ", written at the time that the *Quæstiones* were being translated.   Once the translation was completed and in the press, another attempt at discussion was initiated on a larger scale and with more detailed references ; the outline of it was completed during the year 1931.   Its central concern was to draw out the implications in the concepts of act and potency.   It needed revising fundamentally, as was recognized immediately, but this revision had to be postponed in favour of the quite different work then at hand.

After the writer had been received into the Order of Discalced Carmelites and completed her noviciate she was directed by her superiors to prepare her preliminary sketch for publication. What emerged was an almost entirely new work ; only a few pages of the preliminary sketch (the beginning of the 1st part) have been retained. Thomistic teaching on act and potency still acts as the starting-point, but only as the starting-point : for the central concern lies with the question of Being. It is through a detailed discussion of this question that the relationship between Thomistic and phenomenological thought is elucidated. Because others besides the writer regard this as a crucial issue in philosophy (that is, the search for the meaning of Being, a synthesis between medieval thought and the most vital contemporary philosophy) she has thought it possible that her work may help others towards a solution, despite its insufficiencies.'

Soon afterwards Professor Alexander Koyré from the Sorbonne paid her a visit as he and his wife were on their way back to Paris ; he looked through her work, which was also read by Professor Dempf from Bonn. Both these scholars were extremely impressed by the book, but the next step, which was to find a publisher, proved to be no easy matter. Whenever Sister Benedicta applied to have it published it was refused for one reason or another, although she tried throughout all Germany, Austria and even Switzerland. Eventually the firm of Borgmeyer in Breslau, who had brought out her translation of St. Thomas, said that they would take the risk. On the assumption that Borgmeyer as an experienced business-man had hit upon a way of circumventing the non-Aryan laws, Sister Benedicta entrusted him with her book. Soon the first proofs arrived and she was busy correcting them during the following months.

The final touches had been put to the first volume, and a start had been made on the second, when Sister Benedicta was informed by a confidant that the work was not going to appear under her name but would be issued under the name of another Sister, who was a member of the Reich Literary Institute. Neither Sister would agree to such a proposal. Consequently·

Borgmeyer had no choice but to send the manuscript back and stop the printing. Despite her keen disappointment it did not come as a surprise to Sister Benedicta. She tried to persuade Borgmeyer to arrange for publication in Holland, but even this plan proved unworkable.

IV

THE WAY OF LOVE AND KNOWLEDGE

1937 was a year of thanksgiving for the Cologne Carmel
since it was the tercentenary of its foundation. To
celebrate this great jubilee in a fitting manner all available
hands in the Carmel were turned to preparing for it.
As soon as she was able to walk comfortably without the aid of
a stick, Sister Benedicta was co-opted for this work, and it
naturally fell to her lot to compose a commemorative booklet
describing how this Carmel of the Queen of Peace had been
responsible for twelve other foundations during its three
hundred years of history. She and the Mother Prioress
investigated all the historical sources and collected the necessary documents. Once the manuscript was ready she went
over it, putting it into shape and verifying all the references to
original and secondary works. One result of investigating
the community's history was that Sister Benedicta began to
correspond with the Carmel at Echt, because when the
Cologne Carmelites fled to Echt in Holland at the time of the
Kulturkampf they took with them all the treasures and records
which had belonged to the original community at Cologne.
Very generously the Prioress at Echt sent paintings, chronicles
and other documents to Cologne to be copied.

While the tercentenary festivities were at their height
distant warnings were heard of the storm that was to sweep
away so many communities. In the words of Sister Benedicta,
writing from the Cologne Carmel :

' So far we have been living quite unmolested in the pro-
foundest peace behind our convent walls. But the fate of our

Spanish sisters is an indication of what we have to steel ourselves for. And when these deep rifts in society begin to open up nearer home we can take it as a salutary warning. In any case it is our duty to pray in support of the people who are fighting so hard in the front-line [she was referring to the violent struggle for the schools then in progress]. We celebrated our jubilee from the 30th of September to the 3rd of October. Our guest of honour was the holy statue of the Queen of Peace from our old convent-church, Maria of Peace. It was displayed on the wonderfully decorated high altar where Pontifical High Mass was celebrated every morning. There was also a Sung Mass, several low Masses and three sermons each day. We must be very grateful that such things are still possible.' (5 VI.37).

Clearly Sister Benedicta's literary work was inspired by apostolic enthusiasm, but such intrinsically congenial work did not satisfy her love for her neighbour. Wishing to take her share in works of mercy she asked if she might attend to the needs of Sister Clare of the Precious Blood who was dying of cancer. She was very happy when her superiors allowed her to undertake this labour of love, if only for a few months.

In December, 1937, she was appointed under obedience to an important and responsible office in the community, the office of Turn Sister, which had previously been performed by the sub-prioress. This meant that Sister Benedicta had the job of seeing to the sisters' everyday needs, ordering supplies and giving the extern-sisters their instructions as well as announcing the guests and providing for them. All messages going through the grille came into her province. As our holy Mother insisted in her constitutions, it is an office demanding tact, prudence and, above all, discretion, virtues which Sister Benedicta possessed in the highest degree. She behaved with loving kindness towards the two young girls who used to see to external affairs before extern sisters were introduced into the Cologne Carmel.

THE WAY OF LOVE AND KNOWLEDGE

Yet in spite of such calls upon her from all sides her great philosophical work was now completed. It was entitled *Ewiges und Endliches Sein* (Eternal and Finite Being).

* * * *

Spring of 1938 brought with it two great feasts for Sister Benedicta, her final profession and the taking of the veil, which would mark the end of her education in the Order. The final vows have to be taken exactly three years after the date of temporary vows, which in Sister Benedicta's case meant the 21st of April, Thursday in Easter week. In preparation for her irrevocable surrender to Jesus she made a ten-day retreat. Her happiness this day was very great. It is true that no one could foresee the future calamity, but everyone had uneasy suspicions of its imminence. Since she still wore the white veil of a novice the final seal had yet to be set upon Sister Benedicta's marriage to Christ. She was to receive the black veil, the symbol of sacrifice and of her total consecration to God, on the First of May, Good Shepherd Sunday. The ceremony was to be performed publicly by her friend, auxiliary bishop Dr. Stockums, because the Archiepiscopal Director of Convents, Dr. Lenné, was prevented from coming.

At nine o'clock Sister Benedicta's friends were all gathered in the little convent chapel. The bride herself was kneeling in the Sisters' choir before the wide-open grille so that she could hear the High Mass and listen to the priest who was to preach a special sermon for the occasion. In a rich casket on the altar lay the veil and a wreath of white roses. These were blessed while the sisters sang *Amo Christum*, " I love Christ whose chambers I have entered ; His Mother is a Virgin, His father knew no woman. The voice of His organ sings to me in harmony ; if I love Him then I am chaste, if I touch Him I am pure, if I receive Him I am a virgin. With this ring He has bound me to Himself and has adorned me with treasures beyond price."

Now the Bishop moved towards the grille calling to the

bride : " Come, bride of Christ, receive the crown which your Lord has prepared for you from all eternity." After a slight pause, Sister Benedicta rose from her knees and now gave witness to her vows before all those present : *Suscipe me Domine.* . . .

" Receive me, O Lord, according to Thy Word, and let not my expectations be confounded." Sister Benedicta proceeded towards the open grille and knelt again. The Bishop covered her bowed head with the black veil, set the rose wreath upon it and said : " Receive the sacred veil, the emblem of holy reverence and continence ; carry it before the judgement-seat of our Lord Jesus Christ to gain eternal life and to live for ever, Amen." Shrouded in the black veil Sister Benedicta again withdrew to the middle of the choir and sang, " He has set his seal upon my countenance ".

She sank to her knees while the Sisters responded. " So that I allow no other love but Him." Again she lay prostrate on the floor in the form of the Cross, while the sound of the bells joined with the human voices to glorify God in the *Te Deum laudamus.* After the closing blessing she rose to her feet, dead to this world, but her heart overflowing with that same joy which burst from the heart of her great predecessor, St. John of the Cross, when he sang his great song of triumph : " Mine are the heavens and mine is the earth ; mine are the people, the righteous are mine ; and God Himself is mine, and for me, for Christ is mine and all for me. What, then, dost thou ask for and seek, my soul ? Thine is all this, and it is all for thee. Despise not thyself nor give thou heed to the crumbs which fall from thy Father's table. Go thou forth and do thou glory in thy glory. Hide thee therein and rejoice and thou shalt have the desires of thy heart."

With the taking of her final vows Sister Benedicta became a full member of the community ; she was a member of the chapter having both an active and passive right in voting. Nevertheless she remained what she had always been, a humble and unassuming Carmelite Sister who carried out all her duties conscientiously, living for God alone in God alone. Nothing grieved her more than to find herself held in esteem.   She once wrote to a lady who admired her greatly :

' I do not want to hurt you at all, but I think I must mention something about your last letter, as about many previous ones, which caused me distress.   This is your constant insistence that my life is on a plane immeasureably superior to your own. I should consider myself a pharisee if I were to allow such assurances to be silently accepted, because they have no objective foundation.   You are by no means the only person in whom our grille instils a pious awe.   But this grille does not mean that on that side—" in the world "—everything is wicked, whereas on this side everything is perfect.   We are only too conscious of the human weakness concealed below the habit, and it shames us whenever we find someone scattering incense.   God is merciful and kind-hearted beyond all conception and repays the mere intention of consecrating oneself entirely to Him with incalculable rewards.   When you are here you in some way detect the peace of His House, and for this we give thanks.   But you must not attribute to a poor human being what is, in fact, a pure gift from God.'

News about hostile measures against the Jews began to be heard more regularly :   more and more frequently Sister Benedicta used to receive visits from her god-daughter, Hede Spiegel, wife of a Jewish solicitor, who came to pour out her fears and forebodings, and to discuss how she and her old parents might escape from the bloody persecution then imminent.   She was depressed and confused by rumours that Hitler was demanding a campaign to exterminate the Jews, but Sister Benedicta's rock-like calm and unshakable faith in God acted as an anchor for her bewildered heart.

Quite naturally the suggestion often arose in Sister Benedicta's own mind that she ought to go into exile, especially when she heard of people being boycotted on account of their friendship towards Jews.   This made her fear for the Carmelite family to which she belonged.   However, her superior forbade her to mention the matter, so as to avoid any disturbance which might later prove to have been unnecessary. And then came the decisive day of the Hitler plebiscite.

Chalked up on every tree in the Dürenerstrasse at Lindenthal were the stark words, " Your ' Ja ' for the Führer." The previous elections had already provided their own little comic opera. It had been announced in noisy proclamations that non-Aryans were not to take part in the elections ; so Sister Benedicta stayed behind while the other Sisters, with the Archbishop's permission, set off for the polling-booths to do what little they could for the just cause. But that same evening, just before the voting closed, two gentlemen appeared in the parlour. Having learned that Dr. Stein had not used her vote they had assumed that she was unable to walk to the booth ; and so they had come to drive her there and back in their car. This was the message brought to Sister Benedicta and the Prioress by the turn-sister. Since Sister Benedicta had no mind to declare her ancestry just then, and since there were no other objections, she said very quietly : " Well, if the gentlemen are so keen to have my ' No ' recorded—I cannot bear to disappoint them." Quickly slipping on her shoes she made ready for the journey.

But the 10th of April was no joking matter.

Hitler's method of governing and the fundamental teachings of National Socialism had proved to be so clearly hostile to God and Christianity that even the simplest German could no longer be deceived about Hitler's aim. At the same time, everyone was frightened by the violence and cruelty of the state authorities. Even in the Cologne Carmel, therefore, there was much uncertainty about how one should behave. Already the Gestapo had arrived at many religious houses without warning and simply turned the religious out, leaving them unprovided for on the street. For a long time the Cologne Carmel had been expecting this same fate, which would almost certainly befall them if they displeased the authorities. Well-meant advice to have nothing to do with the elections was therefore unacceptable. Most of the community adopted the attitude that it did not matter how one voted since the election in any case was being engineered by the Nazis, who would concoct whatever results they pleased.

In the passionate attacks which Sister Benedicta made upon this attitude one could scarcely recognize her for the gentle and retiring person she generally was. Time and again she urged the Sisters not to choose Hitler no matter what the consequences either to individuals or to the community. He was an enemy of God and would bring Germany into the dust along with himself. Our bewilderment was great, but it became ever greater just before eight o'clock on the morning of the election ; the Sisters were just getting ready to depart to the polling station when some polling officers carrying an election-urn were shown into the convent parlour. This was quite unprecedented, and Mother Prioress did not hesitate to tell the gentlemen that she found it all very odd. In reply they said they had simply come to oblige the Sisters by collecting their votes, since it was well known that Carmelites are not allowed to leave the enclosure. But Mother Prioress insisted that although voting was a secret act it was also a public duty which the Sisters had always performed publicly in order to set people a good example in citizenship ; the gentlemen were preventing this by coming as they had done. But it was no use arguing, and she had to give in.

The register was called in alphabetical order. At the end the official who held the list of voters said, " There are some who have not voted. Anna Fitzeck's one." " She cannot vote," came the curt answer. " Why not ? " " Because she is weak in the head." A short pause and then the dreaded question, " And Dr. Edith Stein ? She had not voted either." " She has not the right." " Certainly she has—year of birth 1891 ! She must have the right ! " The answer was given with icy calm, " She is a non-Aryan." The three of them started to go away, but one of them turned round and gave the order, " Write in here that she is non-Aryan." That done, they left the Carmel with all speed.

Once Sister Benedicta learned what had happened she again

proposed a transfer. She would have preferred to go to Palestine where a great servant of God, a lay-sister named Miriam of Jesus Crucified, had founded a Carmel at Bethlehem. Most of the Sisters would not hear of such a separation until the events of the 9th of November made it imperative. Order was more or less preserved in the quiet suburb of Lindenthal, but even in Carmel everyone heard how synagogues had been burnt out, how Jews and their friends had been hounded down and their houses wrecked.

Naturally the Sisters were horrified, and Sister Benedicta herself was almost paralysed with grief. " It is the shadow of the Cross which is falling upon my people. If only they would see this ! It is the fulfilment of the curse which my people called upon its own head. Cain must be persecuted, but woe to whoever lays hands upon Cain. Woe also to this city and this country when God's wrath descends upon them for what they are now doing to the Jews."

Now she could enjoy no peace because of her fear that her presence was endangering the community. Since Palestine had refused to allow any more German Jews to immigrate Mother Prioress wrote off to Echt in Holland mentioning that Sister Benedicta needed a change of air. The good Sisters understood immediately what " change of air " meant in this context and warmly invited her to come and join them. Advent was taken up with preparing for the journey, packing and applying for the necessary papers.

To make the passport valid one had to have a photograph on it, and so a photographer was sent for. He came one midday, and Sister Benedicta stationed herself by the open door of the enclosure, since she did not wish to leave the enclosure on any account until it was absolutely necessary. She was wearing her usual shabby Carmelite habit ; but when the Prioress noticed how heavily darned it was she took off her own scapular and placed it over Sister Benedicta, who thanked her. That is the story of the photograph reproduced here, which is marvellously true to life. The feasts of Christmas and its octave were rather subdued this year through grief at the approaching good-bye. Optimists there certainly were who maintained that the separation would not be for long ; those who saw further, including Sister Benedicta, said that it would be for ever.

The preparations for the journey were carried out with great caution. In accordance with Sister Benedicta's own wishes demonstrativeness of any kind was discouraged. Even in the hours just before she left she remained strong and calm. The first sign of emotion was when one of the older sisters, the tears streaming down her face, thanked her for the good example she had set them from the very first. " How can you say that ? It is I who must thank God for having allowed me to live with you." This was the conviction with which she had entered the Cologne Carmel and with which she left it.

Doctor Paul Strerath, a friend of the Cologne community and great servant of God, had offered to transport her across the frontier under cover of darkness. Sister Benedicta had asked if she might have the consolation of praying for a while before the holy statue of the Queen of Peace ; this being granted Dr. Strerath drew up at the presbytery near Siebenburg where Sister Benedicta visited the shrine and knelt for the last time at this sacred spot, the cradle of the German Carmelites. Four years later, during the year of her death, both the Church and the statue of the Queen of Peace went up in smoke and flames. A last farewell to the friendly presbytery, and the car drove into the night, to the Netherlands. At about eight o'clock the travellers arrived at Echt after a comfortable journey. The community had all gathered in the recreation room, and welcomed the refugee with the utmost warmth though not, perhaps, without a certain curiosity. " What immediately struck us as so pleasant about Sister Benedicta was her simple, modest bearing, along with her delicate tact and her heart of gold ", as the Sisters said, when describing her later. " Her features were marked by a deep seriousness, which was very noticeable that evening ; evidently due to her grief at having to leave her beloved Carmel in Cologne."

V

ECHT

THE little Dutch village of Echt in Limburg had offered hospitality to the Cologne Carmelites when they were driven out of Germany during the Kulturkampf. Mother Teresia Alberta, the head of the community, managed to rent a suitable house until she obtained a plot of land in Boovenste Straat where it was possible to lay the foundations of the church and convent. Since all the sisters were German it was only natural that most of the vocations to the Carmel were German girls, with the result that for many years German remained the community's everyday language. But as the National Socialist disease spread, hostility towards foreign ways and speech affected Holland as well ; the Father Provincial of the Dutch Carmelites thought it prudent, therefore, to make Dutch the accepted language for prayers, chapter, refectory reading and conversation in those communities which came originally from Germany—Roermond, Maastricht and Echt. In other respects, however, the Echt Carmel retained its original German character, largely because the two dominating personalities there were German. These were Reverend Mother Ottilia of Jesus and Antonia of the Holy Ghost, one or other of whom was generally either Prioress or Sub-Prioress. When Sister Benedicta was transferred to Echt the Prioress was Mother Ottilia, a truly mystical soul. The sub-Prioress was Mother Antonia, a really Teresian character with a wide outlook and irrepressible energy whom Sister Benedicta had come to know through the Jubilee correspondence of 1937.

The community numbered thirteen choir-members (of

whom ten were German) and four German lay-sisters.   Sister
Benedicta immediately applied herself to the task of learning
Dutch, thus adding another to the six languages she had
already mastered.

' From the very first day she tried to adapt herself to all the
community's customs.   Ever ready to help and wishing to
have a share in all the work, she never refused any favours that
were asked of her.   Often, in fact, she even got in the way
through over-eagerness, because with all her good will she
could never make a thorough job of anything practical.   Even
when she was merely doing the sweeping it was obvious how
unused she was to housework.   The same was true of her
needle-work ; she never progressed beyond the beginners'
stage.   In recreation she was at once serious and cheerful,
though she could laugh heartily and was always glad to tell
stories about her interesting life.'

So runs the Echt Sisters' account of Sister Benedicta.

It had been thought inadvisable for her to take her unfinished
family history to Echt, because if the customs officials at the
frontier had discovered it she might have been caught.   Wishing to continue working on it she sent a message to Cologne
in February, 1939, to see whether one of her friends there
might be ready to risk bringing it through.   Dr. Rhabanus,
C.M.M., a Mariannhill Missionary, offered straight away to
undertake this hazardous task.   At the frontier he was
stopped by officials who searched his car and came across the
voluminous manuscript ; one of them flicked through it and
handed it back with the words, " I see.   Your doctorate thesis.
That's all right."   And so Sister Benedicta was able to continue with this work which was not only dear to her heart but
also a healthy relaxation.

With her charity and unselfishness she did not take long to
settle into her new family circle, and she soon found herself
entrusted with an office in the community.   She acted as
assistant to the portress, Sister Maria Pia, " a real West-

phalian " as she described herself the first time they met, on New Year's Eve. In her own words :

' We felt drawn to each other from the start. As it turned out we had a good deal to do together, and we always got along splendidly. Later, when Rosa Stein came to live in the convent (in a room outside the enclosure) she also used to confide in me a lot. Both of them helped to make life very happy, and what I liked so much was their simplicity, and their unassuming personalities. Sister Benedicta used to eat and drink so little that Mother Prioress had to warn her occasionally not to overdo it. Both of them had such tender hearts, even too tender, perhaps ; Sister Benedicta, for instance, thought it wrong to kill a fly. She took it hard whenever she heard anyone making unfavourable remarks about the Jews ; she would say that they were all calumnies, and that, " People will impute anything whatsoever to the Jews, just as to the Jesuits." '

Although Sister Benedicta, the Carmelite, always remembered that she had been Edith Stein, a member of the Chosen People, it would be a mistake to imagine that she often stressed the fact of her Jewish blood. Before entering into a discussion of such matters she used to wait until she was with someone sensitive to God's ways and not with someone blinded by current opinion. Unhampered by concern for her own self she could quite calmly relate these sufferings to the Source of all Being, which she saw as necessarily springing from a *Person*. The *three-personed* God answered her cry and confirmed her joy at belonging to the people which had worshipped Him as the God of Abraham, Isaac and Jacob, the name by which He will be known to the end of time. Whenever she was discussing the Old Testament this joy used to radiate like a peaceful light from her beautiful eyes, the light which was to shine for her on her own road to Golgotha. One can easily imagine how she suffered with her people in these times. She longed to see once more her favourite sister Erna, who left

Breslau in 1939 and embarked with her family for America. Although she pressed them to visit her in Echt, Erna explains that, " Having bought tickets to go via Hamburg, and hearing how dangerous it was to cross the Dutch frontier, we decided not to risk it." Therefore the sisters had to forego even this last farewell.

Sister Benedicta was all the more pleased, therefore, when her sister Rosa eventually arrived at Echt, after many adventures, in the summer of 1940. Rosa had come to Cologne in 1939 and had been accommodated in one of the rooms outside the enclosure. She had moved all her household goods and her valuables to Aachen where they were stored so that they could be quickly moved to Belgium. Moving furniture over the border just at that time, with war imminent, was both difficult and dangerous for a non-Aryan. Finally, with the help of one of the lay-sisters, Rosa managed to get through to Belgium where she hoped to meet a lady with whom she had been in correspondence. This lady had been advertising in German newspapers to attract members for an Order which she was planning, and which Rosa wished to join. But as soon as she saw the state the place was in and the way it was being run she realized that she had fallen into the clutches of a swindler, and immediately tried to leave. At one time this seemed as if it would be impossible, because she was stranded with no money in a strange land whose language she could not speak ; but Sister Benedicta contacted all her own acquaintances to secure a passport for Rosa to come to Holland. Until the summer of 1940 these efforts were unsuccessful, and even when the passport was granted it was only a personal pass. All her possessions had to remain in Belgium. A certain amount of clothing and linen was all she could bring with her. Everyone was amazed at the equanimity with which Rosa bore the loss of her dearest mementoes and the way in which she had surrendered herself to God's will.

She never allowed a word of complaint to escape from her lips and even joked about how she had become detached from her worldly goods at one swoop ! It was all the more surprising since Rosa was a convert of only three years standing. All the people coming to the convent quickly learned to admire her, and she possessed just the qualities needed for taking charge of the house's external affairs. In addition she had a really noble heart, demanding nothing whatsoever for herself and giving everything she had to others. One of her outstanding qualities was her sound common sense. She was always working, and used to get up very early to spend hours praying in the chapel. In the evening she would be in the chapel again, kneeling for long periods in front of the Blessed Sacrament.

To the relief of their friends both sisters now seemed to be safely hidden away, while in Germany the Church continued to suffer a relentless, though secret, persecution. In their concern for the Cologne Carmel the good sisters at Echt kept advising the Mother Prioress to bring the whole community to Holland for safety, saying that Germany was on the brink of a catastrophe. But in Cologne no one would have dreamed of abandoning the Fatherland in its hour of trial. On the first of September war broke out with the rape of Poland ; followed in 1940 by the criminal occupation of neutral Holland. Although this severely restricted our regular correspondence with Echt we were informed from time to time that Sister Benedicta and Rosa Stein were both quite safe and well. Moreover Sister Benedicta was also allowed to continue with her literary work in Echt, which now included such essays as " St. Elizabeth as a spiritual guide ", " Intellectuals ", " St. Teresa, the teacher ", " Love for love ", " The marriage feast of the Lamb " and " The mystical sufferings of St. John of the Cross ". When the Mother Prioress realized her great devotion to the divine office the instruction of the younger sisters on this subject was handed over to Sister Benedicta, who also taught them Latin. For a considerable period she was provisor as well, which meant looking after the sisters' bodily needs.

ECHT

Early in 1941 Mother Prioress relieved Sister Benedicta of her office as turn-sister so that she might have more time free for her studies in spirituality. She finished her *Ways of knowing God*. But her chief work was her *Science of the Cross*, which she composed in her hours of stillness. and solitude, drawing it from the depths of her intense contemplation and pouring it out again in her own crystal-clear language. In this survey of the sublime mystical teaching of St. John of the Cross she displays a spiritual kinship with that prince of mystics such as one finds nowhere except in the saint's greatest daughter, the Mother of Carmel. A few sentences from her introduction indicate the purpose of the book :

' The following pages form an attempt to grasp the essential unity in the writings and life of St. John of the Cross by adopting a viewpoint specially calculated to bring out this unity. They are neither a biography, therefore, nor an exhaustive account of his teaching, though the unity can only be realized by referring to the facts of his life and the content of his works. Witnesses are called to settle questions of detail, but once they have spoken the author herself intervenes to offer an interpretation in accordance with what she herself has come to believe after a life-time's meditation on the laws of intellectual being and life. This applies particularly to the arguments on spirit, faith and contemplation which have been introduced in different places, especially in the section, " The soul in the realm of the spirit and of spirits ". What is said there about the self, freedom and the person is not drawn directly from St. John of the Cross. For although it contains many points of contact with his teaching most of the arguments deal with matters outside his main theme and are foreign to his way of thought. In the passages mentioned the author has sketched a philosophy of the person, which has only in recent times been acknowledged as a primary task of philosophy.'

Though the whole work[1] was written out within a period of 9–10 months she had in fact been meditating on it for years before the quartercentenary of St. John of the Cross prompted her to it. The concept *Science of the Cross* is worked out in its twofold sense, as a theology of the Cross and as a school of the Cross (i.e. life in the symbol of the Cross). Therefore this book not only offers a modern exposition of St. John of the Cross but Sister Benedicta's personal confession.

Sister Pia tells us :

' Sister Benedicta applied herself so assiduously to writing this book that she seemed to have had a premonition of what was to happen. (The last pages were written on the 2nd of August, 1942.) Every spare moment of the day and even a part of the night were devoted to it. Yet she never neglected her duty of praying ; in the evenings she was to be heard leaving her cell just before the bell rang so as to be in choir punctually for Matins, and in the morning she got up before the time for wakening. Through the open cell-window she could be seen at prayer, on her knees with her arms out-stretched. Rosa Stein, who had now been received into the Third Order of Our Lady of Mount Carmel, used, like her sister in the enclosure, to spend many hours of each day praying in the public chapel. Nor were they praying for themselves alone. They clung lovingly to the people out of whom they were born, and as their predecessors Judith and Esther had once offered their prayers and penances to save Israel from destruction, so these two apostolic souls were now throwing themselves into the arms of divine justice to bring salvation and mercy to both persecutors and persecuted.'

While the furies of war were claiming their victims on all sides the leaders of Germany calculated that the time had come for the convents to be stormed. The Carmelite Order did

---

[1] *Kreuzeswissenschaft*, published 1950 by Nauwelaerts of Louvain as Vol. I of Edith Stein's collected works ; edited by P. Romäus Leuven, O.C.D. and Dr. L. Gelber.

not escape.   The first victims were the sisters in Luxembourg who were driven out of their convent in February 1941 so that it could be used as a club-house and dance-hall for the B.D.M.[1] Scarcely had these homeless sisters found refuge with their sisters in Pützchen before this Carmel also was dissolved in a space of two hours by the arbitrary power of the Gestapo. Aachen was dissolved at the same time in the same way, and Düren followed in August of the same year.

Sister Benedicta's reflections upon this event are contained in a letter written at the beginning of September 1941 :

'It is good to remember, these days, that poverty implies being ready to leave our home in our dear convent.   We have bound ourselves to the enclosure, but God has not bound Himself to protect me in the enclosure-walls for ever.   He does not need to, because He has other walls with which to protect us.   The situation is parallel to the use of the sacraments ; for us these are the pre-ordained means of grace, and we can scarcely be too eager to receive them.   But God is not restricted by them.   At the moment in which we are cut off from the sacraments by external power, He can more than compensate us in some other way ; and He will do so the more surely the more faithfully we have gone to the sacraments beforehand.   Similarly it is our solemn duty to observe the precepts of the enclosure as conscientiously as possible so as to live undisturbed, hidden with Christ in God.   If we have done so faithfully, and if we are driven out onto the street, then our Lord will send His angels to encircle us, and their invisible wings will enfold us in a peace more secure than that of the highest and most solid convent walls.   Certainly we ought to pray that we shall be spared the experience, but only with the deeply sincere addition : " Not mine, but Thy will, be done.'

With this conviction in mind Sister Benedicta entered the last stage of her life.

[1] League of German Girls.

The Cologne Carmel was also expecting to be abolished. Trying to anticipate any eventuality the Mother Prioress ordered all letters and private notes that might have betrayed Sister Benedicta's asylum to be destroyed, which accounts for the loss of her very precious letters. The only letter which has been saved was one addressed to a young friend who had entered the Cologne Carmel eight weeks after Sister Benedicta herself.

Echt, 16*th May*, 1941

' To-day I received Your Charity's letter and must answer it immediately. I believe that it is good for Your Charity to work at something definite. The creative power is there, but needs to be harnessed if it is to be effective. Still it seems to show a good beginning, and these books have not fallen into Your Charity's hands " by chance ". Mother Prioress knows well what happened to myself in this respect, how at the appropriate moment everything that I needed would just " happen " to fall into my hands, often from the most unlikely places. Your Charity already knows the fragments on the Song of Songs by our holy Mother. The " Spiritual Canticle " will also help Your Charity a great deal. Of course Your Charity will derive many lessons from St. Bernard, though I do not know whether there is a translation. If I were there I should be very happy to translate all of it for Your Charity. The exposition by Fr. Anthanasius Miller, O.S.B., may give some idea of contemporary opinions, and the priests who visit the convent will have information about it. For the rest the surest guide is always the Holy Spirit. I shall gladly pray for Your Charity's enlightenment on the subject and ask the same favour for myself, knowing that I have no other refuge. I have moved on to a fresh province of work [she is referring to the *Science of the Cross*] and am stumbling like a little child. Not only must the Holy Spirit be Your Charity's mentor in the present work but He must also be invoked to overcome the fresh crises which will undoubtedly follow hard upon it. No intellectual work is brought into the world without heavy labour.

Furthermore it makes claims upon one's whole person which we cannot possibly comply with ; in itself it is an excellent thing to have a safeguard against becoming absorbed, such as the daily routine and its duties ; but naturally this adjustment cannot be made without its being felt. How glad I would be if we could discuss all these things together sometime. But neither is it mere chance that the opportunity is denied us. So let us be thankful that we are united in that sphere which knows neither frontiers nor limits, neither separation nor distances.

Ever since a young postulant came into the house I have been thinking back over our first days in the Order, and of God's wonderful manner of leading us to Carmel. And yet the history of souls in Carmel is perhaps more wonderful still. Here they are hidden deep in God's heart. And the occasional insights into the mystery which we think we are receiving represent no more than a fleeting glimmer of what will remain a divine mystery until the day when all will be revealed. My greatest joy lies in hoping for the vision which is to come. Our faith in His secret working must also strengthen us in these moments when external events (affecting both ourselves and others) threaten to sap our courage. To-day is the feast of St. Simon Stock. In the early hours of the day we sang his office and, as a May hymn, the *Flos Carmeli*. What promises it holds out to us.

In Caritate Jesu et Regina Carmeli,
> Your Charity's most unworthy
> > SISTER BENEDICTA.'

VI

PLANS OF ESCAPE

SISTER BENEDICTA had good reason to conclude that events in Germany were foreshadowing future developments in the occupied countries. In her account of these days Sister Pia writes, " She was very concerned about her future, and since she was kept abreast of Jewish affairs by Fraülein Rosa she herself spoke to her superiors of what she thought would have to be done if she and her sister were to be saved."

Convinced as she was that they could not stay in Holland indefinitely Sister Benedicta rejected the proposal of petitioning Rome to make her a member of the Echt Carmel, though the fact of having lived at Echt for three years would have been considered sufficient justification. And without waiting for her legal transfer the Prioress had already granted her the privilege of sitting and voting in chapter. Nevertheless Sister Benedicta decided to try writing to some of her friends in Switzerland. Fraülein Nägeli and Dr. Verena Borsinger of the editorial staff of the *Katholische Schweizerin*, Bern, offered to find out whether she could be received into the Carmel of Le Paquier, near Freiburg, and to handle negotiations with the authorities. The impression which Sister Benedicta had made in Switzerland, especially upon the women social workers, remained fresh in their minds. In her lectures at Geneva and Zürich she had talked about Carmel, as she always did, and had been instrumental in drawing many new members to the Third Order. Amongst these tertiaries was a great admirer of Edith Stein's who had since found her vocation in the Le Paquier Carmel. When the Prioress received Sister Bene-

dicta's request to be received at Le Paquier she approached this
novice, who had enjoyed a very wide circle of acquaintances
in the world, and asked her if the name of Edith Stein meant
anything to her. Her enthusiastic reaction to the name was
answer enough, and soon the novice was writing with feverish
energy to interest all her influential Swiss friends in Sister
Benedicta's fate. It was January 1942. There was certainly
no lack of letters of recommendation. In no time Mother
Prioress had moved the hearts of her daughters in Le Paquier
by telling them about Sister Benedicta, and all were in favour
of receiving her.

Fraülein Dr. Borsinger held out the highest hopes and,
after some initial astonishment, the ecclesiastical administrator,
Monsignor Besson, gave permission to carry on. Then the
difficulties began. On no account would Sister Benedicta
leave Rosa behind ; but it would have been impossible for the
Carmel to have taken in two foreign sisters whilst at the same
time having to refuse young Swiss postulants and send them
to Carmels abroad. Once more the Mother Prioress mustered
her powers of persuasion, strongly recommending the Third
Order Carmelites to take in Rosa. In this she was successful,
but the Tertiaries had first of all to apply for sanction to their
mother-house in France, all of which meant constant delays.
Finally permission was given, only to find the civil authorities
making difficulties. Fraülein Dr. Borsinger went from one
court of appeal to another, and with each journey more time
was being lost. The imploring letters from Echt became
more and more urgent ; the Sisters there feared the worst.
Why ? What was going on ? After the first welcoming
words from Le Paquier Sister Benedicta had applied for a
Swiss visa, which seems to have aroused the suspicions of the
police. The result was a summons for her and Rosa to report
in Maastricht, but the Dutch Provincial, Father Cornelius
Lennissen, intervened and very kindly went to answer the
summons himself ; he hoped to be able to save them from
going in person by insisting on their strict rule of enclosure.
The German police, however, were inflexible and ordered

Sister Benedicta to appear in person. When she met them in the Gestapo office at Maastricht she greeted them with the words, " Praised be Jesus Christ ! "[1] Startled by this greeting they simply looked up and made no answer. (Later she explained to Reverend Mother that she had felt driven to behave as she had done, knowing well enough that it was imprudent from a human standpoint, because she saw quite clearly that this was no mere question of diplomacy but was part of the eternal struggle between Jesus and Lucifer.) She had to show them her identity-card, which set them storming and raging at her because it was not stamped with a large " J " to signify that she was Jewish ; nor was her name, Edith Stein, preceded by the name Sara which was prescribed for all Jewish women. They ordered her to write to the Police Bureau in Breslau and to request " very humbly " that her identity-card might be completed as soon as possible. Afterwards both sisters had to report to the Joodsen Raad, where they were very kindly dealt with and were promised that they would be called to Amsterdam within a few weeks.

Another card was sent off to the Cologne Carmel, however, on the 9th of April ; it was full of the spirit of peace and gave no hint of the storm that was gathering over Sister Benedicta's head.

'DEAR SISTER MARIA,

Yesterday evening I received your letter of St. Joseph's feastday. I managed to read it without much bother [a dig at her correspondent's curious handwriting] and it gave me great joy. Precisely because our paths have to be so different I am all the happier that they cross quite often. I am having to go over everything very thoroughly. The ground-plan is simply a gift, i.e. it gradually reveals itself. But the stones I am having to break up on my own, before chiselling them and sliding them into place. Often as I have been at work previously a feeling has come over me, especially when I was

---

[1] *Gelobt sei Jesus Christus*, a form of greeting in Catholic Germany, expecting the response *In ewigkeit* (To all eternity).

worn out, that I should never be able to arrive at what I wish to say. And I was beginning to think it would always be like that. But now I feel as though the strength is flowing back and I can accomplish something. Father John kept giving hints upon the implications of the symbol. When I have finished the MS I may send a copy off to Father Heribert [the German Provincial at that time] to have it duplicated for the convents. The reason I am writing so little is that I need all my time for Father John. I know your Charity will understand this and accept my treatise as if it were letters, just as I take Your Charity's letters for treatises.

Your Charity's most unworthy,
SISTER BENEDICTA '

In May both sisters had to present themselves before the Gestapo and the Joodsen Raad in Amsterdam, and had to wander from one official to another to answer every possible kind of question, filling in sheaves of forms in triplicate without discovering what it was all about. The Gestapo conducted their enquiries quite pitilessly, ordering the two sisters, for example, to stand three yards apart during their cross-examinations. One of these officials, however, did treat them kindly ; he proved to be from Cologne and was able to tell them how the city had been badly damaged by air-raids, and that the church Maria vom Frieden had gone up in flames along with the holy statue on the 28th of April, 1942.

A godchild of Sister Benedicta's, Alicia Reis, was amongst the Jews who had been summoned by the Gestapo. Two years after her conversion, in 1934, she joined the Order of Sisters of the Good Shepherd in Rastatt, whence she was transferred to Leiderdorp in their Dutch Province. Unfortunately she had to leave the Order soon after her clothing because of ill-health. Since it would have been unwise to return to Germany just then she stayed in Holland, serving as a lay-helper in various houses of the Order. She and Sister Benedicta were greatly consoled to see each other once more, never suspecting that they would soon be brought together again in tragic circumstances. Sister Benedicta's own contact with the Gestapo made her all the more eager to act quickly ; because she feared that the Swiss effort to rescue her would not succeed in time she also applied to go to Spain.

Amidst this threatening storm Sister Benedicta in June once more wrote to Cologne :

' For months I have been wearing next to my heart a slip of paper with the 23rd verse of Matt. x. written on it. Negotiations with Le Paquier are still going on, but I am so deeply absorbed in John of the Cross that it is all one to me.'

In Switzerland hopes were running high. During Ember Day in Whitweek one of the pleasantest cells was made ready to receive Sister Benedicta, which meant that two of the Sisters had to share one cell because the Carmel had already reached its complement.

Some weeks later the Chapter held a vote and issued the following announcement :

' On Saturday the 4th of July, 1942, the nuns of Le Paquier held a chapter-meeting at which the Reverend Mother Prioress proposed to accept as a permanent or temporary member of the community, according to the circumstances, Sister Teresia Benedicta of the Cross. in the world Edith Stein, a professed sister of the Cologne Carmel who is now at Echt in Holland.

In 1938, because of her Jewish blood, Sister Benedicta was forced to leave the Carmel where she had made her profession. The German rulers who have conquered Holland are now compelling her to leave that country. The Sister in question has obtained the necessary permission for her transfer from the Father Provincial in Holland ; our Right Reverend Lord Bishop has agreed to her reception into our Carmel, and our Right Reverend Father General is now arranging for the Indult.

On the fifth Sunday of the same month the nuns were assembled once again and the Reverend Mother Prioress made the same proposal, after which it was unanimously resolved by a secret vote to receive Sister Teresia Benedicta into the community for an indefinite time.

We, the undersigned, testify to this act,

Sr. Marie Agnes of the Immaculate Conception, Prioress ;
Sr. Marie Françoise of the Most Sacred Heart, Clavary.
Executed on the 5th July, 1942, at Le Paquier.'

Now that the Swiss Carmel had made all preparations the next step was to get the consent of the Swiss civil authorities. As it happened Dr. Etter, President of the Federal Council, paid a visit to the little Carmel at Le Paquier on the 29th of July. The Reverend Mother seized the opportunity to interest him in Sister Benedicta, whereupon he promised to take the matter into his own hands. In her latest letter to the Reverend Mother, Verena Borsinger had spoken of how depressing it was to be held back by so much red-tape, even though she had replied " Yes " very definitely when the Federal Council had asked whether the non-Aryan applicant stood in danger of her life. She had been on holiday at the time but had returned to Zürich to speed negotiations.

In Holland ever fiercer regulations against the Jews were continually being issued.

Already in August 1941 the Dutch Hierarchy had found themselves in conflict with the German authorities. On the Reichskommissar's instructions Professor van Dam had published a decree by which Jewish school children were to be taught by none but Jewish school-teachers, which would have meant excluding Catholic children of Jewish parentage from Catholic education. Mgr. de Jong, in the name of all the bishops, protested against this injustice and declared that Catholic teachers would never allow children to be sent away from school on account of their race.

Soon afterwards a proclamation was issued that bills should be posted on all public buildings, " Voor Joden verboden." The Bishops refused to allow this either. Yet the exclusion of Jews from public life was of little significance compared to the mass-deportations of men, women and children, indeed of whole Jewish families, which began in 1942. As was generally feared, many of them went to meet certain death in the Polish concentration-camps, where they were either gassed or driven to do inhuman work in the salt, lead or tin mines.

On the 11th July 1942 the representatives of all religious denominations sent a telegram to the Reichskommissar expressing their indignation at these measures, which offended the deepest moral feelings of the Dutch people, and, above all, denied the divine precepts of justice and mercy. It meant that Jewish Christians were cut off from sharing in the life of the church : consequently the combined churches urgently requested that these measures be cancelled.

Replying, in the name of the Reichskommissar, General-Kommissar Schmidt gave an assurance that Jewish Christians would not be deported so long as they had been members of a Christian community before January 1941.

Immediately the Bishop of Roermond wrote to Sister Benedicta, quoting this exception in order to set her mind at rest. But the exception did not remove the churches' objection to the deportation of Jews, and so they resolved to issue a joint protest on Sunday, the 26th July 1942, to be read out in all churches.

It was agreed that the protest should contain a literal reproduction of the telegram sent to Seyss-Inquart on the 11th July 1942 ; but before the appointed day Seyss-Inquart and Schmidt got to know what was in this joint letter. They sought urgently to persuade Dr. H. J. Diykmeester of the Nederlandse Herformde Kerk to omit the telegram from the prepared text, alleging that it had been confidential. The Synod of the Nederlandse Herformde Kerk agreed to this concession, but the Gereformerde Kerk and the others refused to be taken in. The Archbishop of Utrecht also refused on the ground that he could not countenance a secular power's influencing, or interfering with, a pastoral letter. Apart from anything else, from the technical viewpoint it would prove impossible to make alterations, since the pastoral had already been sent off.   Therefore the pastoral was read in all Catholic churches on Sunday the 26th of July.[1]

After the usual preliminaries the text of the letter ran as follows :

' All of us are living through a period of great distress, both from a spiritual as from a material standpoint.   But there are two sets of people whose distress is deeper than that of others, the distress of the Jews and the distress of those who are deported to work abroad.

Such distress is the concern of us all ; and it is the purpose of this pastoral to bring it before your minds.

Such distress must also be brought to the notice of those who exercise power over these men.   On account of which the hierarchy of the Netherlands, in combination with almost all the other religious bodies in the Netherlands, has made representations to the occupying powers : the following telegram in favour of the Jews and others was despatched on Saturday the 11th of July.

" The undersigned religious organizations of the Netherlands, deeply shaken by the measures against the Jews which have excluded them from the normal life of the people, have learnt with terror of the latest regulations by which men, women, children and whole families are to be deported to the territory of the German Reich.

" The suffering which has thus been imposed on thousands of people, the awareness that these regulations offend the deepest moral convictions of the Netherlands people, and above all, the denial in these regulations of God's precepts of justice and mercy, forces the undersigned religious organizations to request most urgently that these regulations shall not be carried out.   On behalf of those Jews who are Christians we wish to emphasize further that these regulations will cut them off from the normal life of the church."

[1] Taken from the book : *Het verzet van de Nederlandsche Bischoppen tegen National-Socialisme en Doitsche Tyrannie* by Dr. Stokman, O.F.M., Utrecht, 1945.

As a result of this telegram the General-Kommissar, in the name of the Reichskommissar, has conceded that Jewish Christians shall not be deported so long as they belonged to a Christian organization before January 1941.

Dear Brethren ! When we survey the frightful misery of body and soul that has for three years been threatening the whole world with destruction, we cannot help thinking of that event portrayed for us in today's Gospel.

" In those days, as Jesus drew near and caught sight of the city, he wept over it, and said : Ah, if thou too couldst understand, above all in this day that is granted thee, the ways that can bring thee peace ! As it is, they are hidden from thy sight. The days will come upon thee when thy enemies will fence thee round about, and encircle thee, and press thee hard on every side, and bring down in ruin both thee and thy children that are in thee, not leaving one stone of thee upon another ; and all because thou didst not recognize the time of my visiting thee ". This prophecy of Jesus was fulfilled to the letter : forty years later the city of Jerusalem was visited by God's judgment. It had not recognized the time of grace.

And now once more everything around us points towards divine punishment. But, thank God, for us it is not too late. We can still avert that judgment, if we recognize the time of grace, if we will only see the path to peace. And that is none other than a return to God, from whom a part of the world has turned away for so many years. All human remedies are now in vain—God is our only help.

Dear Brethren ! Let us in the first place examine our own selves in a spirit of deep repentance and humility. For do we not share the blame for the catastrophes we are enduring ? Have we always sought first the kingdom of God and His justice ? Have we always fulfilled our duties towards our neighbours, treating them justly and loving them ? Have we not perhaps harboured feelings of gnawing hatred and bitterness ? Have we always sought our refuge in God, our heavenly Father ?

When we reflect upon ourselves we cannot but confess that

we have all failed. *Peccavimus ante Dominum Deum nostrum ;* we have sinned before the Lord, our God.

But we also know that God does not despise a humble and a contrite heart. *Cor contritum et humiliatum non despicies.* Therefore let us turn to Him and filled with child-like trust beseech Him for mercy. He himself tells us, " Ask and you shall receive, seek and you shall find, knock and it shall be opened up to you."

In the Introit of today's Mass the Church calls to us in the words of the Psalmist—" For behold God is my helper : and the Lord is the protector of my soul. Turn back the evils upon my enemies ; and cut them off in Thy truth," and in the epistle she repeats those ever comforting words of the Apostle, " May no temptation come upon you that is beyond man's strength. Not that God will play you false ; He will not allow you to be tempted beyond your powers. With the temptation itself, He will ordain the issue of it, and enable you to hold your own."

And so, dear Brethren, let us implore God, through the mediation of the Mother of Mercy, to grant to the world a just peace. May He strengthen the people of Israel who are being so sorely tested in these days, and may He bring them to the true redemption in Christ Jesus. May He shelter those whose lot it is to work in a strange land far from their loved ones. May He guard over them in body and soul, protecting them from bitterness and loss of courage, keeping them true in the Faith and strengthening their families at home. Let us implore His help for all those in tribulation, for prisoners and hostages, for so many over whom hang clouds of peril and destruction—*Pateant aures misericordiæ tuæ, Domine, precibus supplicantium*—Open the ears of Thy Mercy, O Lord, to the prayers of those who fly to Thee.

This joint pastoral shall be read out on Sunday the 26th of July in all churches within our province and in all chapels where there is a rector, at every appointed Mass and in the customary manner.

Given at Utrecht on the 20th July in the year of our Lord 1942.'

This pastoral aroused great excitement in Holland, and the populace became very apprehensive over the effects it was likely to produce.

In Carmel, however, the sisters breathed again, and their hearts beat less quickly because some lines from the Bishop of Roermond had assured Sister Benedicta that the threatened punishment was now lifted. So she was thought to be safe, and thanksgiving was offered to God for this favourable turn of events, which seemed so appropriate to the Liturgy of the day. For it was the feast of St. Peter's Chains (1 Aug.), about which Sister Benedicta had written earlier,

" It is a specially dear feast for me, not because it commemorates anything particular in my life, but because of the chains being loosened by angels' hands. How many chains have already been loosed, and what bliss it will be when the last ones fall." (July 1938.) St. Peter's Chains was to be the last day of quiet life in Carmel for Sister Benedicta.

Already God had despatched his angel to end the exile of this truly free individual whose only attachment to earth was through her body. Since everyone believed that the dreaded disaster had been averted, the sickening blow came the more suddenly.

On the 2nd of August all non-Aryan members of every Dutch religious community were arrested and carried off. At Echt there was no hint of what was about to happen. At five in the afternoon the Sisters had assembled in choir for meditation ; Sister Benedicta was just reading out the theme for meditation when two knocks on the grille were heard, the signal that Mother Prioress was wanted in the parlour. When she asked at the grille who wished to speak with her she was told that there were two officers seeking Sister Stein. So the Reverend Mother signalled for Sister Benedicta to leave the choir and sent her into the parlour alone, thinking it was about the exit permit for Switzerland which the two sisters had been expecting daily.

" Two convents situated close to each other in Freiburg Canton had each offered them hospitality, and the Swiss on their side had already granted their entry permits, so I thought that they could get on without me," reports Mother Prioress :

' Rosa was already waiting in the outer part of the parlour. Speaking through the choir-window I said to the community, " Sisters, please pray. I think it is the Gestapo ! " Then I stationed myself beside the parlour door in order to follow the conversation. To my horror I discovered that it was something much worse. They were members of the " S.S." One of them, the spokesman, ordered Sister Benedicta to leave the convent within five minutes. She replied, " I cannot. We are strictly enclosed." " Get this out of the way [he meant the iron grille] and come out." " You must show me how to do it first." " Call your superior." Having heard it all myself I made a slight detour to go to the parlour while Sister Benedicta returned to the Choir.

She knelt imploringly in front of the Blessed Sacrament and then left the Choir with the whispered words, " Pray, please, sisters ! " She signed to Sister Pia, who hurried after her and asked anxiously, " What is it, Sister Benedicta ? " " I must leave the house in ten minutes." " But where to ? " " He didn't say." '

Only then did Sister Pia realize that it must be the S.S. Mother Antonia meanwhile had been speaking to the S.S. man. He said, " Are you the Superior ? " " Yes." " Sister Stein must leave the convent in five minutes." " That is impossible." " Then in ten minutes. We have no time ! " " We have taken steps to have the two sisters received into Swiss convents and are only waiting for sanction from the Germans. On the Swiss side everything is arranged." " We'll see about that later, but now Sister Stein must come out. She can either dress up or come as she is. Give her a blanket, a mug, a spoon and three days' rations." Again the anguished Superior protested. The S.S. man replied, " You don't need me to tell you what will happen to you and your convent if you refuse to send Sister Stein out." Thinking that he was trying to frighten her the Prioress said, " Give us half an hour at least." " We will not. There's no time." Seeing that nothing would move him she said, " If we must give way to force, then we do so in the name of God." She left the parlour and went upstairs to Sister Benedicta's cell, where several of the Sisters were already helping her to pack. Sister Benedicta said quickly, " Please write straight away to the Swiss Consul at the Hague for the entry permits." (They had been in contact with the consul for some time now.) She was still convinced that the transfer to the Le Paquier Carmel was a hope. Then she scarcely spoke again, and her mind seemed to be far away.

Mother Antonia continues :

' I went from her cell to the enclosure door, where Fraülein Stein was kneeling to receive a farewell blessing. A lady, one of her friends, was standing close by. Soon Sister Benedicta appeared. The other sisters were running here and there to make up a parcel of food for her. Sister Benedicta could only take away a few odd scraps because time was up.

After the two of them had gone outside the enclosure, I could still hear Sister Benedicta explaining her plans for leaving the country to the S.S. men, one of whom had never spoken a word the whole time. While they had been waiting in the parlour the two S.S. men had remained perfectly quiet, and we, on our side, had behaved as calmly as possible in spite of being so sorrow-stricken at this sudden farewell.'

Naturally the whole street was full of people loudly protesting against this barbarous injustice, for Rosa Stein was deeply loved and admired by the local people. But it would have gone hard with anyone who had shown active sympathy. At the street corner the police-van was waiting to move off ; the two sisters climbed in and found several more victims there already, two of them pensioners from the Institut Konings-bosch. Then the van drove off, no one knew where.

PLANS OF ESCAPE

That very day General-Kommissar Schmidt announced in a public speech at Gravenhage that this was a reprisal against the pastoral letter of the 26th of July. He ended with these words :

' Even in Protestant churches declarations were made in which they took up an unmistakable standpoint. However, the representations of the Protestant churches have informed us that this announcement was unintentional, but could not be withdrawn in the time for technical reasons. Since the Catholic hierarchy, on the other hand, refuses to enter into negotiations, then we, for our part, are compelled to regard the Catholic Jews as our worst enemies and consequently see to their deportation to the East with all possible speed.'[1]

This announcement by Schmidt, with its untruths and false suggestions, called forth a vigorous protest on the 23rd August 1942 from Archbishop de Jong writing to Seyss-Inquart in the name of the hierarchy. To begin with, various Protestant churches had read out the whole text of the joint letter and had never even considered omitting the telegram of the 11th July. Furthermore, this was the first that anyone had heard about these " negotiations into which the Catholic hierarchy refuses to enter."

Neither Dr. Diykmeester nor General-Kommissar Schmidt, at their meeting on the 24th July, had breathed a word about the attitude of the Catholic Church or the other religious bodies towards omitting the telegram. At the same time the Archbishop said what he thought of the Germans' pretence that the telegram was " confidential ". " There is nothing ' confidential ' about a message sent by public telegraph and referring to publicly proclaimed regulations. Moreover, the Catholic population has every right to know what steps their bishops have taken in face of such an important issue as the deportation of the Jews."

In his deep distress at the Catholic Jews and religious being

[1] *De Tijd*, 3 August 1942. (Holland's Catholic daily newspaper.)

made victims for the slaughter the Archbishop tried desperately to have the same exception applied to them as applied to all other Jewish Christians. This request was repeated in a telegram of the 27th August. But Seyss-Inquart made no reply either to the letter or to the telegram.[1]

Commenting upon this announcement Fr. Hopster, S.V.D., writes :

' From Schmidt's declaration one can conclude with confidence that all these religious, both men and women, really died *testimonium fidei*, because their arrest was an act of reprisal for the Bishops' pastoral letter. It was an attempt to strike at the Bishops and the Church by arresting Jewish members of Catholic religious orders.'

[1] Dr. Stokman, O.F.M.

VII

THE WAY OF THE CROSS

THE days passed, leaving the Echt Carmelites to bitter grief and the torments of waiting. Had she gone, never to be heard of again ?

It was on Wednesday the 5th of August that a telegram arrived from Westerbork, a tiny place beside the railway in Northern Holland. The Joodsen Raad had sent it at the same time as they sent a similar telegram on behalf of Ruth Kantorowicz to the Ursulines in Venlo, which ran : " Send warm clothing, blankets and medicaments immediately by messenger for Ruth Kantorowicz at Westerbork assembly-camp near Hooghalen."

' It was the signal for a positive contest in loving kindness on the part of the Sisters. Each of them wished to do something for their dear ones, each to sacrifice some object which they needed. Everything was collected in the chapter-room to be packed, so that the whole of this big room looked just like a shop, full of blankets and parcels. Books, candles, eatables and goodness only knows what else, all whisked away ' [Mother Antonia].

While clearing out Sister Benedicta's cell they had found a small picture on the back of which she had written down her wish to sacrifice her life for the conversion of the Jews. As it was sent on to her with the other gifts we have unfortunately lost this written testimony of her readiness for this heroic sacrifice. One precious memento of her is still kept, however, in the Echt Carmel, a used post-card on which Sister Benedicta had addressed a petition to her Prioress as long ago as March 1939. It is a fresh proof of how obediently and loyally she responded to the renewed graces pouring into her soul, of her unconditional service of Christ, of how she looked reality squarely in the face and had foreseen what later came to pass. She wrote :

' Dear Mother, I beg your Reverence's permission to offer myself to the Heart of Jesus as a sacrificial expiation for the sake of true peace : that the Antichrist's sway may be broken, if possible without another world-war, and that a new order may be established. I am asking this today because it is already the twelfth hour. I know that I am nothing, but Jesus wills it, and He will call many more to the same sacrifice in these days.

Passion Sunday, 26.III.1939.'

The Sisters' main concern was to find a suitable messenger. Two Echt men said they were willing to take the various articles ; early on Thursday morning they set off loaded with cases and parcels. As the camp lay at a considerable distance they blessed their good luck when they were picked up on the way by a lorry which was carrying sand to the camp.

Later these men gave the following account of what happened :

' We arrived at Hooghalen dead on five o'clock. There we met two gentlemen who had been sent from Venlo by the Ursulines to contact Dr Ruth Kantorowicz. The camp itself lay about five kilometres away from Hooghalen. In front of the camp, which consisted of thousands and thousands of huts, we came to a little building where we had to report to the Dutch police. We showed them the telegram ; we exchanged cigarettes with them and were soon chatting to each other in a friendly way. The police did not like their job one little bit. When they learned why we were there they sent a Jewish youngster with the telegram to the hut where Sister Benedicta and Rosa were billeted. After a few minutes excited waiting the high barbed-wire fence was opened and immediately, in the distance, we could see the brown habit and black veil of Sister Benedicta, who was accompanied by Fraülein Rosa.

The Dutch police-guards outside the camp were greatly surprised to learn that they were nuns whom we wished to see. They said, " There are no nuns in this camp ! " It was the first they knew about it.

Our emotions when we met the sisters were a mixture of sadness and joy. After we had shaken hands it was some time before anyone could get any words out, they were so over-joyed to see Echt people again. But the ice was soon broken and we handed them everything the Carmelites had given to us. Sister Benedicta in particular was glad and thankful when she heard of her sisters' greetings and prayers ; through the kindness of the Dutch police she was not made to open any-thing for examination, not even Mother Prioress's letter. Sister Benedicta told us at once that she had found many of her acquaintances in the camp, even members of her family. On their journey their route had been as follows : In the police-van they went from Echt to the headquarters at Roermond. In the evening they left in two police-vans, one carrying thir-teen and the other seventeen people. The destination was Amersfoort, but the driver missed his way and they did not arrive till three in the morning.[1]

Between Echt and Amersfoort the German S.S. were very obliging and friendly towards the prisoners, but in Amersfoort Camp they were treated very brutally, the S.S. beating them on their backs with truncheons and driving them into a hut

---

[1] Usually this journey takes 3–4 hours. Apparently the driver took the good road through Nijmegen, Arnhem, and then followed the main road from Utrecht to the Hague. Between Arnhem and Utrecht they left the main road and did not get back again, which is understandable enough in view of the black-out. The prisoners remained in the Amersfoort Camp from early on Monday until Tuesday evening. Then they set off for Westerbork, where they arrived in the night. The transport went through Apeldoorn, Zwolle, Meppel, Hogeveen, Hooghalen. Westerbork lies to the side of Hooghalen station.

where they had to sleep without having a meal. The non-Catholic Jews ate what provisions they had, and then, after they had tried to sleep a little while in beds piled in tiers one over the other, the prisoners were transported to Westerbork Camp near Hooghalen. Through the intervention of the Jewish Council, which was looking after the prisoners, they were allowed to send telegrams. The Council is very kind, especially to Catholic Jews. But the German camp-commandant ordered the Catholic Jews to be isolated from the rest. So now the Council can do nothing for them. They are all together in one hut.

As Sister Benedicta was telling us all this she was perfectly calm and composed. Her eyes shone with the radiance of a saintly Carmelite. Quietly and calmly she described everyone's troubles but her own. We had specially to remember to assure the Carmelites that she was still wearing the habit of the Order and that all the other nuns in the hut—there were ten of them—intended to keep on wearing their habits. She explained how glad everyone in the Camp had been to find Catholic nuns and priests there. The latter were the one hope and support of all the poor folk in the camp who had been forced to abandon everything, everything whatsoever.

Sister Benedicta was happy at being able to help and comfort people by words and by prayer. Her deep faith created about her an atmosphere of heavenly confidence. Several times she assured us that as far as they were concerned Reverend Mother could set her mind completely at rest. The whole day was free for prayer except for three breaks to collect their food. Never a word of complaint about the food, or about the soldiers' behaviour. She did not know how long they would be staying in the camp. There was a rumour that they would be leaving today (Friday the 7th of August) for Silesia, their native province, but no one knew for certain. Another transport of Jews from Amsterdam was expected that very night (Thursday to Friday). Fraülein Rosa is also bearing up well, being encouraged and strengthened by the shining example of Sister Benedicta. No matter where they go or what kind of work they are given (and this is still not known) nothing will be allowed to take precedence over prayer. Sister Benedicta did write a short letter, but does not know if it got through.'

So ends the account of their visit which the two good men wrote down in 1947, but the two messengers sent by the Ursulines from Venlo to Ruth Kantorowicz also made a report.

' On Thursday the 6th of August, 1942, Mr. Philipsen and myself [1] set off loaded with cases for the Hooghalen Jewish Camp. On the way we made several changes ; at one station we fell in with two gentlemen and a nun who were on the same errand, and therefore travelled with them. At the terminus the two gentlemen from Echt went along with us to reconnoitre the transport situation and we all managed to get a lift in a sand-lorry which used to go backwards and forwards from Westerbork to Hooghalen. The lorry-driver warned me that it would be as well not to take the baggage with me in case the S.S. patrol happened to discover us. So we drove towards the camp with anxious hearts.

The lorry stopped right outside a kind of pavilion, a glass-house from which you had a clear view on all sides. Here were the quarters of the Dutch police-guards. We had been advised by the driver to get in there as quickly as possible because the guards would see to it that we were all right. It could not have worked out better. The police were obviously astonished when they heard that the people in the camp whom we wished to meet were nuns. They called in a little Jewish boy, some sort of orderly it seems, and explained our business to him. He knew straight away which hut (No. 7, I believe) these people were billeted in, and so he was sent off to fetch the persons asked for. Meanwhile the nun had arrived in a private car and we learned that she was the Mother Superior of a Community (Sisters of St. Joseph, Roermond, I think) seeking one of her nuns in the camp. The boy returned with everyone

[1] Mr. Schlütter.

we wanted. Fraülein Ruth spotted me while they were still a long way off and she waved vigorously. Each of them wore the Star of David. Fraülein Ruth was an old friend of the Carmelite, and they came to us together. But we arranged with the police to go with Fraülein Ruth to a bench at the back of the guard-house where we could talk to her privately and give her the parcels. So far as I know all the other visitors were allowed a similar privacy. Fraülein Ruth outlined for us the story of the treatment they had had to endure so far. After their arrest they were carried off to Amersfoort, and then bundled into a goods-train for the journey to Hooghalen. But the train stopped in an open stretch of country before Hooghalen and they had to get out, after which they were herded across fields, through the woods and hedges to the Camp. Here the Catholics had been isolated from the rest, which in one way pleased Fraülein Ruth because she was now amongst members of religious orders. In the morning they used to get up very early to say their morning prayers together. There were also several Trappist monks and lay-brothers, three or four of them, who, as a matter of fact, were brothers in the flesh ; they all came to see the visitors, wearing their habits and the Star of David. Whether they had their own visitors as well I cannot say for certain.

Fraülein Ruth expressed the hope that they would soon be allowed to celebrate Holy Mass every morning. Then the S.S. patrol blew a shrill blast on their whistles as the order for the prisoners to go back to their huts, but Fraülein Ruth quickly called the Carmelite to come across and introduced her to us. Even those few moments proved edifying to me ; this Sister was so recollected and calm.

When I offered her my sympathy the brave Sister said : " Whatever happens I am prepared for it. Our dear Child Jesus is with us even here." Warmly shaking my hand she wished God's blessing on me and mine. After I had tried to say how I hoped everything would turn out all right she begged me not to worry about them, because they were all in God's hands. When it came to wishing them all good-bye the words just stuck in my throat. The prisoners walked away in a group to their huts, but kept turning to wave to us, all except Sister Benedicta, who went resolutely on her way.

Since we could not get back to Venlo that same day, we preferred to stay overnight in Hooghalen. We were on the road early next morning. At the little railway-station I noticed two gentlemen wearing the Star of David and said to Mr. Philipsen, " I'll have a word with them " ; and though he thought it might be dangerous to talk to a Jew openly, I did so nevertheless. On my asking whether they came from the camp they said " Yes " ; and when I enquired if they knew Hut 7 they informed me that all the Catholics, lay and religious, had been taken away the night before, apparently to the East.'

These accounts are supplemented by a few lines which were written by a Jewish business-man from Cologne, Julius Markan. In the Westerbork Camp he had been put in charge of the prisoners and, along with his wife, had been spared deportation.

' Amongst the prisoners who were brought in on the 5th of August Sister Benedicta stood out on account of her calmness and composure. The distress in the barracks, and the stir caused by the new arrivals, was indescribable. Sister Benedicta was just like an angel, going around amongst the women, comforting them, helping them and calming them. Many of the mothers were near to distraction ; they had not bothered about their children the whole day long, but just sat brooding in dumb despair. Sister Benedicta took care of the little children, washed them and combed them, looked after their feeding and their other needs. During the whole of her stay there she washed and cleaned for people, following one act of charity with another until everyone wondered at her goodness.'

Their stay in Westerbork lasted from early on Wednesday the 5th of August until the night of the 6th to the 7th of

August. Altogether 1,200 Catholic Jews were interned in the barracks of whom ten to fifteen were members of religious orders. A thousand of them, including Sister Benedicta, were deported during the night. Before leaving, however, she had managed to write two notes which eventually reached the Reverend Mother. The first, with no indication of either date or place, runs :

' Dear Mother, If Your Reverence has been allowed to see Father ——'s [the name is illegible] letter you will know what he thinks. There is nothing more for me to do in the matter. I leave it all in the hands of Y.R. to decide whether Y.R. should do anything about it. I am quite content in any case. One can only learn a *Scientia Crucis* if one feels the Cross in one's own person. I was convinced of this from the very first and have said with all my heart : *Ave crux, spes unica !*
Y.R.'s grateful child, B.'

The second note took some days to arrive at Echt, and was written the same day that the messengers brought the articles asked for in the telegram.

' J. & M. Pax Xti ! Drente—Westerbork. Hut 36. 8.VIII.42.
Dear Mother, The Superior of a Convent came yesterday evening with some parcels for one of her daughters and is going to take this note with her. Early tomorrow the first transport will leave (Silesia or Czechoslovakia ?). Most urgent are woollen stockings and two blankets. For Rosa all her warm underclothes and whatever was in the wash. For both, hand-towels and face-cloths. Rosa has neither a tooth-brush, crucifix nor Rosary. I should be glad to have the next volume of the Breviary. (Prayer going marvellously so far.) Our identity-cards, race- and bread-cards.
A thousand thanks and greetings to all,
Y.R.'s grateful child, B.
   1 Habit and apron.
   1 small veil.'

The third note, to the Swiss Consul at the Hague, merely contains her address and a few words : " Try to have us taken out as soon as possible. Our convent will pay for the tickets."

How deep is the desire, expressed in the second letter, to continue living the life to which she was dedicated, as far as possible. The third was intended, perhaps, as an S.O.S. to be telegraphed to the Consul. A letter from Rosa to the Prioress at Echt was unfortunately lost.

News gradually filtered in about other convents that had been the victims of the S.S. visitation on the same day ; experiences were exchanged and so were the letters smuggled through by the kidnapped nuns.

The first note from Alice Reis was written after the whole group had been transferred from the barracks at Amersfoort to the Westerbork assembly-camp, and it reached the Sisters of the Good Shepherd at Almelo on the 6th of August. Although she was not a member of this Order she had worked in the convent as a lay-helper. At five o'clock on the morning of August 2nd she had been carried off by the Gestapo, even though the Superior protested vigorously and pointed out that Alice suffered from severe asthma. In her note she asked for them to send warm garments, bandages, etc. straight away, because they had absolutely nothing. A telegram arrived at four o'clock the same evening asking for the same articles, which the Sisters sent off by express delivery before nightfall. Alice had also informed them that the prisoners would not be kept in Holland but were to be deported further away. Consequently the Sisters tried to find someone who could go personally to Westerbork via Assen in order to deliver the articles. But when the Dean of Almelo phoned up the priest at Assen he learned that the entire group had been transported to the East at half past four that very morning.

We can form an even clearer picture of this whole group from a letter which Fraülein Dr. Meirowsky addressed to her confessor in Tilburg, again on the 6th of August. Dr. Meirowsky and Sister Benedicta had only been slightly acquainted previously, but during the first months of 1942 they had exchanged several letters. Since 1940 Dr. Meirowsky had lived at the lodge of the Trappistine Abbey near Tilburg, acting as door-keeper for the community besides rendering valuable service as the community-doctor. She was a member of the Dominican Third Order and regarded by the Trappistines as one of themselves. Her letter reads :

Transfiguratio, 6.VIII.42.

' You know already where we are, and that we are expecting to be sent to Poland. To-morrow morning is the time fixed. There are two Trappistine nuns with me here, as well as two Trappist monks and a lay-brother from the same abbey [1] ; all of us were driven to the camp at Amersfoort on Sunday morning, before being brought to Westerbork near Hooghalen on the Feast of our Holy Father, St. Dominic. I know, dear Father, that you are heart and soul in this with me, with us all. Your spiritual child, Sister Judith, is also here, and so is the Carmelite from Echt whom I met that time in Amsterdam. Now I want to send you my last greetings and to tell you that I have complete confidence in God and have surrendered myself entirely to His Will. Even more—I regard it as a grace and privilege to be driven along this road under these conditions, a witness to the words of our good fathers and shepherds in Christ.

If our sufferings have been increased somewhat then we have received a double portion of grace, and a glorious crown is being prepared for us in heaven. Rejoice with me. I am going forward unshaken, confidently and joyfully—like the Sisters who are with me—to testify to Jesus Christ, and to bear witness to the Truth in company with our Bishops. We are going as children of Our Holy Mother, the Church ; we will unite our sufferings with the sufferings of our King, our Saviour and our Bridegroom, sacrificing ourselves for the

---

[1] These five brothers and sisters were the children of Dr. Lob, a lecturer in mining at Bergen op Zoom.

conversion of many, for the Jews, for those who persecute us, so that all may know the peace of Christ and His Kingdom.

In case I do not survive, would you please be so good as to write later on to my beloved parents and brothers, telling them that my life is being offered for them—may God grant them the light of faith and happiness both on earth and in heaven, if that is His Will. Pass on my love and gratitude to them and ask them to forgive me for any wrongs and sorrows I have caused them. Tell them also that my mother's sisters and my father's twin-sisters left here for Poland full of faith and trust, wholly given to the will of God. And send my best wishes to my sister-in-law and my little nieces—from the depths of my heart I pray for the good of their souls. Tell Fr. Stratman that he must not be troubled, but rather join me in thanking God for this great favour by singing an exultant Magnificat ; the work that we started together [she refers to the Peace Movement] will only be fruitful when, where and how God wills. And this is the best and surest way for me to co-operate ; either through my slight sufferings, which are not to be compared with the eternity of happiness which awaits us —or to continue by his side helping him from beyond the grave.

If you have the opportunity to visit Tilburg Abbey later on, please do so, or write to Father Willibrordus van Dyk that I gratefully pray for him always. I myself shall be writing to Mother Abbess and Father Rector, who was my confessor. All our good friends are brought into my prayers and sacrifice. Please write also to Frau Schmutzer in Utrecht ; and please pray very hard for Dr. Lazarus, who has been imprisoned in Amersfoort Camp because he did not wear the Star. I am praying much for him.

And now I want to thank you from my heart for all your goodness towards me, for your compassionate brotherly love. How often you have given me courage.

Here our greatest trial is that we do not have Holy Mass and Communion ; but if Jesus does not wish it, neither do I. He dwells in my heart, walks with me and gives me strength.   He is my strength and my peace.

As soon as I can write again you shall hear from me. Would you also be so kind (if you think it advisable) to write to me on an international card (but not prepaid).   May Mary protect you and God sanctify you with His Love.   Once more I humbly ask for your prayers and your priestly blessing.

In Jesus and Mary,
Your Sister M. Magdalena Dominica.
(In the world Doctor Meirowsky).'

The community at Echt waited anxiously for some fresh communication, but the only news was of the deportation of the entire barrackful of Catholics to Poland on the First Friday.   The vans were full to suffocation, with the result that many of these poor creatures died on the journey.   Moreover they were all dressed in prison-uniform.   The two sisters, so it seems, had been put into a group of forty Catholics which included some recently converted Jews.   Perhaps they had already acquired their martyrs' crowns before anything was heard of them in Cologne Carmel, whose communications with Echt had necessarily been curtailed by the strict censorship imposed on foreign mail.   The awful news eventually came, a few words written on a plain postcard : " B. & R. taken away 2.VIII.   Destination unknown.   Probably to the East."

Meanwhile the Carmel at Le Paquier had successfully surmounted all the difficulties about their passports, and Switzerland was now offering the two sisters refuge.   To their grief the Carmelites learned that all their trouble had been in vain. For a long time the cell set aside for Sister Benedicta stood empty, awaiting her coming, but with heavy heart the Mother Prioress had to make the following entry in the Chapter book :

' Sœur Teresia Benedicta ayant obtenu, ainsi que sa sœur Rosa, l'entrée en Suisse, grace a la bienveillante intervention de

Mons. Etter, président de la Confédération, fut emmenée soudainement avec elle (en dix minutes) de son Carmel d'Echt par la police allemande pour destination inconnue vers l'est. Nous faisons des démarches de plusieurs cotés pour la retrouver, sans vrai espoir, hélas ! [1] '

[1] In translation : Sister Teresia Benedicta, who with her sister Rosa had obtained an entry permit for Switzerland, thanks to the good offices of Mons. Etter, President of the Confederation, was suddenly (in ten minutes) abducted with her from the Carmel at Echt by the German police, and taken to an unknown destination in the East. We are making enquiries in various places to find her, but, alas with no real hope.

VIII

THE LAST NEWS

SECRET investigations were set on foot in all quarters to discover where they had vanished to, but without much likelihood of success, for no one could give the exact name of the concentration-camp and everything had to be done under cover. Rumours circulated plentifully but never proved reliable. Then just before Christmas 1942 Sister Bonaventura from St. Magdalena Convent in Speyer visited the Cologne Carmel with a piece of information that she had not dared to send by letter. On the 6th of August (actually it must have been the 7th) a young married woman was standing on the platform at Schifferstadt when she suddenly heard someone call her by her maiden-name. On looking round she saw her former teacher, Fraülein Dr. Stein, in one of the stationary trains. Dr. Stein called to her, " Give my love to the Sisters in St. Magdalena—I am on my way to the East." Despite endless enquiries this lady's name could not be discovered. But, on the same day, according to La Fouqué, the station-master at Schifferstadt, one of the female prisoners from a train going East introduced herself to him as a Carmelite named Sister Benedicta, and asked whether by any chance there happened to be a priest on the station. He was sorry, but there wasn't ; having learned this she simply asked him to give her regards to the parish priest and tell him that she was on the journey to Poland. It seems that the last word from her came to a Lioba Sister in Freiburg who received a tiny note from an unknown quarter ; the note was written in pencil and said no more than, " Greetings from the journey to Poland. Sister Teresia Benedicta."

THE LAST NEWS

In the early days the friends and Sisters of the two victims cherished the hope that they were still alive and would come back. True and false rumours sprang up which no one could get to the bottom of because everyone had enough troubles of their own to keep them busy during these terrible years of bombardment. At one time Sister Benedicta was reported to be in Auschwitz, on another occasion that she had been moved to Teresienstadt, from where, some said, she had volunteered to work in the hospital at Litzmannstadt. Last of all, a Quaker in Speyer who had been released from the Ravensbrück concentration camp, declared that she had seen Sister Benedicta in that camp. Such were the vague rumours nourishing the hopes of all who had loved Sister Benedicta and longed to see her, and who still continued to pray for her.

Meanwhile the Cologne Carmel had also met its doom. For four years the Church and Convent seemed to have been miraculously protected from the countless air-raids, because, although it was hit time and again, no external damage could be seen ; the Carmel still remained, like an oasis of peace in a desert of ruins. Then on the evening of October 30th, 1944, came a sustained air-attack which in an hour of screaming bombs reduced Lindenthal to a heap of ashes and rubble. At the end of it the Carmel was completely destroyed except for a room in the cellar where the Sisters were on their knees expecting death at any minute. But the Lord was not in the earthquake which shook the foundations. He was not in the storm of bombs which swept away the convent, nor in the fire which devoured it from all sides. He led them unharmed out of the place of horrors, out of the burning city into the welcoming peace of their Sisters at Welden Carmel near Augsburg.

All contacts with the Carmel at Echt were brought to an end, as Holland was occupied by the allies. Already the Sisters in Echt had suffered a great deal during the stubborn defensive campaign of the German troops, on one occasion having to abandon their convent for a short time. Fortunately they had previously put Sister Benedicta's posthumous papers into good order and stored them away. Here the papers remained in safety until the Sisters were suddenly forced to flee from Echt, on the 6th of January, 1945, before the wave of retreating troops. All of them were driven off to Herkenbosch in German military vehicles. But three days later one of the Sisters managed to return to Echt to salvage something, and at the same time brought Sister Benedicta's writings back with her in two sacks.

' We wanted to hide them in the cellar of the convent which had given us shelter, but the convent was so tiny that the Superior would not permit it owing to lack of space. So the sacks were left lying in the open. We asked at the big Franciscan House in Vlodrop whether we might store them there, but severe shelling prevented the request from being delivered for three weeks. Long before this we ourselves had been driven out of Herkenbosch, and although Sister Pia was left behind to look after Sister Francisca, who was wounded, she could do nothing. Danger and destruction were everywhere. Once we were in Leinarden, communication with the south was out of the question for months. We were powerless ' [Mother Antonia].

Eventually, in March 1945, Professor Father Hermann van Breda, O.F.M., of Louvain, and the Carmelite Prior of Geleen borrowed a military vehicle and took Sister Pia and Sister Francisca to Echt in search of the manuscripts. Finding nothing there, they drove on through the ice-bound countryside to Herkenbosch, to the tiny convent mentioned by Mother Antonia. It was now nothing more than a ruin, but they found what they wanted, Sister Benedicta's papers, three-quarters of which lay scattered about, very dirty and torn.

During 1945 the country was beginning to return to some sort of order, which enabled the Sisters to establish contact with America through the Red Cross. Frau Biberstein was informed of the forcible abduction of her sisters, Edith and Rosa, and knowing what such news meant she also started making what investigations she could. It was all in vain.

Neither the head of the Order in Rome nor the Carmelite convents in either Germany, Holland or Switzerland was able to discover any trace of them. All the more startling, therefore, for everyone concerned was a notice which appeared in the *Osservatore Romano* in 1947, which ran :

From Judaism to the University, and thence to Carmel
' Before she entered the religious life, the Carmelite Sister Benedicta a Cruce was known throughout Germany as Dr. Edith Stein, a woman philosopher converted from Judaism to Catholicism.

Sister Benedicta was born in 1875 and executed in 1945 by the Nazis. In October 1933 she entered the Carmelite convent at Lindenthal in Cologne. On account of her ancestry she was secretly transferred to the Carmel at Echt in Holland during 1938. One of her superiors testifies that she was as obedient as St. Thérèse of Lisieux. On the 2nd of August 1945 a Nazi police-van drove up to the convent. Sister Benedicta was given five minutes in which to get ready to leave. This delay was extended to ten minutes as a special favour. Then she was led away, together with a Sister Rosa and other unknown victims.

On arriving in Germany she was beaten with cudgels, thrown into prison and then killed, either in a gas-chamber or, as some think, by being thrown down a salt-mine.'

This newspaper-notice was taken up and reprinted in Catholic diocesan magazines both at home and abroad, despite the very obvious errors which it contains. It proved impossible to trace the source of this announcement. The only reliable news was a report sent from Echt to Cologne by one of the men who had taken the cases to Sister Benedicta and Rosa in the camp ; on the 13th of March 1947 he had received an official intimation from the Joodsen Raad, Amsterdam, to say that none of those from the transport which contained the two sisters had ever returned.

A veritable flood of letters asking for more information and for accounts of Sister Benedicta now began to inundate the Cologne Carmel (which had once more returned to Cologne in order to rebuild the convent Maria vom Frieden near Siebenburgen, being housed temporarily in Junkersdorf). The only possible answer to all these questions was to send off the rapidly composed sketch of this great Carmelite's life, a hundred thousand copies of which went to all parts of the globe. At the time this was very much a case of casting one's bread upon the waters, but it was greatly rewarded when letters and favours came pouring in from all quarters of Germany as well as from abroad. The writers represented every conceivable grade of society, every profession, every age, every level of education, all with one voice acclaiming this heroine as venerable, as a model for everyone, as a saint. One of the letters even contained a manuscript entitled, " The ontic structure of the person and its bearing on epistemology ", a copy of the lectures which Sister Benedicta had delivered in Münster during the Winter term 1932–33 ; she had given the manuscript to Frau Dr. Schweitzer just before entering Carmel.

Besides this precious find the memorial card unexpectedly brought to light the sole survivor who had witnessed Sister Benedicta moving along the last stages of her Via Crucis.

In February 1947 Professor Dr. Max Budde came across the memorial card quite by accident and having read it, wrote to say that his friend, Director General Doctor Lenig, had been interned in Amersfoort camp just about the same time. This was the third time that Dr. Lenig had been arrested since the Nazis seized power, but the fact that he had led the Resistance movement against the Third Reich from outside was his salvation. His friends in the Resistance movement had rescued him from the Nazis, and therefore he was the one survivor, so perhaps he could add something to the picture.

By the next post a letter of enquiry was sent to Dr. Lenig, from whom the following reply arrived on the 27th of February 1947 :

THE LAST NEWS

' Reverend Mother Prioress,

At the request of my dear friend, Professor Max Budde of Gelsenkirchen, I have the honour to inform you as follows :

Time and again in their pastoral letters the Dutch Archbishops and Bishops made vigorous but thoroughly justified attacks upon National Socialism. For a long time I had been aware of the danger overhanging all Catholics who refused to fall into line with the political ideology of the new German Empire. But I must confine myself to details of personal interest to the Carmel Maria vom Frieden. I met Sister Teresia Benedicta a Cruce, known in the camp as Edith Stein, on the 2nd of August, 1942, when she came into the transit camp at Amersfoort, into Hut No. 9, if I am not mistaken. On this Sunday all Catholics of Jewish, or partly Jewish, ancestry were arrested by the German hangmen as a reprisal for the pastoral letter which had been read from the pulpits of all Dutch Churches the previous Sunday. They were thrown into vans and assembled at Amersfoort before being carried off to the gas-chambers and crematoria. When your Sister and the other three hundred men, women and children were once behind the barbed-wire of the camp they had to stand waiting for a roll-call on the barrack-square, just as a pleasant welcome. As a punishment, so far as I remember—one of the starving internees had " stolen " some dry bread that had been thrown away—the whole camp was being made to stand there for several days. That is to say, part of them were still standing, the rest had collapsed and were being continually mishandled to get them on their feet again. Amongst those still standing I noticed an inflexible opponent of the Third Reich, Ministerial Director Dr. Lazarus, who, like the new arrivals, was an active and ardent Catholic. Nor can I forget how the day was one long series of kickings and beatings, although these were tolerable. The most distressing thing was the condition of the women. It was in this that Edith Stein showed her worth. It must be mentioned to begin with that all were released who had been brought in by mistake, Protestants, Greek Orthodox, etc., and then the routine of camp-life set in. Roll-calls and nightly deportations. They devoted themselves to reading the *Imitation of Christ*, which someone had smuggled in, a Trappist faithfully said Holy Mass for them—his six brothers and sisters who had all joined the same Order were with him, all awaiting transportation. Holy Communion was distributed, and despite the cat-calls of the S.S., everyone of this host destined for death steadfastly sang the *Confiteor* daily, until the last of them had gone their way. . . .

It was very moving also to see the response of this community of believers when they heard that there were priests somewhere in the camp ; immediately they gave up their meagre rations, their tobacco, their money, etc., which were now useless to them but might help the priests to placate the sadistic guards and so stay alive until the day of liberation.

Many of these night transports went to the death-camp at Drente and others went straight to Auschwitz. Mothers had to send off home for prams in which to take their children, or to order trucks for their baggage, which was usually left behind. I have never heard anything more of any of them. There was one lady of some religious Order who was claimed by the Swiss Consulate—and yet was gassed. I would like to emphasize that the Dutch convents all took endless trouble to try to ease the lot of their Brothers and Sisters. I myself, partly on my own initiative and partly at the request of different convents, including Echt, have tried to discover the fate of all the deportees. Everywhere I have had people trying to help me. So far I have heard nothing of any of the religious, man or woman, nor of any wife or husband, of neither old nor young, except that all their lives on earth were ended in a few weeks.

Amongst the first to be carried off by night was your lamented Sister, Edith Stein. Like them all she went calmly to her death, fully assured of rising again to eternal life. It is impossible for me to say definitely whether it was the night of the 4th or the 5th of August. May God be merciful to her, and to all the victims of German Race-" Christianity " ; may

THE LAST NEWS

He grant them eternal peace and may His eternal light shine upon them.   Amen.

With my respectful regards,
Yours,
Lenig.'

This terrifying picture raised doubts in the Cologne Carmel about whether some of the facts mentioned in the sketch of her life on the memorial card were correct.   Also some of the Sisters wondered whether the testimony sent by Dr. Lenig was sufficient ground for accepting Sister Benedicta's death as certain.   When these doubts were placed before him Dr. Lenig replied again, on the 8th of April, 1947 :

' The statements on the memorial card are as accurate as human judgment allows.   It is quite certain that the death-transports were directed through Schifferstadt.   We know from accounts of other transports that the condemned persons sometimes managed to attract the attention of acquaintances whom they happened to see ;   consequently the suggestion that your lamented Sister was seen and heard definitely falls within the bounds of possibility.

From the legal viewpoint your Sister must be regarded as dead.   And it is morally certain that she was murdered in Auschwitz, not in the Low Countries.'

On the strength of this news Sister Benedicta was reported to the General in Rome as dead.   From Rome the sad message was passed round to all Carmelite houses so that they might each offer to God the customary suffrages offered for all departed members of the Order.

In the little oratory of their temporary Carmel at Junkersdorf her Sisters sang a solemn Requiem for her.   No one outside the community was present.   No note of real sadness entered in, nor did bitterness cloud the holy sorrow and just anger which were called forth at the memory of the wrongs inflicted upon our dead Sister.   It was Easter again, the high feast, the one which she loved most of all the feasts in the Church's year. And now she was singing her alleluia to the Easter Lamb in Heaven.

But the earth sounded with a chant of sadness : *Libera me Domine . . . dum veneris judicare sæculum per ignem.*

Some words of Sister Benedicta's, true to the spirit of one who had acquired so deep a vision into finite and eternal being, seemed to sound a quiet accompaniment to the Requiem :

> Let us judge not that we be not judged.
> Since, blinded by earth's outward show,
> We see in shadows and in images
> The truth which God alone can know.

POSTSCRIPT

THIS little book was presented to the public on the feast of Christmas 1948 by Glock und Lutz, the Nüremberg publishers. The demand for it was so great that by the Spring of 1950 the fifth edition was already being prepared, as well as translations into four foreign languages. But the present edition embodies considerable alterations. For we have been able to fill in this sketch of our beloved Sister, and bring out the light and shade, by quoting from her friends' letters and reminiscences, as well as from her own contributions, which were recently discovered contrary to all expectations. But questions about the when, where and how of her end remain shrouded in as much mystery as ever, and this uncertainty has driven her friends on to tireless investigations. So far these investigations have produced no indisputable results. But we can give the following stories and assertions for what they are worth, without trying to reconcile their contradictions, in the sad hope that they may provide the clue to a reliable explanation.

In *Frauenland* (No. 3/4 1950) the Lioba Sister Placida Laubhardt writes that authentic witnesses prove how Edith Stein died a violent death in the gas-chambers of Auschwitz on the 9th of August 1942. A similar assertion is found in the biographical sketch for the first volume of Edith Stein's works, *Kreuzeswissenschaft* : On the 7th of August 1942 she was deported to Auschwitz (Silesia), where she was gassed, and her body burnt, on the 10th of August 1942. These details have been culled from a document which we had quoted, an official form from the Dutch Red Cross specially prepared for answering questions about deportees who have not returned ; its form is so general and imprecise that it could not be treated as authentic testimony. And therefore considerations were soon raised throwing doubt upon the date given for her death.

A lady from Berlin (formerly a prisoner in Ravensbrück-Auschwitz, her prison no. 279) writes :

' Having read about Edith Stein I feel in duty bound to give the following information : From the end of March 1942 (to be precise, the 27.III.42) drafts of a 1,000 Jewish women used to come into the camp every day. The first transports came from Slovakia, Bohemia and Hungary. Until the beginning of 1943 they came mainly from these lands. Afterwards from Holland, Belgium, France and Greece.

Not until the middle of 1943 did we get mixed Jewish transports (i.e. a mixture of German and others). The vast majority of these transports came from the camp at Theresienstadt.

According to my calculations, therefore, Edith Stein cannot have come to Auschwitz in 1942. If she had come to Auschwitz in 1942, it would be known for certain, since the writer of these lines was a prisoner in Auschwitz from 27.III.42 until 18.I.45, and was working until the end of 1943 in the Prisoners' Bureau at Auschwitz, and later at Auschwitz-Birkenau. All the prisoners were registered there, and Edith Stein would have stood out immediately as a Catholic Jewess when she was questioned as to her denomination.

Moreover there was a very active resistance movement in the women's camp at Auschwitz. They used to take away almost all the German Jewesses who arrived to a distant barracks where they would be in less danger. Those who escaped in this way would be able to give information. But I am certain Edith Stein was not one of them.

If Edith Stein did not come directly to Auschwitz in 1942 where was she in the meantime ? That will have to be determined by exact detailed investigation.'

A nursing sister writes :

POSTSCRIPT

' Unfortunately I cannot give you any definite information about Sister Benedicta. But I can at least pass on to you something that might be relevant. For four years I was medical attendant in a large factory at Augsburg (Michel-Factory). In October 1944, on instructions from the authorities, we had to clear out one floor of the factory so that it could be turned into a concentration camp. On the 5 Sept. 1944 we received 500 Jewish Hungarian women who had come straight from Auschwitz. They were all cultured people, teachers, doctors, nuns and university types. Though it grieved me to do so, I refused at first to take charge of the medical side, because many demands were made upon me which I as a Catholic nurse could not reconcile with my conscience. The commanding officer of the camp forced me to do so, however, which meant that I could go in and out of the place regularly. Despite its many difficulties this task brought me great joy, because my charges soon discovered how tender-hearted I was. As soon as I knew that the S.S. guards were out of the building we used to gather together and try to comfort one another. It was on one such occasion that a teacher, her eyes filled with tears, described to me how Edith Stein had already trod her way of the Cross ; she had been gassed the same day that her name was called. There were many Catholics amongst those whom I had to look after, though I do not know whether they all were. But one thing I can say for certain—that I and my charges used often to pray together to our Lord, and to our dear Edith as we used to call her ; we asked for strength and blessing from Christ for prisoners who are always so dear to Him. They were hours of peace on which we drew for interior strength. A fortnight before the Nazi collapse they were all taken off to the assembly-camp at Kaufbeuren. Here most of them were shot, but a few managed to escape, including two who came to see me ; that is why I know their fate after leaving Augsburg. One of them went to America, and one back to Hungary. Unfortunately they have not written to me at all. At one time I had occasion to go to Theresienstadt concentration-camp, but I never heard mention of Edith Stein. I am inclined to believe that Auschwitz was the scene of her death, because in October 1944 a great clear-out took place there. Orders were given to clear the place out entirely, though I do not know whether they were actually executed. Perhaps it rests with dear Edith herself to give us some clue about the manner of her end. Certainly all those from Theresienstadt were taken to Auschwitz to be gassed. The gas-oven in Theresienstadt was only completed a few days before the Russians arrived—I know, for I saw it ; all those killed in Theresienstadt were shot.'

The third letter offering an explanation comes from a parish priest in Würtemberg :

'Yesterday I showed the picture of your dear Sister Benedicta Teresia in her black veil to one of my parishioners who was in Auschwitz. He maintained through thick and thin that he had seen her there dressed as in the photograph. I contradicted him immediately, because he had admitted that he only arrived there in October 1942. Yet he stuck to his original statement.

Today he came back again and corrected the dates he had given for his stay there. In fact, he arrived at Auschwitz no later than the end of July 1942 and stayed there about a year. He could just about swear that this Sister had looked fixedly at him and another guard as if she guessed that the two of them were talking about her—" she's not weak in the head anyway " they had said, in reference to the story in the guard-house that the whole transport was mad.

Although I rather mistrust this fellow on account of his past and his family circumstances I am very much inclined to accept his version, because he quite spontaneously claimed that he recognized the Sister the very moment I showed him the picture, and before I had explained my reasons for showing it to him. He would not have it that Sister Benedicta must have been wearing prisoner's clothes when she arrived ; that was not the case with any of the transports to Auschwitz. On the same day at the beginning of August—he cannot remember the exact date—two transports arrived from Holland, one of men in the morning and one of women about ten at night. Both were ticked off at the guard-house as transports of insane people. The SD. sealed these transports off so effectively that no one was able to speak to the victims.

The train had taken him further into the camp than he was usually supposed to go. Finding himself alone he risked going further still, and noticed the Sister in the middle portion of the train ; around her were people who seemed to know her, but who were not wearing religious habits. Possibly there were more Sisters further forward. At other times lists of people for working-parties were drawn up even from transports of women, but no one from this transport was noticed in the following days ; it was therefore believed that all these victims had stripped off their clothes at the usual spot and then been herded naked about a quarter of a mile to the place of slaughter. Here they had been burnt in the crematorium—immediately after they had arrived. He had never heard whether these victims were Jews or not.'

One might very well echo the sentiments of the nursing Sister, who wished that S. Benedicta herself would give us some sign by which to confirm our guesses. But perhaps she wishes us to be content with her last recorded words, " I am on my way to the East ", for they echo in our minds like words spoken to me from another world, recalling the *kalon to dynai* of Saint Ignatius of Antioch. He found it so wonderful being on his way to the West with death before him, for so he could sink down with Christ, the sun, to rise again with Christ. Are these not Sister Benedicta's signs to us ? tokens of her risen, glorified life in Christ.

A great many letters have been received which report striking favours obtained through her intercession. She especially helps those searching for jobs. The following letter from Nymwegen gives an account of a cure attributed to her mediation.

EDITH STEIN

Nymwegen. S. Marcus 1950.

' REVEREND MOTHER PRIORESS,

I cannot wait any longer to give you the news about that man for whom I asked you to start a Novena. This man was given up by the doctors who said he would only last another day or two. Then we prayed to Sister Benedicta ; and this is what happened. To everyone's amazement he has been let out of hospital and is back at work. He has already been home a week and feels fine. His one kidney is functioning well, even better than before—normally, in fact. His love of life has returned, he eats well (though still on a diet) ; he goes for walks, and smokes, and everything agrees with him. All of this to everyone's astonishment, and to the great joy of his wife and his four kiddies, and everyone who knows him.

But of course we must be very prudent, i.e. he must go back to his doctor for another examination in a few weeks. I told him, you get the doctor to put it down in writing, what you were like at first, then after a week, and now ; because this is all to do with God's glory.'

Countless people are praying for Sister Benedicta's beatification, as we are assured in many letters. The Order of our blessed Lady of Mount Carmel has introduced the Informatory Process. But was Dom Raphael Walzer, O.S.B., not right when he said : "We do not know what God's providence has in store for her now. Will she one day be raised to the altars of the Church ? Or will she only go down to history as an ideal personality ? The latter would not surprise me. But one thing is certain : her example, her prayer and her works, her silence and suffering, and her last journey to the East will not easily fade from the memory of future generations. They will always radiate strength, and will awaken the longing for ever deeper faith, hope and love."

COLOGNE CARMEL
    PENTECOST. 1950